In the Footsteps of Abraham Ulrikab

The events of
1880–1881

France Rivet

POLAR HORIZONS

Researcher, author, editor, French-English translations, layout designer	France Rivet
German-English translation of Abraham's diary and a subset of the other related texts	Hartmut Lutz and his students from Greisfwald University
German-English translation of Johan Adrian Jacobsen's diary	Hartmut Lutz
Editing and proofreading	Line Fortin

Cover by Sumit Shringi. Abraham's portrait byJacob Martin Jacobsen, 1880 (Moravian Archives, Herrnhut).
Background photo of Saglek Fjord © France Rivet, Polar Horizons, 2009.
Author's portrait © Rémi Laprise, 2013.

Bibliothèque et Archives nationales du Québec and Library and Archives Canada cataloguing in publication

Rivet, France, 1963-

[Sur les traces d'Abraham Ulrikab. English]

In the footsteps of Abraham Ulrikab : the events of 1880-1881

Translation of : Sur les traces d'Abraham Ulrikab.

Includes bibliographical references and index.

ISBN 978-0-99367-406-8

1. Inuit - Europe - History - 19th century. 2. Ulrikab, Abraham, 1845?-1881 - Death and burial. 3. Human remains (Archaeology) - Repatriation - Newfoundland and Labrador. 4. Human zoos - Europe - History - 19th century. I. Title. II. Title : Sur les traces d'Abraham Ulrikab. English.

| E99.E7R58313 2014 | 305.897'124094 | C2014-941525-7 |

Legal Deposit - Bibliothèque et Archives nationales du Québec, 2014
Legal Deposit – Library and Archives Canada, 2014.
Also available in electronic format (PDF): ISBN 978-0-99367-403-7

Polar Horizons Inc.
27 de Cotignac Street, Gatineau (Quebec) J8T 8E4
info@polarhorizons.com / www.polarhorizons.com/en

To the memory of:

Abraham
Maria
Nuggasak
Paingu
Sara
Tigianniak
Tobias
Ulrike

To all Nunatsiavummiut:

May this book provide
the essential elements to allow you to
reclaim a part of your history
and enable you to close the loop on the fate
of eight of your fellow countrymen.

TABLE OF CONTENTS

List of Figures 7

Foreword 11

Preface 15

A Few Notes 21

The Beginnings of Carl Hagenbeck's Ethnographic Shows 25

The Search for a New Ship 31

Jacobsen Attempts to Recruit in Greenland 33

The Arrival in Hebron, Labrador 37

Nachvak Fjord 41

The Departure for Europe 49

The Crossing of the Atlantic 57

The Arrival in Hamburg 61

The Stay in Hamburg 65

The Stay in Berlin 69

Abraham's First Letter to Brother Elsner 89

Meeting With Moravian Brothers and Sisters in Berlin 95

The *Eskimos* Studied by Rudolf Virchow 105

The Stay in Prague 135

The Stay in Frankfurt 139

The Stay in Darmstadt and Nuggasak's Death 149

The Stay in Bockum and the Deaths of Paingu and Maria 153

The Arrival at the *Jardin d'acclimatation* in Paris 163

Abraham's Last Letter to Brother Elsner 171

The *Eskimos'* Death in Paris 173

The Autopsies Results 185

The *Eskimos'* Death in the Press.. 195

The Commission of Inquiry on the *Eskimos'* Death..................................... 201

The Debate on Compulsory Vaccination.. 213

The *Eskimos'* Belongings Return to Labrador 219

Paingu's Skullcap.. 229

Three Eskimo Brain Casts 233

The Exhumation of the *Eskimos'* Remains.. 245

Were the Skeletons Exhibited in Paris?.. 251

What Happened to the Remains of Nuggasak, Paingu and Sara?...... 261

The Collection of Artifacts.. 265

The Impacts of the *Eskimos'* Death 273

Next Steps….. 277

Appendix A – Abraham's Diary 279

Appendix B – Chronological Summary of Events 287

Appendix C – Study of the Brains by Théophile Chudzinski 293

Appendix D – Broca's Gyrus 299

Appendix E – Various Mentions of Abraham's Story 303

Acknowledgments 305

Bibliographic References 317

Index of Names Cited.. 339

LIST OF FIGURES

Fig. 1 Poster *Die Eskimos von Lavrador*, 1881 10
Fig. 2 Saglek Fjord, Torngat Mountains National Park 14
Fig. 3 Nachvak Fjord, Torngat Mountains National Park 14
Fig. 4 Carl Hagenbeck, ca 1890 24
Fig. 5 Heinrich Leutemann, ca 1880 25
Fig. 6 Emperor Wilhelm I observing the Greenlanders 28
Fig. 7 Johan Adrian Jacobsen, 1881 30
Fig. 8 The *Eisbär*, 1880 36
Fig. 9 Moravian settlement in Hebron, Labrador, mid-19th century 40
Fig. 10 HBC post at Nachvak Fjord, ca 1910 43
Fig. 11 George Ford and his first wife Harriet Merrifield 46
Fig. 12 Hebron's Moravian church 47
Fig. 13 Nuggasak, Paingu and Tigianniak, 1880 48
Fig. 14 Geographical map of locations in Labrador or Greenland 54
Fig. 15 Geographical map of locations in Europe 55
Fig. 16 Abraham's family, 1880 56
Fig. 17 Heligoland, ca 1890–1900 58
Fig. 18 Tigianniak calming the storm, 1880 60
Fig. 19 Cuxhaven's new and old Kugelbake, 1867 61
Fig. 20 Hamburg Harbour, 1883 62
Fig. 21 Carl Hagenbeck's residence at 13 Neuer Pferdemarkt 64
Fig. 22 Tobias' *carte de visite*, 1880 66
Fig. 23 Adolf Schoepf (left) and J. A. Jacobsen (right), 1909 67
Fig. 24 Berliner train station in Hamburg 68
Fig. 25 The hall of the Berliner train station 68
Fig. 26 Hamburger train station in Berlin, ca 1850 70
Fig. 27 Map of Berlin zoo, 1873 72
Fig. 28 Kaiser Gallery housing Castan's Panopticum, Berlin, 1900 76
Fig. 29 Scenes from the Berlin zoo, 1880, Part 1 80
Fig. 30 Scenes from the Berlin zoo, 1880, Part 2 81
Fig. 31 Abraham and Tobias in their kayaks, 1880 82
Fig. 32 Adolf Stöcker 94
Fig. 33 Heinrich Bodinus 98
Fig. 34 Location of 136 Wilhelmstraße, Berlin 103
Fig. 35 Illustrations of the eight *Eskimos*, 1880 104
Fig. 36 Rudolf Virchow 105
Fig. 37 Table of colour names 112
Fig. 38 Drawings on Paingu's forearm 120
Fig. 39 Contour of Tobias' right hand and right foot (Fig. 2 and 3) 127

Fig. 40 Contour of Ulrike's right hand and right foot (Fig. 4 and 5) 128
Fig. 41 Labrador spear-thrower 131
Fig. 42 Greenlandic spear-thrower 131
Fig. 43 Advertisement, *Bohemia*, November 15, 1880 135
Fig. 44 Advertisement, *Bohemia*, November 19, 1880 137
Fig. 45 Frankfurt Zoo, 1878 139
Fig. 46 Map of the Frankfurt Zoo, 1875 140
Fig. 47 Frankfurt Zoo's Pond 145
Fig. 48 Nuggasak, 1880 148
Fig. 49 Internal and external views of the Orpheum, ca 1905 152
Fig. 50 Section II-J, Darmstadt cemetery 152
Fig. 51 Bockum Zoo's Pond, 1906 154
Fig. 52 Concert hall where Christmas was celebrated, Bockum 155
Fig. 53 Paingu, 1880 157
Fig. 54 Site of Bockum's cemetery where Paingu was buried 158
Fig. 55 Alexianer hospital, Crefeld, 1883 159
Fig. 56 Gare du Nord, ca 1921 165
Fig. 57 1877 Greenlanders at the *Jardin d'acclimatation* 167
Fig. 58 Inuit sod house in Hebron 167
Fig. 59 The 'big lawn' and the stables, *Jardin d'acclimatation* 168
Fig. 60 *Hôpital Saint-Louis*, front of the courtyard entrance 174
Fig. 61 *The Eskimo's Departure* 175
Fig. 62 Hôpital Saint-Louis Plan 176
Fig. 63 *Hôpital Saint-Louis'* admission logbook for Maria. 177
Fig. 64 *Hôpital Saint-Louis'* admission logbook for the five adults 177
Fig. 65 *Hôpital Saint-Louis* Death Records – Maria's death record 178
Fig. 66 Tigianniak, 1880 179
Fig. 67 Paingu, Tigianniak and Nuggasak, 1880 184
Fig. 68 Dr. Émile Landrieux 185
Fig. 69 Ulrike and Maria, 1880 190
Fig. 70 Tobias, Abraham, Ulrike, Sara, and Maria, 1880 194
Fig. 71 Tobias, Abraham, Ulrike, Sara, and Maria, 1880 200
Fig. 72 Dr. Léon Colin 201
Fig. 73 Dr. Henri Liouville 218
Fig. 74 Poster *Amerikanishe Völkertypen* 228
Fig. 75 Paingu's portrait 228
Fig. 76 Tigianniak, Paingu and Nuggasak, 1886 232
Fig. 77 Dr. Paul Topinard 233
Fig. 78 Théophile Chudzinski... 236
Fig. 79 Refectory of the Cordeliers' Convent 238
Fig. 80 *Musée Broca*'s skeleton and brain casts collection 239
Fig. 81 Aleš Hrdlička 240
Fig. 82 Abraham, J. A. Jacobsen's interpreter, 1880 244
Fig. 83 Armand de Quatrefages 245
Fig. 84 Paul Brouardel.. 247
Fig. 85 Abraham, 1880 250
Fig. 86 Exterior view of the *Bâtiment de la baleine*, 1892 251
Fig. 87 General view – Comparative anatomy gallery, 1880 252
Fig. 88 Group of European skeletons, 1880 253
Fig. 89 Ernest Théodore Hamy, 1883... 254

Fig. 90 Anthropology and paleontology galleries 256
Fig. 91 René Verneau 257
Fig. 92 Eskimo Race. Anthropology gallery, *Musée de l'Homme* 260
Fig. 93 Rudolf Virchow in his laboratory, 1891 264
Fig. 94 *Musée d'ethnographie du Trocadéro* 265
Fig. 95 Armand Landrin 266
Fig. 96 Berlin Royal Museum of Ethnology, ca 1900 272
Fig. 97 Herman Frederik Carel ten Kate 286
Fig. 98 Poster *Amerikanische Völker* 292
Fig. 99 Nuggasak and Tigianniak's portrait 292
Fig. 100 Entrance door to the Berlin Zoo in 1880 302

Fig. 1 Poster *Die Eskimos von Lavrador*, 1881
Illustration by J. H. Fischer. Published in *Deutsche Illustrirte Zeitung*.
N° 13, p. 196. (Collection Hans-Josef Rollmann)

Foreword

Vicomte DE CHALLANS
Chronique parisienne, *La Presse*, Paris, February 10, 1881

Obituary

If you do not mind, let's not talk about divorce. [...] Let's not touch either on the front page news, the sensational trials, or the week's *premieres*. All these things represent the job's benefits; there will be no shortage of columnists to exploit them.

Let's talk, if you wish, about a simple fact which caused neither surprise nor resulted in any protest.

The thing happened in a public place, in the *Jardin d'acclimatation* in the Bois de Boulogne; the place where you go to admire a number of exiled creatures, most of which have that sad and dreamy look of people hit by nostalgia!

All these creatures are beasts or rather animals – the word beast is too easily given to fools for it to not be an insult.[1]

But in the midst of these animals doomed to the miseries of forced civilization, I do not know who was the fierce scholar who had the unfortunate idea to bring an Eskimo family.

What type of bait was used to attract them here?

I do not know! In any case, they were here. In any case, they are no longer here.

They are dead, all of them! From the first to the last. They died of smallpox, it seems; smallpox is so serious when complicated by acclimatization.

---

[1] In French, there are two distinct definitions for the word 'bête' used by the author: the noun meaning 'animal' and the adjective referring to a stupid, not very bright person.

After the first loss, the survivors must have ardently aspired to their motherland.

Oh, I understand that by representing their snow-covered country, their smoky huts in the open, the sad vegetation of lichens and some culinary preparations that would turn a Frenchman's stomach, we can exclaim like the legendary soldier: "They call it a home!..."

But each area has its splendours. Walks of snow and ice, wonderfully irradiated by the sun, may have their charm too.

And the Eskimos, accustomed to the fantastic lights of the aurora borealis, the eternal mirage of glittering ice floes did not easily get acclimatised to our beautiful land of France, where very often the sky looks macadamized.

To think that there may be, over there, near the pole, rather naive creatures to believe that their countrymen settled in the land of Cockaigne.[2]

Certainly, those who watch us from afar, and who see us through the fanciful tales of vain sailors and of acclimatization philanthropists, believe we live in the best of all possible worlds.

Now, what would be useful from the standpoint of future acclimatizations, would be to fully know the impressions of the poor dead Eskimos. They have not, as far as I know, left behind a sentimental notebook as the heroines of the courts of assize do. They must have died, like most variolous people, quietly, in the state of prostration which usually follows the great fever. It is true that they did not need to show their faces in public.

What if we did a little investigation? What if we appointed a commission, a sub-commission and ad hoc agents to establish, after examination, what part of the responsibility each person should bear?

Because they are dead, poor souls, and it is someone's fault if they are not, at this time, gathered in the hut where they were born.

Since you were bringing them here, in our friendly and peaceful Republic, you needed to plan for these probable downsides. Why did you not have them vaccinated? Let this be a lesson.

---

[2] An imaginary land of easy and luxurious living.

What a chance that they were put up in this beautiful garden, where the air was not lacking. At least they did not experience the sad existence of large cities.

I have never been to the *Jardin d'acclimatation* without, along the way, a great expenditure of emotion and pity. Whenever I hear the voice of a wild beast, whenever my eyes meet those of the antelope, the aurochs[3] or bison, it seems that all these exiles must miss their native air. [...]

I come back to the Eskimos. Do you want me to tell you what I really think?

Despite our grand ideas about the brotherhood of man, I bet that many French stopped in front of the Eskimos simply out of curiosity and as if there were just a few new animals over at the bois de Boulogne.

Also, when these poor people succumbed to the terrible evil that has befallen them, the newspapers were satisfied with publishing this short snippet:

"The Eskimos of the *Jardin d'acclimatation* are dead!"

Just as it is written from time to time: "The giraffe died of consumption."

Oh sorry! Not so long ago, every morning, the health report of a phthisic monkey was published. But the Eskimos!...

Listen, the toys are so sophisticated that there is nothing new to see. We now need toys made of flesh and bone. When will a young Samoyed be displayed in Alphonse Giroux's window[4] ?

---

[3] Ancestor of the current breeds of cattle, now extinct.

[4] Alphonse Giroux (ca 1775–1848) specialized in paintings restoration and was an art dealer. He worked on the restoration of the Notre-Dame de Paris Cathedral.

Fig. 2 Saglek Fjord, Torngat Mountains National Park
(© France Rivet, Polar Horizons, 2009)

Fig. 3 Nachvak Fjord, Torngat Mountains National Park
(© France Rivet, Polar Horizons, 2009)

PREFACE

One hundred and thirty-three years will have been necessary for the Vicomte de Challans to finally get answers to the various questions he raised following the death, amid public indifference, of the *Eskimos*. How did they manage to attract the Eskimos to Europe? Why were they not vaccinated? Who is responsible for their demise?

The Vicomte de Challans would have been pleasantly surprised to learn that Abraham, one of the *Eskimos* and a 35 years old father, has indeed left a diary describing his thoughts and states of mind. Originally from the community of Hebron in Labrador, Abraham was a Christian and had been educated by the Moravian missionaries.[5] He was literate, played the violin, spoke English and some German words. Among the 35,000 individuals[6] who were exhibited in major European cities during the decades of ethnographic shows (1800–1958), Abraham is, to our knowledge, the only one who left a written testimony of his experience as an 'exotic showpiece.'

Shortly after his death, the diary Abraham had written in Inuktitut, his mother tongue, was returned to Labrador. Brother Kretschmer, a Moravian missionary in Hebron, translated it to German. English and French translations were also produced by the Moravian Church who printed them in some of its publications. Then, the story fell into oblivion for a century.

In 1980, the tragedy of the *Eskimos* resurfaced when Canadian ethnologist Dr. James Garth Taylor discovered a copy of the German translation of Abraham's diary in the Moravian Church

---

[5] The Moravian Church or the *Unity of the Brethren* is a branch of the Protestant Church that began in 1457 in Moravia (a region that is now part of the Czech Republic). Its main settlement is in Herrnhut, Germany. The first Moravian settlement in Labrador was established in Nain in 1771. The one in Hebron was established in 1830.

[6] Human zoos: The Invention of the Savage. [n.d.].

archives located in Pennsylvania (United States). It is through the article Dr. Taylor published in 1981 in *Canadian Geographic*[7] that the story of the eight Labrador Inuit who died in Europe was unveiled to the 20th century public.

Over the next 25 years, a few individuals looked into this tragedy, including German ethnologist Hilke Thode-Arora and Professor Hartmut Lutz and his students at the University of Greifswald in Germany. They studied Abraham's diary and tallied it with the diary of Norwegian Johan Adrian Jacobsen, who recruited the *Eskimos*. They searched in the Moravian archives, in 19th century newspapers as well as in the archives of Johan Adrian Jacobsen and Carl Hagenbeck.[8] Their work was published in English and in German, in scientific journals or in book form.

But to this day, nobody had conducted research in Paris where five of the eight individuals died. No one had yet tried to answer the questions: What happened in Paris? Where were the *Eskimos* buried? They had to have left evidence of their presence in Paris. Where were these traces?

These are some of the questions I have been trying to answer since 2010.

My adventure began in the summer of 2009, during a cruise along the Labrador coast. As the Lyubov Orlova was leaving St. John's harbour, I noticed a photographer with two Canon cameras around his neck. The next day, when he appeared with a woolen 'Pang hat' identical to mine, I knew I had to talk to him. It turned out that it was Hans-Ludwig Blohm, a master photographer who had been travelling across the Arctic for more than 30 years. Hans and I became friends instantly (and we live a mere twenty kilometers from each other!).

As the ship approached Hebron, Hans briefly told me about the tragic story of Abraham and invited me to read the copy of *The Diary of Abraham Ulrikab: Text and Context*[9] he had donated to the ship's library. The book had been written by his friend Hartmut Lutz, the German version of it had been published by his sister and Hans' photos of Hebron and Nunatsiavut appeared in both the English and the German editions.

---

[7] Taylor, James Garth. (1981).

[8] The instigator of ethnographic shows and Jacobsen's partner in this venture.

[9] Lutz, Hartmut, Alootook Ipellie and Hans-Ludwig Blohm. (2005).

I was stunned by the story of these two families. I did not remember hearing about such practices where human beings were exhibited in zoos simply because they came from faraway lands.

In 1880, Abraham had agreed to cooperate in such a scenario to earn income that would allow him to pay the debts he and his late father owed the Moravian Church for the purchase of basic necessities. For him, this offer represented his best hope for the betterment of his family once back in Labrador. Unfortunately, they would never see their homeland again. The whole group was decimated by smallpox, less than four months after they set foot on European soil. Three of them died in Germany. The remaining five, including Abraham, died in Paris.

I was fascinated by this story, but it seemed incomplete. Since the book merely indicated that the *Eskimos* had been admitted to the hospital and had died, I sought, in vain, the chapter describing what had happened in Paris.

As we were disembarking, Hans was stunned to see Zipporah Nochasak, our Parks Canada guide, approach him with the ship's copy of *The Diary of Abraham Ulrikab* in hand. She had recognized Hans from a photo appearing in the book. Having recently discovered the book herself, Zipporah was still shaken by her reading of it. For her, it was clear that this group, especially 15 years old Nuggasak, had to be members of her family. Hans was simply astonished to be standing in front of a person who could possibly be related to the individuals who died in Europe 128 years earlier.

A few months later, Zipporah came to Ottawa. The three of us met and discussed Abraham's story. French being my mother tongue, and as I have always enjoyed conducting research and digging in archives, I promised them that I would try to trace information about the *Eskimos* in Paris.

Four years and three research trips to Europe later, you will find in the following pages the result of my work. What began as a fun activity to be conducted when time allowed, actually took an unexpected turn and became my full-time occupation.

I would never have imagined that this research would lead me to meet the curators, and to visit the reserves, of two French national museums; to cross the doorsteps of institutions that are usually closed to the public; to travel not only to Paris, but also to Hamburg and Tromsø with stops in Krefeld, Darmstadt, Frankfurt,

Berlin and Oslo; to meet with Nunatsiavut's Minister and Deputy Minister of Culture, Recreation and Tourism, ambassadors as well as other Canadian, French, and German diplomats; to run a crowdfunding campaign.

Every day I pinch myself to make sure this is all real. All those hours dedicated to researching the past have definitely resulted in increasing our knowledge of the 1880–1881 events. Isn't uncovering and telling the whole story the least that could be done so that the deaths of Abraham, his wife Ulrike (24 years old), their daughters Sara (3 years old) and Maria (9 months old), a young man, Tobias (20 years old), Tigianniak (45 years old), his wife Paingu (50 years old), and their daughter Nuggasak (15 years old) were not in vain? In Europe, the *Eskimos* entertained the crowds, and enabled entrepreneurs to pocket profits. They were studied by anthropologists who were thrilled to have 'savages' from these distant lands in their midst. Unfortunately, these eight individuals paid the ultimate price for their desire to improve their living conditions, and to see 'civilized' Europe.

What makes me most proud is that this effort spent searching for information in museums and archives, among other places in Canada and Europe, has led to an opportunity that could potentially change the course of Abraham's story. Such a possibility never crossed my mind when I initiated the research in 2010.

On more than one occasion, in his diary, Abraham expressed his desire to return home to Labrador:

> It is too long until the year is over because we would very much like to return to our country, because we are unable to stay here forever, yes indeed, it is impossible! [...]
>
> I do not long for earthly possessions, but this is what I long for: to see my relatives again, who are over there [...]

By the time you read these lines, the news of the discovery, in Paris, of the skeletons of Abraham, his wife Ulrike, their daughter Maria, Tobias and Tigianniak will have been made public. The possibility to turn Abraham's dearest wish to come home into reality is now conceivable. In addition, 133 years after their deaths, Abraham and Ulrike could be reunited with Sara, the 3-year-old daughter they had to entrust to a hospital in Germany when the group had to continue its journey to Paris. Sara's skull was located in Berlin.

In June 2013, during my visit to the Canadian Embassy in Paris, I was most surprised to learn that Canada's Prime Minister Stephen Harper and France's President François Hollande had signed, on June 14, 2013, the *Canada-France Enhanced Cooperation Agenda*[10] in which we find the following commitment in the 'Arctic and North' section:

> Work with the appropriate authorities to help to repatriate Inuit bones from French museum collections to Canada.

This statement was included specifically with Abraham and his group in mind. Therefore, the story does not end with the publication of this book. Instead, this book represents the beginning of a totally new chapter to be written in the months, or years, to come, as the descendants, the Labrador Inuit, Canadian, French and German authorities discuss the possibility of repatriating the human remains in Canada.

Reading through the following pages, you will discover the events that took place in the 19th century, both before and after the group's death. I hope to have respected my commitment to not judge these past events which may seem highly reprehensible when we look at them through our 21st century's eyes.

My goal in publishing this book is to consolidate the many documents, at least those I have found so far, associated with the sad story of Abraham Ulrikab and his family. May the original documents containing Abraham's own moving words, and those of his contemporaries, be of benefit to the Labrador Inuit community in their quest to learn the whole truth about — and finally close the loop on — the tragic events of 1880–1881.

My hope is for this book to enable us all to better understand the past and to allow the decision makers to make an informed decision on the potential repatriation.

I hope you will find this sad chapter in late 19th century history — a journey shared by Inuit, Canadians, French people, Germans and Norwegians — of interest.

May all participants involved in future decisions give a positive and constructive end to this story, and may this book inspire the

---

[10] Harper, Stephen. Prime Minister of Canada. (2013, June 14).

Inuit youth to learn about their past and to tell the stories of their predecessors. There has to be many more fascinating tales waiting to be uncovered and brought to light.

Thank you! Nakkumek!

France Rivet
Gatineau, Quebec
May 2014

A FEW NOTES

Before you move on to reading Abraham's story, I would like to make a few clarifications which may prove useful.

MORAVIAN DOCUMENTS

First, it should be noted that the present book provides only a portion of the documents preserved in the archives of the Church of the Unity of Brethren (Moravian Church). It was unrealistic for me to tackle such a task since these archives are mostly written in German and I have no knowledge of the language. Furthermore, for the past few years, other researchers have already been going through them with a fine tooth comb. For the time being, I have limited myself to include the English and French language Moravian documents I have uncovered. I must express my appreciation to Professor Hartmut Lutz for allowing me to reproduce the English translations of the Moravian records he published in his book *The Diary of Abraham Ulrikab: Text and Context*. Although not exhaustive, together, these documents nonetheless provide a good overview of the Moravian vision of the events. Hopefully, a comprehensive Moravian view of the story will be published in the not too distant future. One of the outcomes I am most looking forward to is to read a profile of the eight individuals, their families, and their communities before their departure for Europe.

THE SPELLING OF NAMES

In 1880, the Inuit did not have a last name. To distinguish individuals with the same first name, the custom was, for unmarried people, to append the first name of their father to their own and, for married people, to append the first name of their spouse. Abraham Ulrikab therefore means 'Abraham, husband of Ulrike.'

That said, when the group arrived in Europe, the adults of the Christian family were assigned the name of their father as a surname. On European soil, Abraham became Abraham Paulus (although he continued to sign his letters and his diary Abraham followed by the name of his wife). Ulrike became Ulrike Henocq. Tobias, Tobias Ignatius. Abraham's daughters took the last name that was assigned to their father and became Sara Paulus and Maria Paulus.

As for the non-Christian family, no last name was assigned to them in Europe. They were known by their first names only. After consultation with the Inuktitut specialists of the Torngâsok Cultural Center in Nain, it was decided that, for our purpose, we would spell their names as per the new Labrador Inuktitut writing system: Nuggasak, Paingu, and Tigianniak. That said, to respect the authenticity of the historical documents, we have reproduced the names as they was spelled by the author. You will therefore see them spelled in a multitude of ways whenever a document is being quoted.

Nuggasak: Nochasak, Noggasak, Nokassak, Nogasak, Nogosak, Roggasack, etc.

Paingu: Paingo, Pangu, Bairngo, Bangu, Baignu, Beango, Paieng, Paceng, Païeng, etc.

Tigianniak: Terrianiak, Terrianniak, Teggianiack, Tiggianiak, Tigganick, Teregianaik, Täggianjak, Tereganiak, etc.

When the spelling might cause some confusion, the name is followed by the Inuktitut spelling placed within square brackets.

QUOTATIONS

Since my goal is to provide access to the original writings, this book contains a large number of quotations.

To allow a quick visual identification of these excerpts, quotations from Johan Adrian Jacobsen's diary are surrounded by simple lines; those from Abraham's diary are surrounded by a shaded box, while the ones from newspapers are surrounded by double lines. Quotations from other sources are simply indented.

In all extracts from Jacobsen's diary, parentheses (...) are Jacobsen's own. So are words that are crossed out, underlined or written in larger font.

Similarly, all parentheses that appear in extracts from Abraham's diary are those of Brother Kretschmer.

JACOBSEN'S DIARY

When Johan Adrian Jacobsen started writing his diary in 1880, he decided to write it in German, a language he did not fully master. Even though he did his very best, the result is a unique mixture of German, Norwegian and Danish. In order to ease the understanding of the text, we took some liberties with our English translation. For example, we corrected the spelling and syntax errors, and made sure to spell people and places' names consistently. Nevertheless, the phrasing still reflects Jacobsen's somewhat chaotic language.

This book contains only a selection of the most significant excerpts from his diary. For those of you who would like read the many other details Jacobsen provides, Polar Horizons has published his entire diary separately under the title *Voyage With the Labrador Eskimos, 1880–1881*.

ESKIMO VERSUS INUIT

All 19th century texts included in this book reflect that era's common usage of the term *Eskimo*. In the hope that readers will remain in the atmosphere of past centuries throughout the book, whenever our own words refer to the group of Inuit who were exhibited in Europe, we also use the word *Eskimos*, but we made sure to write it in italics.

The term Inuit is used in all other circumstances.

PHOTOGRAPHS OF THE *ESKIMOS*' REMAINS

Should any visual representation of the remains of the 1880 Labrador Inuit be released publicly? How would the community, and potential descendants, react if such images were to be released? To help answer the question, Nain's elders were asked to provide their advice. The consensus was quickly reached: No!

So, if you are hoping to find a photograph of the Inuit's remains, you will be disappointed. There are none in this book. A couple of photographs showing anonymous skeletons have nevertheless been included for the purpose of giving a feel of what the anthropology galleries looked like at the end of the 19th century or early 20th century.

Fig. 4 Carl Hagenbeck, ca 1890
(Wikimedia Commons)

The Beginnings of Carl Hagenbeck's Ethnographic Shows

Hamburg (Germany), 1874. Carl Hagenbeck, a merchant of exotic animals and a menagerie owner, was preparing to bring to Hamburg a herd of reindeers from Lapland. His revenues had dropped and he needed to find a solution. His friend, wildlife painter Heinrich Leutemann, proposed the idea that it may be quite picturesque to also bring a Lapp family. Hagenbeck loved the idea and immediately sent the order for the reindeers to be accompanied by their breeders.[11]

Fig. 5 Heinrich Leutemann, ca 1880
(Wikimedia Commons)

---

[11] Elliot, Hugh S.R. and Thacker, A.G. (1912). p. 16.

A few months later, three men, one woman and two young children arrived in Hamburg with the reindeers. Hagenbeck described them as follows in his autobiography:[12]

> Our guests, it is true, would not have shone in a beauty show, but they were so wholly unsophisticated and so totally unspoiled by civilization that they seemed like beings from another world. I felt sure that the little strangers would arouse great interest in Germany. [...]

> My optimistic expectations were fully realized; this first of my ethnographic exhibitions was, from every point of view a huge success. I attribute this mainly to the simplicity with which the whole thing was organized, and to the complete absence of all vulgar accessories. [...] The Laplanders themselves had no conception of the commercial side of the venture, and knew nothing of exhibitions. They were merely paying a short visit to the hustling civilization which they saw around them, and it never occurred to them to alter their own primitive habits of life. The result was that they behaved just as though they were in their native land, and the interest and value of the exhibition were therefore greatly enhanced. They took up their abode in the grounds behind my house at Neuer Pferdemarkt, and lived entirely out of doors. All Hamburg came to see this genuine 'Lapland in miniature.'

This first experience with ethnographic shows having proven to be quite lucrative, Hagenbeck brought a group of Nubians from Sudan, as soon as the Laplanders left. The Laplanders had impressed the crowds with their interactions with the reindeer. In summer of 1876, the Nubians impressed Europeans in Hamburg, Düsseldorf, Paris, and Breslau with their ability to ride horses and camels. Hagenbeck asked the Nubians if they would come back for the winter 1877–1878. They accepted and were exhibited in Frankfurt, Dresden, London, and Berlin (where more than 62,000 people came to watch in a single day).[13]

In the spring 1877, wanting to ensure that his exhibitions could be presented year round, Hagenbeck hired a young Norwegian, Johan Adrian Jacobsen and sent him to Greenland with the mission to bring back *Eskimo* families.

---

[12] Elliot, Hugh S.R. and Thacker, A.G. (1912). p. 16-17.
[13] Rothfels, Nigel. (2008). p. 84.

Jacobsen, 23 years old, was born and raised on the island of Risøya[14] in Norway. He was familiar with the challenges of navigation on the Atlantic and Arctic oceans. He had been sailing between the islands since his childhood and, in his adolescence, had spent many summers fishing and hunting in Svalbard in the High Arctic. Jacobsen's desire to travel the world had been awakened by his older brother, Jacob Martin who, at the age of 15, had left home to travel for several years before settling in Hamburg.

When he met Hagenbeck, Johan Adrian had recently returned from a 3-year stay in South America and was staying with his older brother in Hamburg.

"One day I heard of a countryman who had sold six polar bears to Mr. Carl Hagenbeck in Hamburg. Hagenbeck had given orders to make ethnographic collections of artifacts used by the Eskimo and to bring an Eskimo family from Greenland. But the captain was going to Novaya Zemlya,[15] where he could not get Eskimos; so I went to Hagenbeck and introduced myself and told him that I knew where the Eskimos were and could get them for him," wrote Jacobsen.[16]

"Do you trust yourself to do that?" Hagenbeck asked.

"Why not?" replied Jacobsen.

"You are my man. You shall travel!"[17] Hagenbeck said to the man who was to become one of his main collaborators for his ethnographic shows.

Jacobsen immediately boarded a Danish ship heading to Greenland. After unsuccessful attempts in Disco Bay, it was finally in Jakobshavn[18] that Jacobsen managed to hire six individuals: a young family of four, Caspar Mikel Okabak (36 years old), his wife Juliane Maggak (24 years old) and their two daughters Anne (2½ years old) and Katrine (1¾ years old) and two young single men, Heinrich Kujanje (28 years old) and Hans Kokkik (41 years old).

---

[14] Island located on the 70th parallel north, near the city of Tromsø.

[15] An archipelo in the Arctic Ocean north of Russia.

[16] Jacobsen, Johan Adrian and Adrian Woldt (1977). p. 220.

[17] Fienup-Riordan, Ann. (2005). p. 3-5.

[18] Now known as Illulisat.

The group moved into Hagenbeck's backyard, where the Laplanders had stayed three years earlier, before they went on tour to various European cities: Paris, Brussels, Cologne, Berlin, Dresden, Hamburg, and Copenhagen. In Berlin, Emperor Wilhelm I marveled at their ability to handle their kayaks.

Fig. 6 Emperor Wilhelm I observing the Greenlanders
Illustration by M. Hoffmann (Courtesy of Tierpark Hagenbeck Archives)

In mid-July 1878, the *Eskimos* were returned to Greenland while Jacobsen was already on his way to Lapland to gather another ethnographic collection and to recruit new subjects to exhibit. Nine individuals accepted his offer and were exhibited in Hamburg, Hanover, Paris, Lille, Brussels, Düsseldorf, Berlin, and Dresden. The group was still in Europe when Hagenbeck asked Jacobsen to go to Le Havre to greet three Patagonians.

Hagenbeck's ethnographic shows were doing well and offset the losses of his trade of exotic animals which was suffering.

In the fall of 1879, Johan Adrian Jacobsen wrote in his diary that he and Carl Hagenbeck were discussing recruiting *Eskimos* once again in the hope of repeating their 1877–1878 success. They considered recruiting Hans Hendrik,[19] a Greenlander who partic-

---

[19] Hans Hendrik (1834–1889), known under his native name *Suersaq*, was a Greenlander interpreter hired as a guide by various Arctic explorers. As far as we know, he would be the first Inuk to have published his

ipated in various Arctic expeditions. But, eventually, the two men realized that, if they wanted 'wild Eskimos,' they had no choice, but to get them themselves. At the same time, Jacobsen's older brother, Jacob Martin, was planning to acquire a ship to fish *haakjerring* (Greenland shark) along the coast of Iceland. So why not also use the ship to travel the world in search of exotic ethnographic objects and people to bring to Europe? Jacob Martin believed that he could acquire a ship for 15,000 marks. If they could get a ship for that price, Hagenbeck offered to use the ship to recruit *Eskimos*. He was willing to pay a third of the cost, and in return, collect a third of the revenue. He was confident their *Eskimos* would allow them to make huge profits.

Jacobsen accepted Hagenbeck's offer and the quest for a ship began.

---

memoirs (*Memoirs of Hans Hendrik, the Arctic traveller, serving under Kane, Hayes, Hall and Nares, 1853–1876*) in 1878. *Hans Island*, this tiny island disputed by Canada and Denmark was named in his honour.

Fig. 7 Johan Adrian Jacobsen, 1881
(Courtesy of Mrs. Anne Kirsti Jacobsen)

The Search for a New Ship

The Jacobsen brothers first headed to Glückstadt, on the Elbe River, to look at a ship. As they could not agree on a price with the owner, they decided to try their luck in Norway.

Johan Adrian left Hamburg on November 14, 1879. His first stop was in Stavanger[20] where he spent eight days. Unfortunately, all available ships were too expensive or simply could not be moved as they were already frozen in the ice. He had made his way to Bergen[21] when a telegram arrived requesting that he head to Kristiansund[22] to have a look at a ship that was for sale.

> I had already started to think that the whole thing was a venture that would ruin us, but my brother would not hear about my worries. As always, he had set his mind on something, he had no concerns and would not even think about whether or not it would pay off. So I had to go to Kristiansund where I arrived on December 1. Eight days later, I had bought the ship named the *Hevnegutten* (the revenge boy). (J. A. Jacobsen's diary, page 79)

Jacobsen purchased the ship, but was unable to bring it back to Hamburg, the Elbe River being frozen and the forecast calling for several stormy days.

Jacobsen, who renamed the schooner *Eisbär*,[23] hired captain Bang, a veteran skipper from Tønsberg with sailing experience on the Arctic Ocean. In an attempt to turn the trip to Hamburg into a lucrative business, Jacobsen purchased a shipment of gua-

---

[20] City located on the south-west coast of Norway.
[21] City located about 200 km north of Stavanger.
[22] City located about 500 km north of Bergen.
[23] *Eisbär* means 'polar bear.'

no.[24] One night, the ship took in a huge amount of water and more than 100 bags of ruined guano had to be thrown away. The ship was brought back to the shipyard to find the leak. The repairs took about a month.

Finally, on February 18, the ship was ready and left Kristiansund. En route for Hamburg, they faced several storms forcing them to often stop in search of shelter. They arrived in Hamburg on March 18, the date they had originally intended on leaving for their expedition.

Before they could be on their way, the ship had to be insured and equipped with different types of fishing gears. Also, now that the ship was under the German flag and in German possession, Jacobsen had to go to Berlin to get permission to keep Bang as the ship's captain. Taking all these unexpected expenses into account, the ship ended up costing them 28,000 marks, almost double the initial estimate of 15,000 marks.

On board the *Eisbär*, there were at least three other crew members: Mr. Gulliksen, a captain from Tønsberg who had sailed for a polar company, Mr. Christensen, who had several years of experience sailing the Arctic Ocean, and a navigator who remains unnamed.

Finally, on April 27, 1880, the *Eisbär* and its crew left Hamburg with the mission to recruit twelve to fifteen *Eskimos* ('wild' and 'tame'[25] ones) who would agree to come to Europe.

---

[24] Guano, the excrement of seabirds or bats that is used as fertilizer. In the 19th century, guano trade played a pivotal role in the development of modern farming practices.

[25] They mean 'Christianized.'

Jacobsen Attempts to Recruit in Greenland

The *Eisbär* headed to Greenland. At first, Jacobsen intended to participate in seal and whale hunting off the coast of Greenland. Unfortunately, their efforts yielded meager results, the temperature was uncomfortable with lots of fog and rain, ice prevented them from advancing and Jacobsen began experiencing health problems.

After a short stay on the East Coast of Greenland, they set sail for the West Coast. On July 6, the *Eisbär* finally arrived in Jakobshavn, where Jacobsen had assembled the group in 1877. His arrival did not go unnoticed and Jacobsen took up with his acquaintances.

> The ship was besieged by Eskimos from morning until evening; everybody from Jakobshavn knew me, of course, and wanted to welcome me, many to get schnapps. Okabak and his family, Kokkik was now married, and Kujanje (Hendrik) [Heinrich] had moved north to Rittenbenck and married there. (J. A. Jacobsen's diary, July 7, 1880)

According to Jacobsen, many of them were ready to follow him to Europe, but the Danish government refused him permission to bring anyone back.

> Today I received a letter from Godhavn. [26] It sounds rather unfavourable. I am not allowed to take along Greenlanders, because the inspector's office is not allowed to concede such a thing. However, I received permission to

---

[26] Now known under the name *Qeqertarsuaq*.

> buy 6 dogs, probably because there is a kind of dog dis-
> ease here, and he knows that most of the dogs will die
> anyway. Furthermore, I am allowed to buy 2 kayaks and
> 12 pairs of kamikker (boots) and up to 6 furs. But they
> were not available, because I asked for them every day.
> It is a shame that these poor Eskimos are tyrannized in this
> manner, because they all wanted to come along gladly.
> The woman[27] who had been in Europe cried almost daily,
> because she could not come along. Little Kujanje had
> gone to fetch his wife, he lived 9 miles from the colony,
> and he was fully determined to come along, but when
> he heard that the inspector had forbidden it, he was
> scared. If someone had gone along, they would have been punished.[28] (J. A.
> Jacobsen's diary, July 18, 1880)

A hypothesis to explain the Danish authorities' refusal is related
to problems caused in the community following the return of the
individuals who had travelled to Europe in 1877–1878:[29]

> Richly laden with gifts of every kind and with wonderful
> pay, the Eskimos returned to their home. Okabak invited all
> his fellow tribesmen in the Disko harbor to a huge party. He
> had purchased so much coffee, tea, sugar, flour and zwie-
> back that he could have hosted for days. Atop a large
> stone he lectured on his trip to Europe, which had, in fact,
> even led him to Paris; the lectures had no end. Who can
> wonder that no one wanted to go hunting anymore and
> that they all lay on their lazy skins and dreamed of travels in
> the South. Things got so bad that the Danish government
> prohibited taking Greenland Eskimos to Europe again.

Jacobsen went with his plan B: to try his luck in Cumberland
Sound[30] on Baffin Island.

---

[27] Jacobsen refers to Juliane Maggak, Okabak's wife.

[28] Extracts from Jacobsen's diary which appear as a superscript are
insertions that were subsequently added between the lines, most likely
by Jacobsen himself.

[29] Quote from author Günter Niemeyer from the book *Hagenbeck:
Geschichte und Geschichten*. See Rothfels, Nigel. (2008). p. 139.

[30] Cumberland Sound is an Arctic waterway located on Baffin Island,
west of the Labrador Sea. Pangnirtung is the only community established on the shores of this sound.

Thick fog until 11 o'clock in the morning. Then, it cleared up a little. Unfortunately, it revealed so much and such tightly packed ice that all penetration to the land had to be given up. I suggested we should bear west along the [coast] towards south, but the captain was of the opinion that there was nothing else to do but get out of the ice in the same direction and then try again further south. The ship was turned south to get out of the ice. All afternoon we drifted and sailed among ice, because it had grown foggy again. It has turned into a fresh breeze and the last two days were so cold that all the ropes are full of ice; the water freezes on deck. Thus, our high hopes were thwarted again. I have no high hopes either to reach land; the ice conditions are too difficult. All my courage is gone. Ruin remains the only prospect on returning home. (J. A. Jacobsen's diary, August 2, 1880)

From Cape Walers[31] to Leopold Island we have tried to reach the coast. Further south on Cumberland there is no hope to reach the coast. I have made the decision to steer south towards Labrador and make an attempt to reach the coast. (J. A. Jacobsen's diary, August 5, 1880)

An additional five days were needed for the *Eisbär* to reach the coast of Labrador. At 7 o'clock in the evening of Tuesday, August 10, 1880, Jacobsen's ship anchored in the port of Hebron, a small community of about 200 souls.

[31] Would Cape Walers actually be the Cape Prince of Wales located on the Ungava Peninsula near the village of Kangiqsujuaq (61° 37' 0" N, 71° 30' 0" W)? As for Leopold Island, it is located near Cumberland Sound (64° 58 '0 "N, 63 ° 23' 0" W). (Canadian Geographical Names Database)

Fig. 8 The *Eisbär*, 1880
Illustration by M. Hoffmann.
See Hagenbeck, Carl and M. Hoffmann. (1880). p. 10.

The Arrival in Hebron, Labrador

Upon his arrival in Hebron, Jacobsen visited the community and met with Brothers Kretschmer, Haugk and Schneider, missionaries of the Moravian Church. To his dismay, the missionaries did not take kindly to his project.

> The missionaries here do not seem to want to further my enterprise, as I had hoped. When I told them that I had brought Eskimos from Greenland to Europe, they all insisted that the people must have been spoiled for life, because taking a trip to Europe appears to be the same as ruining ~~the souls~~ of these people. (J. A. Jacobsen's diary, August 10, 1880)

> [I] Talked today to several Eskimos about going to Europe. Two families seemed to me to have decided to come along, if the missionaries were not opposed. I then asked those gentlemen missionaries. They said it would never work, because, first of all, they had no permission from their superiors in Germany; secondly, because of the Labrador or the Hudson's Bay Company and they then insisted firmly, that the people would be spoilt by it because the Eskimos are, as they said, a reckless people, etc. All of my counter arguments were in vain.
>
> However, the Eskimos are a people who possess no independence. Whatever the Europeans living in the country tell them is the law. Therefore, the missionaries had nothing more pressing than to forbid the Eskimos the voyage, and of course their order was lent a better ear than my offer, because I was, after all, a foreigner. However, there is one family who would come along, in spite of the prohibition, but they cannot persuade another to

come as well, and one family is just too little. I have made the proposal to him [the head of the family?], to penetrate further north with me and, if possible, to persuade the wild Eskimos to come along. But he said it would be of no avail, because the savages are spread out everywhere across the rocky mountains on caribou hunts and therefore difficult to find. They are also mistrusting suspicious of foreigners, because they are often cheated in trade with the schooners which come from Newfoundland ~~Labrador~~ to barter. (J. A. Jacobsen's diary, August 12, 1880)

Again, I spent all day trying to persuade the Eskimos to come along, promised a lot to the people, but still one is too scared to come along, because the missionaries have forbidden it. It is sad to see the people under the stick, suppressed so slavishly, and even more so, now that the Europeans show their power in such a manner. If our cause were not so well recognized and honorable, but thus it is a shame, because the missionaries all know Hagenbeck by name, and I have also shown them my power of attorney, all in vain. (J. A. Jacobsen's diary, August 14, 1880)

Finally, on August 15, after several days of efforts, Jacobsen managed to hire an interpreter, Abraham, to go to Nachvak, a fjord to the north, to try to recruit non-Christian families. As they were not under the influence of the Moravian missionaries, Jacobsen was hoping they would be persuaded more easily.

Our Eskimo interpreter is one of the most intelligent Eskimos I have met so far. He possesses a lot of knowledge, he writes a good hand, plays organ, violin fiddle, guitar, knows most countries and larger cities, speaks a bit of English, is a good sealer, dogsledder, etc. (J. A. Jacobsen's diary, August 16, 1880)

During his stay in Hebron, Jacobsen took the opportunity to visit ancient graves and gathered artifacts to constitute an ethnographic collection.

I got to know that very close by there are some old graves and, together with two of my crew members, I paid them a visit. They were old graves from pagan times, and I received explanations for a lot of things I did not know. Next to each grave, and partly also inside of it, the things are buried laid down, occasionally also inside the grave which had belonged to the deceased. It seems, however, that the items were broken before, because all containers were broken apart, even in places that were otherwise entirely secure. It is the custom among the Eskimos, that an item which belonged to a deceased, will never be used by others. Therefore, everything is carried to the grave and deposited on top of it. There, one finds remnants of kayaks, tents, omiaks (larger boats), and household items; in short, all the possessions left behind by an Eskimo. One could therefore still gather a rich collection in Labrador, if one has time to search, because the missionaries do not care about it. It is different in Greenland, where everything has been searched through by Europeans. I was quite surprised that all implements were made of wood and iron, only few of bone or stone. Indeed, I only found one spearhead of stone, and only a few insignificant implements of bone.

On margin: [32] I had examined the graves at various places in Labrador and taken along everything suitable for a museum. (J. A. Jacobsen's diary, August 11, 1880)

Jacobsen was satisfied with the quantity of items he mustered. Although he was initially surprised to feel no reluctance on the Inuit's part, he later admitted that he finally realized they did not like his practice.

On margin: Have noticed that, after all, the Eskimos do not like to see one messing around near the graves of their ancestors, probably more because of the spirits of their ancestors. (J. A. Jacobsen's diary, August 13, 1880)

[32] Extracts from Jacobsen's diary which are marked 'On margin' are insertions that were subsequently added on the margins, most likely by Jacobsen himself.

HEBRON IN LABRADOR.

Fig. 9 Moravian settlement in Hebron, Labrador, mid-19th century
A reproduction of a lithography by Moravian missionary Levin Theodor
Reichel. (Courtesy of the Archives of the Centre for Newfoundland
Studies – *Labrador Inuit Through Moravian Eyes.*)

NACHVAK FJORD

Monday, August 16 at 7 a.m., the *Eisbär* set sail towards Na-chvak Fjord. That same day, the Moravian missionaries in Hebron wrote a letter to the Unity's Elders' Conference[33] informing them of Jacobsen's visit and seeking guidance on how to react should such a situation arise again:[34]

Letter from the Hebron conference to UAC.[35]

August 16, 1880

To our astonishment, on August 10, a schooner flying the German flag entered our port. It was a Mr. Jakobsen from Hamburg who is travelling on behalf of Hagenbeck, the menagerie owner, and is looking for antiquities, etc., but at the same time, also for Eskimos in order to exhibit them in European cities. Originally, he had wanted to get heathens from Northumberland, but could not reach the coast be-cause of the huge amount of drift ice; so, he came to us from there within nine days.

We resolutely explained to him that we are neither allowed nor willing to help him so that our christened people are exhibited outside and looked at like wild animals in ex-change for money. But he could not share our reservations and could not see why we did not want to be useful in the interest of science, because the Eskimos would be gener-ously rewarded like those from Greenland, whom he took with him three years ago. In spite of our resistance, the re-

---

[33] An executive board (located in Germany) of twelve members elect-ed to oversight and administer all general affairs of the Moravian Church.
[34] Lutz, Hartmut *et al.* (2005). p. 3-5.
[35] Abbreviation for *Unitätsaeltestenkonferenz*: Unity's Elders' Conference.

cruitment took place and one family had already agreed. But, because he did not want to take with him only four persons, but from eight to ten, nothing happened yet. He will now try his luck in the Nachvak region. However, we would like to know how to behave in cases like this.

G. Kretschmer, W. Haugk, A. Hlawatscheck

P.S. The Eskimos' contribution to the mission £ 2.12 s. 4 d.

The three missionaries also recorded this visit in the mission's log, which, at the end of the year, was shared with all Moravian settlements. They wrote:[36]

August 10th. The *Meta*[37] arrived with Br. and Sr. Schneider[38] on board, on their way to Ramah to relieve Br. and Sr. Weitz.[39] On the same day the *Ice Bear*, a Norwegian ship sailing under the German flag, reached the harbor. The master, Mr. Jacobsen from Tromsø in Norway, was employed by the well-known collector of objects for ethnographical museums, Hagenbeck of Hamburg, who a few years ago exhibited some Greenlanders in Germany. After a few days he informed us that he wished to engage some eight or nine Eskimos from Labrador for the same purpose, and could not see why we should object to our people accepting his offer. We were, however, very glad when he left us on the 16th to proceed to Nachvak, where he hoped to procure some heathen natives to take with him to Europe.

Three days of navigation were required for the *Eisbär* to reach Nachvak Fjord where it arrived in the evening of August 18.

Steered into the fjord. The maps are totally useless here, because they are designed totally wrong, and our interpreter has never come as far north. At 12 o'clock mid-

---

[36] *Periodical Accounts Relating to the Missions of the Church of the United Brethren Established Among the Heathen.* (1881, December). p. 448.

[37] The *Meta* was mainly used by the Labrador Moravian Mission for keeping up the communication between its local mission settlements.

[38] Missionary Johann Georg Schneider and his wife.

[39] Missionary Samuel Weiz and his wife.

night we anchored at 8 fathoms depth. We fired several gunshots at first to see if any people were nearby. We soon saw light and received an answering shot, and since the depth was alright, we dropped our anchor. So there must be Eskimos in the vicinity. [...] Will therefore make new attempts tomorrow, to acquire people. (J. A. Jacobsen's diary, August 18, 1880)

Fig. 10 HBC post at Nachvak Fjord, ca 1910
(McCord Museum MP-0000.637.8)

Went on land at 7 o'clock with my interpreter and one sailor in a direction where we saw smoke. There were four families present and we learned from these people that they are the only inhabitants of Nachvak because the others had moved inland and would only return in October. They were now hunting caribou; the meat and fat are dried and kept for the winter. These were all older people; only the young ones go into the inner land. Because hunting is too tiring, they are left behind. They now subsist on catching trout, of which there are many here, and in exchange for tobacco and matches you can get a lot of trout. I invited the people to visit our ship, and at noon had all four families on board. I fed them well, and after that I made them the proposal to come along to Europe. In the beginning no one would, but my interpreter knew how to persuade the people (I had promised him a new suit if he could convince somebody to travel with us) so one family at last decided to come along. It was a man, an older woman, and their daughter. But from where will I get the others? (J. A. Jacobsen's diary, August 19, 1880)

In his book *Eventyrlige Farter, Fortalte for Ungdommen*[40] published in 1894, Jacobsen offered a slightly different version of his first encounter with the Inuit from Nachvak and provided additional details.

One stormy evening we were in Nachvak Fjord. None of the indigenous villages were marked on the map, so we did not know if the region was inhabited or not. It was dark, the fjord was full of violent waves, and black clouds chased each other in a mad race across the sky. Every once in a while a giant rain shower would rush in. We constantly took soundings /and moved [?]/ with reefed sails. Finally, I hit upon the idea to fire a rifle shot. To our delight it was answered a short while later, and /from close by/, from the coast on the right. We fired again, and after several shots and answering shots from the land, we could finally drop anchor in a small bay, where the water was fairly calm.

Soon after, a boat filled with Eskimos came out to us. They immediately climbed on board without showing the least sign of fear. They were wild guys, at least judged by their looks. The men wore their hair long, hanging down to their eyebrows, and in the back it flowed unkempt and wild over their shoulders. Short jackets of reindeer skin and sealskin trousers were their traditional costume. The women wear a jacket of sealskin which reaches down to their ankles in the back somewhat in shape like a beaver's tail. The hair is braided and rolled up around the ears; braided into the hair they wear a long dangling tassel of pearls, which often hangs down over the shoulders in more than half an ell's length.[41] The forehead is

---

[40] Jacobsen, Johan Adrian. (1894).

[41] An ale (in Danish) or Elle (in German) is the length between wrist and elbow. Half an ell would be about 6 inches (15 cm). (Translator's note)

tattooed with stripes, running parallel with the eyebrows. The rest of the traditional costume: pants and short boots.

Since the language of these Eskimos is rather similar to that of the Greenlanders, we could soon make us understood to each other, and so we learned that we were in the vicinity of a trading post belonging to the Hudson's Bay Company, and because of that, all the Eskimos were supplied with weapons.

We treated them to salted meat, hardtack, butter and tea. One after the other of the savages tasted the salted meat, but all of them together spat it out again immediately, exclaiming: "Tara juk!" (Too much salt!). But the tea and the hardtack they seemed to enjoy excellently.

In the afternoon of August 19, Jacobsen visited the Hudson's Bay Company (HBC) post manager in Nachvak, George Ford.[42]

The two men quickly hit it off and Ford took such interest in Jacobsen's project that he had a long discussion with Abraham and managed to convince him to go to Europe with his family. However, Abraham imposed a condition: for Jacobsen to ensure that food would be delivered to his mother during the year he would be away. Jacobsen exulted:

Mr. Ford has now talked at length to my interpreter and he obtained his promise to go to Europe with me, provided I supply his mother with provisions until he returns next year, which, of course, I promised immediately. So we have to return to Hebron to fetch his family. I am very pleased about that and I am convinced that, despite my many efforts, I would not have succeeded in persuading him to come along without Mr. Ford's help. He speaks the language well because he was born in Labrador of English parents. In the afternoon I was at an old burial site, also found a number of things like household utensils, etc. Returned to our ship, only Ford accompanied us on board, where we arrived at 9 o'clock at night. Mr. Ford

---

[42] George Ford was born in Labrador in 1857, a year after his parents arrived from the United Kingdom. George joined the HBC in Nachvak in 1877. He remained there until 1908. He died of the Spanish flu in 1918 in St. John's, Newfoundland and Labrador.

spent the night on board. I bought various items from him, like clothes, etc. Calm and clear sky in the evening.

On margin: In my delight about Abraham's promise to come along to Europe with his wife and two children, Mr. Ford and I got solidly drunk. I was well equipped with wines, cognac, rum, and aquavit, and even though my captain Bang had secretly stolen a lot of it, there was still enough. I have repeatedly had the good luck to find people who helped me with all their might. In 1877 it was Fleischer [Carl] in Greenland and now it is Mr. Ford here. Only his powers of persuasion succeeded in changing Abraham's mind. (J. A. Jacobsen's diary, August 20, 1880)

Fig. 11 George Ford and his first wife Harriet Merrifield (Courtesy of Them Days[43], extracted from Vol. 25 No. 4)

---

[43] Ford, Henry. (2000).

On August 21, accompanied by Abraham, Jacobsen fetched the non-Christian family who agreed to go to Europe. The family consisted of Tigianniak, a 45-year-old shaman, his wife Paingu, aged about 50 years old, and their daughter Nuggasak, aged 15. They boarded with, among other things, four dogs, a kayak and an old tent. The *Eisbär* weighed anchor on August 22 at 8 a.m. and was back in Hebron on August 25 at 3 a.m.

Fig. 12 Hebron's Moravian church
(© Hans Blohm, 1993)

Fig. 13 Nuggasak, Paingu and Tigianniak, 1880
Photo by Jacob Martin Jacobsen.
(Nederlands Fotomuseum)

THE DEPARTURE FOR EUROPE

The Moravian missionaries were appalled by Abraham's decision, but they could not force him to stay.

In a single day, the *Eisbär* was prepared for the Atlantic crossing and Jacobsen greeted five more individuals on board the ship. They were: Abraham,[44] 35 years old, his wife Ulrike, 24 years old, their two daughters Sara, 3 years old, and Maria,[45] 9 months old, and a young bachelor, Tobias,[46] 20 years old.

> At 9 o'clock in the evening we were ready, and at 11 o'clock our Eskimos came on board 'with gown and gear' as the saying goes, and all the Eskimos of half of Labrador came to the rendezvous; I believe, because the ship was filled with Eskimos. I had all of them be hosted well to put us in a good reputation memory among the Eskimos. Came to rest very late.
>
> On margin: The missionaries were not very pleased that Abraham, his family and his nephew Tobias were travelling with us. I, on the other hand, was totally enraptured.

---

[44] Abraham was born in Hebron on January 29, 1845, to Paulus and Elizabeth. He was baptized on February 25, 1845, and had at least four other siblings: Jonas born on January 19, 1848; Sabine born on November 5, 1850; Niccodemius born on February 4, 1854, and Niccodemius born on September 27, 1855 (the assumption is that the first born to this name died). See Microfilm 510, Library and Archives Canada.

[45] Maria Clara was born on November 9, 1879, and was baptized in Hebron on December 26, 1879. See Microfilm 510, Library and Archives Canada.

[46] Some writings indicate that Tobias is a nephew of Ulrike, others a nephew of Abraham, others that he is simply an unmarried young man from Hebron. Further research is under way to confirm if there is a relationship between Tobias and Abraham or Ulrike.

It came very close for the great financial investment we made to be wasted (the cost of the expedition had amounted to something like 30,000 marks). My feeling of honor was also at risk, as I, who had so to speak, planned and organized the whole project, should never have miscalculated so badly. Often during the summer I had been close to despair. (J. A. Jacobsen's diary, August 25, 1880)

The *Eisbär* weighed anchor for its transatlantic crossing on August 26 at 7 a.m. with eight new passengers as well as 9 adult dogs, 8 puppies and 5 kayaks plus the crew.

That same day, Brother Kretschmer wrote a letter to Brother Connor in Germany:[47]

August 26, 1880

Dear Brother Connor,

Now something quite new and special. The vessel *Eisbär* (Polar Bear) from Hamburg, which was here recently, returned from Nachvak yesterday and got only one family from there. Now, however, one family from here decided to go along after all, the married couple Abraham and Ulrike (brethren in the Lord's Supper). I told them that we absolutely cannot allow our baptized people to be exhibited like wild animals outside in Europe to gain money. They could not, however, understand our reservations, did not want to upset us, but were unable to refuse Mr. Jakobsen. In addition, they were promised daily earnings of three shillings per man, two shillings per woman, and one shilling per child. That will make quite a lot, if the promise is kept and they would return next year with a payment and presents. I told them that we did not in the least begrudge them to see so many beautiful and great things in Germany, but that we had to despise this way towards the goal. But no Eskimo can understand that it should be bad for him to receive pay from somebody who wishes to see him. Moreover, the desire for European splendours is too strong, and besides, Abraham intends to see all Labrador missions and the congregations Herrnhut, Niesky and '...' In any case, you will be informed from Hamburg about their arrival. Since we

---

[47] Lutz, Hartmut *et al.* (2005). p. 5-13.

were entirely opposed to this, we neither could nor would
sign a contract with Mr. Jakobsen. Therefore, we are not responsible for any good or bad consequences that may still
occur. Mr. Jakobsen regretted not to have bought it[48] before and to not have previously inquired in Berthelsdorf (he
had not even wanted to come to Labrador, but to Cumberland). Now, however, there was no time. I briefly asked
him not to give them any alcoholic beverages and to su-
pervise them so that they may not see anything evil, etc.
This morning he sailed away with them, very happy not to
have made the voyage in vain. Last night an unmarried lad
reported that he should and would go along as well. He also went along this morning, and is of an audacious character, anyway. But they are free people and we cannot hold
them.

Without doubt the dear brethren and friends in and outside
the congregation will be rightfully indignant when it is
made public in the newspapers that Eskimos from Hebron
are exhibited publicly in the zoos of Berlin, Dresden and Paris. We can attest, however, that while it is happening with
our knowledge, it is entirely happening against our will. To
excuse the Eskimos it must be stated that they cannot understand our reservations against the trip; they are upset
that we could not say yes, but it is too much for them to let
go of all the pleasure and riches hoped for. Last winter
Abraham and his family suffered great poverty and would
still not be helped from the alms box. Next winter he will be
in for the same since he gained very little in the spring and
could not repay his debt of 10 £. Therefore, he now wants
to be given money in Europe for a net so that he can then
repay his debts. He also wishes to see Herrnhut, Niesky, and
Schalke (?) together with his wife, and Mr. Jakobsen has
promised him this. Should he really make it there, we would
like to ask you not to treat them in any repulsive manner as
disobedient ones, etc., which would do more harm than
good because they would only think that we begrudged
them the good luck to see so much beauty. We would like
best if they could be spoken to by brethren from Labrador
(Abraham is personally known to Brothers Kern, Elsner,
Linder, Sister Erdmann). He plays the violin, the clarinet, the

---

[48] This sentence is not clear. What did Jacobsen regret not to have purchased?

guitar, understand a little English. His wife Ulrike, aged 24 years, a well-behaved person, was never excluded, served for four years with us as housemaid, a good pupil with Brother Erdmann, knows a little German.

The heathen family from Nachvak were planning to move to Rama next winter to be converted. The man is called Terrieniak (fox), the woman Paingu (homesickness), the child Nachosak, about whom you can read in the diarium of Rama for the year 1876. Eventually, we shall learn next year whether these people or ours were considered alike, whether a difference was observed between the baptized and the heathen. The fact that the Eskimo know that Greenlanders were in Germany three years ago also added much to make such a visit desirable, and, had the ship stayed longer, many more would have registered to go along, because they are children and suspect no evil, but always expect the best.

Shouldn't it be good if some of this were made public in the *Herrnhut*?[49] Please act accordingly to what you deem best. May the Saviour protect them in the world and may He let serve for the best even this crooked way. We fear they will be difficult people for us afterwards, but even in this, His will be done.

Best wishes to you and all your dear colleagues.

Your humble Brother B. G. Kretschmer

A few days later, on August 30, it was missionary Samuel Weiz's turn to express his concerns:[50]

[...] I did not manage to see these people before their departure, but my colleagues have done all that was in their power to retain them in Labrador. Everything was useless, and we cannot and do not want to use force. The only thing left for us to do is to recommend them to the Good Shepherd, begging Him to watch over their souls. In all likelihood, these poor people will be, after their return, a pernicious element among our herds, and create many difficulties for the missionaries.

---

[49] Moravian magazine.
[50] *Les Esquimaux en Europe.* (1881, March 6). p. 105.

The 1881 *Periodical Accounts* provide additional information on the fears haunting the Hebron missionaries as they watched the *Eisbär* sail away:[51]

[...] We regret to have to add, that a number of Christian Eskimoes from Hebron, comprising a man with his wife and two children, and an unmarried man and three heathen natives from Nachvak, have been brought to Europe, and are at present being exhibited in the Zoological Gardens at Berlin. The prospect of seeing something of the world, and earning plenty of food and money without hard work, was more powerful than the arguments and exhortations of the missionaries. The head of the Christian family, Abraham, is an unusually clever Eskimo, who plays the violin, and has already picked up some knowledge of German: he is said to have imposed upon his employer the condition that during his stay in Europe he shall be taken to Herrnhut. For the degrading side of such an exhibition of themselves they had no feelings; still less was it possible for the missionaries to open their eyes to the moral dangers to which they would be exposed in Europe, and which proved very injurious to a company of natives of North Greenland similarly exhibited in Germany some three years ago. The future of such persons is very gloomy. Unaccustomed to daily toil for their food in the fashion of the country, with constitutions more or less unfavourably affected by the unwonted clime and mode of living, such travellers return to their home all but incapacitated for the resumption of the old life. As long as his money lasts, the Eskimo will, on his return, probably revel in idleness, and then sink into poverty and misery. In view of these present and future dangers, the anxiety of the missionaries on behalf of these members of their flock cannot be surprising, and we may be sure that they will be the subject of many prayers at Hebron.

---

[51] *Periodical Accounts Relating to the Missions of the Church of the United Brethren Established Among the Heathen.* (1881, December). p. 448-449.

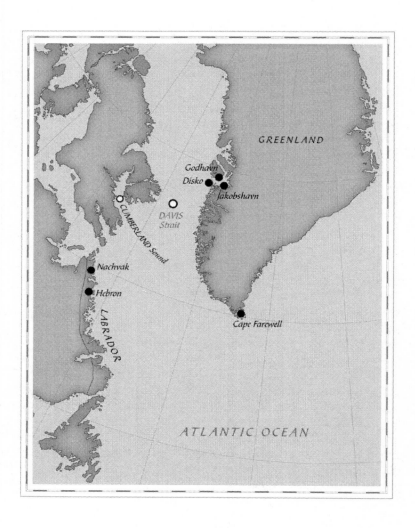

Fig. 14 Geographical map of locations in Labrador or Greenland
(illustration by Diane Mongeau, 2014)

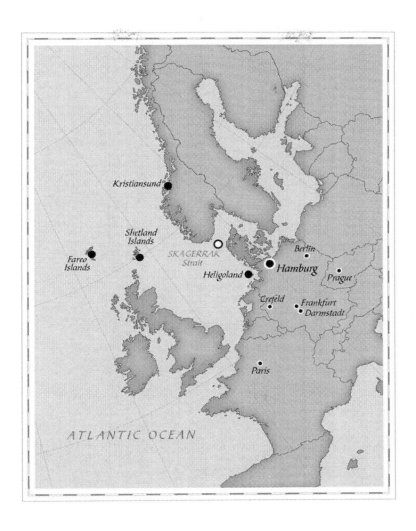

Fig. 15 Geographical map of locations in Europe
(illustration by Diane Mongeau, 2014)

Fig. 16 Abraham's family, 1880
Ulrike holding Maria on her knees, Tobias, Abraham and Sara.
Photo by Jacob Martin Jacobsen. (Moravian Archives, Herrnhut)

THE CROSSING OF THE ATLANTIC

Seasickness rapidly affected the *Eskimos* and Jacobsen thought they had to greatly regret having been persuaded to leave their beloved Labrador. Nuggasak was the one suffering most from the effects of the sea.

The journey was barely in its fourth day when the *Eskimos* started asking Jacobsen how much longer the trip would last.

> Even with this beautiful wind, if it continued to blow like today, we could not be in Hamburg for another month. [...]
>
> On margin: I tried everything to solace/comfort my Eskimos. We have installed a comfortable (living) room below deck for the people. Instead of the hatch, we have fashioned a so-called 'Kashpe,' so that the people can go up or down at any time. We have also constructed a good staircase instead of the previous ladder, so they can walk well on it. (J. A. Jacobsen's diary, August 30, 1880)

On September 1, 1880, they passed Cape Farewell, the southern tip of Greenland and, September 4 was the first quiet day during which no one suffered from seasickness.

> The Eskimos are beginning now to exchange their seasickness for boredom, and they are forever asking whether we are not going to see land soon. They also see daily that we are fixing our position, and asked one of the sailors, who was at the helm, what there was to see in it [the sextant]. The good-for-nothing said that one could see Hamburg through the octant and how far it was. The Eskimos tried it as well, could not find out where Hamburg was located. (J. A. Jacobsen's diary, September 13, 1880)

On September 9, they passed the western tip of Iceland, the 23rd meridian west of Greenwich, and on September 15, they sailed along the Faroe Islands. Three weeks to the day after their departure, they saw land for the first time. It was Foula, the westernmost of the Shetland Islands, an archipelago located in the north of Scotland.

Europe was so close; yet, another week of sailing was required before they could finally make their entrance into the Elbe River.

On September 22, 1880, at 7 a.m., Johan Adrian Jacobsen reported that Heligoland, an archipelago in the North Sea located 62 km from the mouth of the Elbe River, was in sight. Twelve hours of navigation were required to reach it.

Fig. 17 Heligoland, ca 1890–1900
(Wikimedia Commons)

It started storming and it was likely we would run aground on the coast of Schleswig.[52] The reason for our coming so far east was that our chronometer was not working correctly. We travelled with as much sail as possible and we

[52] Refers to the Duchy of Schleswig located in north-western Germany near the Danish border.

succeeded to reach Heligoland at 7 o'clock in the evening, where we dropped anchor. Right afterwards the
wind jumped to NNW. Strong wind. Decided to wait until
2 o'clock in the morning, so we would not enter the Elbe
River too early. I had told the Eskimos that we were in the
danger of running aground. Right afterwards I went into
the cabin, and all of a sudden I heard a terrible screaming. I hurried on deck fast because I thought that someone had gone overboard or had been hurt some way.
Here I was presented with a rather surprising spectacle.

The pagan Eskimo ^{Terrianiak} stood at the bow of the ship,
gesticulated with his arms, and uttered one howl after
the other. At first I thought that he had suddenly turned
mad. We stood all around him and did not know what to
do with him. His voice sounded through the howling of
the storm, like that of an unfortunate person in extreme
danger of death. Then one of the other Eskimos stepped
forward and said we should leave him in peace, because he was in the process of making magic, namely
for good wind. At the same time his wife sat in her cabin
and made the most wondrous gestures with her hands,
but uttered no sounds. After he had finished howling his
hexing formulas, he calmly went to his cabin with the
prophecy that we would have good wind. A few hours
later we really had good wind ^{north wind}, and Terrianiak
(that is his name and he is supposed to be well known in
his homeland as a great magician, an Angakok[53]), insisted firmly, that it was his own doing <sup>meaning that he had called the
north wind</sup>. I was really highly pleased that the guy had not,
^{contrary to what we had believed}, turned mad in the process, of
which I had been convinced in the beginning. But after
that our sailors believed that Terrianiak was a real magician because the wind had turned so suddenly into a
north wind from a SW storm. (J. A. Jacobsen's diary, September 22, 1880)

In his book *Eventyrlige Farter, Fortalte for Ungdommen,*[54] Jacobsen recounted this episode.

---

[53] Jacobsen used the Greenlandic spelling of the word. In Inuktitut, it is
spelled *angakkug*.
[54] Jacobsen, Johan Adrian. (1894).

In the stem of the ship stood the shaman – Terrianiak, the old red fox, was his name – with wild gestures, with his face turned against the storm, so that his long hair whipped like a mane in the wind, with raging shrieks and incantations, which again and again drowned out the storm's thundering. At the same time, another of the Eskimo sat in the hatch and made the most surprising movements with the hands, but in the deepest silence. Only after the shaman had carried on for a long time, so that he could hardly seem to have any more voice in his life, did he stop with his screaming and his gestures. When I asked him what his surprising behavior should mean, he answered ceremoniously that he had conjured the storm and that it would soon turn to our advantage.

Fig. 18 Tigianniak calming the storm, 1880
Illustration by M. Hoffmann.
See Hagenbeck, Carl and M. Hoffmann. (1880). p. 15.

THE ARRIVAL IN HAMBURG

The *Eisbär* weighed anchor and left Heligoland at night. Darkness preventing them from venturing into the Elbe River unmanned, they stopped at the lightship which stood at 7.5 km from the river's mouth.[55] A pilot boarded at 8 a.m. on September 23 to lead the group safely.

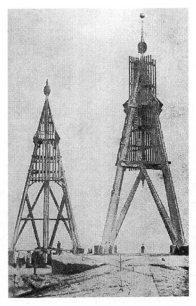

Fig. 19 Cuxhaven's new and old Kugelbake, 1867
(Wikimedia Commons)

---

[55] Back in those days, pilots would wait at the *Feuerschiff* or light (signal) ship lying at anchor before the mouth of the Elbe River. Since 1816, the lightship was positioned at the geographical coordinates 54° 0' 0" N, 8° 10' 40" known as 'Elbe 1.' In 1880, the lightship was the *Gustav-Heinrich*, a wooden three-masted schooner build in 1879 and named in honor of Gustav Heinrich Kirchenpauer, a bailiff in Hamburg. See Feuerschiff Elbe 1. [n.d.].

Around noon, the *Eisbär* made a stop in Cuxhaven, at the mouth of the Elbe River, where Jacobsen sent a telegram to his brother Jacob Martin in Hamburg informing him of their arrival.

Undoubtedly, they must have noticed the Kugelbake, the 30 meter high wooden structure, the main landmark of Cuxhaven marking the spot where the North Sea ends and the Elbe River begins. In 1880, the structure had been guiding sailors for almost 200 years.

At 4 p.m., they passed Glückstadt, a city on the right bank of the Elbe River, located approximately halfway between Cuxhaven and Hamburg, their destination.

At 9 p.m., Jacob Martin Jacobsen and Claus Gottfried Carl Hagenbeck, Carl Hagenbeck's father, boarded and accompanied the group until their arrival in Hamburg, on September 24, 1880, at 6 a.m.

Fig. 20 Hamburg Harbour, 1883
Photo by Georg Koppmann. (Wikimedia Commons)

The *Eskimos*, their luggage and the dogs were immediately unloaded and brought to Carl Hagenbeck's residence, at 13 Neuer Pferdemarkt Street, in the St. Pauli district; the same location where the Laplanders and the Greenlanders had been exhibited in 1874 and 1878, respectively.

Summoned by Carl Hagenbeck to come immediately to Berlin to meet him, Jacobsen left in the evening of his arrival. He met his partner the next morning at 6 a.m. at the Topfers Hotel. They briefed each other on the recent months' events and started planning the European tour.

> But Hagenbeck was happy beyond all measures that I had brought the Eskimos after all, and we forged plans, where we would be able to set up our Eskimo village first and with the greatest profit. After Hamburg we wanted to start first in Berlin, where we had been so very lucky in 1878 with the Greenlanders that Emperor Wilhelm I had looked at them. (J. A. Jacobsen's diary, notes added to page 139)

The two men headed to the Berlin Zoological Garden and paid a visit to painter and writer M. Hoffmann, hired by Hagenbeck to write and illustrate an account of Jacobsen's journey based on his diary.[56] Jacobsen headed back to Hamburg that same evening.

---

[56] Published under the title *Beiträge über leben und treiben der Eskimos in Labrador und Grönland*. See Hagenbeck, Carl and M. Hoffmann. (1880).

Fig. 21 Carl Hagenbeck's residence at 13 Neuer Pferdemarkt
(Courtesy of Tierpark Hagenbeck Archives)

THE STAY IN HAMBURG

For the next week, Carl Hagenbeck's backyard, a 6,226 square meter lot[57] and home to his menagerie, was buzzing with activity. All were working to build huts, to erect tents, and to set up the artifact collection assembled by Jacobsen.

A big sign *Carl Hagenbeck's Thierpark* adorned the front of his private residence. Visitors entered by the main door, went through a large corridor decorated with horns, skulls and antlers, and exited onto his backyard designed specifically to accommodate a wide variety of animal species. Small songbirds were present alongside tigers, polar bears and elephants. Usually, the animals were present for a few days or weeks, in other words, for the length of time needed by Hagenbeck to find them a new owner. It was not uncommon for his backyard to be the temporary home of nearly a thousand animals. Therefore, it was surrounded by wildlife from around the world that the eight *Eskimos* started their European tour.

The first visitors were greeted on October 2, 1880. Unfortunately, few details have been uncovered so far regarding the exhibition in Hamburg. Abraham had not yet started his diary. As for Jacobsen, his diary is silent for the period of October 4 to 27. He had been admitted to the hospital during that time to recover from various ailments that had affected his health during the summer.

The exhibition in Hamburg lasted twelve days. It was during this period that Jacob Martin Jacobsen took the official portraits of the group's members. These photos became the *cartes de visite* purchased by visitors in the various locations where the *Eskimos* were shown.

---

[57] Von Kuenheim, Haug. (2009). p. 58.

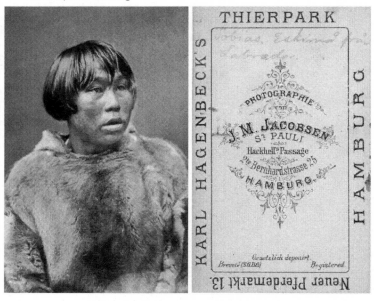

Fig. 22 Tobias' *carte de visite*, 1880
Photo by Jacob Martin Jacobsen. (Courtesy of Kenn Harper)

Carl Hagenbeck hired two other persons to accompany and take care of the Labrador people: Adolf Schoepf, a good friend of Johan Adrian Jacobsen from Dresden, and a lady, Mrs. Jacobsen,[58] who prepared their meals, did their laundry, etc. Jacobsen said of her:

> [...] she cares for the people like a mother. Since she has been travelling with them for years (she was also with our Greenlanders), she has received the name 'Anthropologenmutter' (anthropology mother). (J. A. Jacobsen's diary, September 25, 1880)

Since Jacobsen was incapacitated by health problems, it was Adolf Schoepf who took charge of the group in Hamburg. He

---

[58] In his diary, Jacobsen calls this lady, Mrs. Jacobs. However, based on various newspaper articles and other records, this person's name was Mrs. Jacobsen. We're assuming Jacobsen used an abbreviation in his diary. The identity of this person has not yet been fully uncovered, but for consistency purposes, we have therefore adopted the name Jacobsen.

followed them throughout their stay and Johan Adrian Jacobsen joined them when his health allowed it.

Fig. 23 Adolf Schoepf (left) and J. A. Jacobsen (right), 1909
(Courtesy of Dresden Zoo Archives)

Fig. 24 Berliner train station in Hamburg
(Wikimedia Commons)

Fig. 25 The hall of the Berliner train station
(Wikimedia Commons)

THE STAY IN BERLIN

On Friday, October 15, 1880, the *Eskimos* accompanied by Adolf Schoepf and Mrs. Jacobsen went to Hamburg's Berliner train station for the overnight trip to Berlin. Built in 1846, the station was, at the time, one of the most important wooden structures in Germany. The group departed at 9 p.m., covering the 284 km trip in nine hours. Abraham, who began his diary in October, wrote about his first experience with the railroad system:

> When we were travelling with steam, we were faster than flying. We always occupied (places) that are reserved for grand gentlemen. The train was so long[59] that there was a great distance between both ends. We were in the middle in a very nice house (a wagon), we could not close the windows in order to see, looking out was impossible because of the wind; my eyes were bad and swollen with seeing, although I hardly stuck my head out.
>
> [While we were travelling, our countryman Fox (Terrianiak) worked [his] magic quite exceptionally. Although he was in the beautiful steam wagon, he was extremely distressed by his witchcraft and could not smile at anyone, when we arrived.][60]

---

[59] Abraham was right to say that the train was long. On Wikipedia, we read that on this line, locomotives were pulling 33 passenger cars (first and second class), 43 third-class cars and one luxury car for VIPs. When Abraham said he travelled in the section reserved for grand gentlemen, we can image the group was seated in this unique luxury car. See Berlin-Hamburg Railway. [n.d.].

[60] The following note can be found in the right margin of Brother Kretschmer's manuscript: "The passage in square brackets [...] was

At 6 a.m. on Saturday, October 16, the train arrived at the Hamburger Station in Berlin.

Fig. 26 Hamburger train station in Berlin, ca 1850
(Wikimedia Commons)

An article published in the *Charlottenburger Zeitung* tells us that despite the gruelling overnight journey, on arrival, the *Eskimos* were in a good mood:[61]

The Hagenbeck Eskimo caravan has arrived. The caravan consists of 8 persons, who consider Labrador as their home, which science as of yet has little explored, and who differ in an essential way in shape, in habits and in customs from the Greenland Eskimos, who were presented to us by Hagenbeck two years ago.

crossed out, perhaps with an eye to readers in Europe. It is also possible, however, that it was crossed out in the original. (?)". This note suggests that the manuscript is not that of Kretschmer, but a copy by a third party (another Moravian brother?) who did not have access to Abraham's original diary.

[61] *Charlottenburger Zeitung*. (1880, October 19).

The caravan is divided into two groups, of which one consists of 34-year-old Abraham, his 24-year-old wife Ulrike, their daughters Sarah and Maria, and the 21-year-old still unmarried Tobias, who come from the Moravian colony of Hebron and already have acquired a pretty high degree of civilization; while the 44-year-old Teregeniak [Tigianniak] (German for fox), his 50-year-old wife Tägnu [Paingu] and 15-year-old daughter, Nokassak (reindeer) are native to Nachvak, lying far to the north, are still in a completely primitive state. Despite their strenuous travel during the night, the people were in the best mood and observed carefully everything that they encountered on the trip to the zoo. They were especially surprised by the tents with the row of beer gardens, and, shaking their heads, they repeated again and again with questioning looks the word 'beer.'

The zoological garden with its fine facilities made a noticeably surprising impression on the people, and Abraham, apparently the most intelligent of the caravan, said in a loud voice "A jong gni" (this is nice) while quiet Teregeniak expressed his feelings with a pleasing "Ananak" (good). Abraham is rather capable in English, can count in German and recite the days of the week. "Oblone Saturday" (today [is] Saturday), he said, and as he heard mentioned in passing the word Sunday. The caravan has 3 Labrador and 9 Greenland Kingmik (dogs) with them, enabling them to drive their sleds. They have also brought numerous kayaks (boats). Characteristic for the woman's costume is a peculiar tailcoat-like fur coat[62] and the hair decoration made of pearls, Zapangat, into which the front braids flow.

The caravan has moved into huts in the zoological garden, which are pitched by the pond near the restaurant area, and their interior arrangement characterizes the cultural state of each family.

---

[62] In Inuktitut, this 'peculiar' coat is called an *amauti*.

Fig. 27 Map of Berlin zoo, 1873
(Wikimedia Commons)

As for Abraham, he describes their arrival in Berlin as follows:

[...] We arrived in Berlin by means of the marvelous steam. At 9 p.m. we had left Hamburg, at 6 a.m. we arrived in Berlin at our house that we built ourselves; a beautiful house although only of boards. To wipe the floor of our house was nearly impossible because of all the people. Although they were thrown out by our masters, others quickly took their place. Between some trees we have a house. Nearby is a music house, a cause for astonishment. A lot of people wish to see our house, but it is impossible to be seen by all of them. Only a few have seen it, our masters even did not know whether we should ask someone in (or not). When the teachers came they were the first ones in, but not immediately, because it was impossible due to all those people. Our enclosure was often broken by the throng.

One day a great gentleman from Berlin came to see us and had many gentlemen with him. They all came into our enclosure to see the kayak, but immediately everything was filled with people and it was impossible to move anymore. Both our masters Schoepf and Jacobsen shouted with big voices and some of the higher-ranking soldiers left, but most of them had no ears.

> Since our two masters did not achieve anything, they came to me and sent me to drive them out. So I did what I could. Taking my whip and the Greenland seal harpoon, I made myself terrible. One of the gentlemen was like a crier. Others quickly shook hands with me when I chased them out. Others went and jumped over the fence because there were so many. Several thanked me for doing this and our masters also thanked me very much. Ulrike had also locked our house from the inside and plugged up the entrance so that nobody would go in, and those who wanted to look in through the windows were pushed away with a piece of wood.

It did not take long for the crowds and the constant noise to start bothering the *Eskimos*. This fatigue was actually the first thing Abraham noted in his diary when he started it around October 22.

> In Berlin, it is not really nice since it is impossible because of people and trees, indeed, because so many children come. The air is constantly buzzing from the sound of the walking and driving; our enclosure is filled up immediately. [...]
>
> Our fellowmen, the fox family (Terrianiak) stopped to be cheerful, because they are tired of the people. And we in the other house have been very patient, although we have also been greatly tired. Constantly in the evenings, we pray, wanting to be helped. This thing (our praying) also seems to achieve something within us.
>
> Some *Kablunat*,[63] some Catholics (?) laugh at us, but this did not make us tired, as their souls are also to be laughed at. To some of them, who were talking about us, I have even given answers often, as they could

[63] Inuit term to mean 'people who are not Inuit, typically white people, considered as a group.'

> speak English. Often, some of them were even horrified by our Northlanders[64]. Every day I have consistent work drawing people, Labrador and Nain.

Abraham also reported on a few of their interactions with the Berliners.

> The *Kablunat* (the audience) always take delicious things with them to treat us with; all kinds of things to chew, which they give to us, and big fruits, which even have juice (fresh fruits).
>
> On some days I have also played the violin outdoors, as the *Kablunat* wished it so greatly, even if I am not very good at it they don't mind. I was constantly told to write my name, occasionally, there were many voices, one always took it away from the other; to please them all was impossible, there were too many. [...]
>
> Sometimes we are given some money, sometimes two pence, sometimes one mark, sometimes 50 pence, sometimes 20 pence, also cigarettes every day.
>
> It is too long until the year is over because we would very much like to return to our country, because we are unable to stay here forever, yes indeed, it is impossible! It buzzes and roars day and night because of the rattling of the sleighs and the constant voices of the steam whistles.

Abraham's diary sheds light on their working conditions: the cold that makes them sick, the food that does not offer much of a variety, and, certainly, would not make any of us envy them.

> On Oct. 23, snow was falling all the time, the *Kablunat* are freezing; even we are freezing very much. [...]
>
> Daily we heard the voices of the canons very loud. But it is very easy to get sick with a bad cold; I am still quite well, although I have a badly running nose. But the daily work is getting hard due to indisposition, because our

---

[64] Abraham refers to Tigianniak and his family.

child Sara is ill, and because we all have to suffer; that is certainly difficult. That (Sara) has to stay alone is regrettable, but she herself does not complain, because she is already able to understand that it can't be any different. [...]

Nov. 7. Had sorrow again. Our companion, the unmarried Tobias, was beaten with a dog whip by our master, Mr. Jacobsen. (Mr. Jacobsen) was immediately furious because, as he said, Tobias never obeyed him and had got himself into trouble too often. He was nearly not taken and sent away. If Mr. J. does that twice I shall write to England as I am told. Afterwards, he was very friendly towards me so that I don't write. Even our two wives were immediately bought silken ribbons. If Tobias is frequently as stubborn, he won't get paid, but if he is nice, he will get greatly paid. After this incident, Tobias was very sick.

The pond on which we kayak around is very cold; we always have to get rid of the ice before we can kayak. At times there is a great cold. [...]

Meat (seal meat) we miss very greatly, let be, some of it is probably not very good, but that's what we mostly eat: coffee and rusk in the morning, codfish, potatoes, beer and ship cookies for lunch. Coffee and ship bread at 4 p.m. Tea, herring, beer and ship bread at 6 p.m.

Nov. 11. Few people. We got no money, because they were too few.

The episode where Tobias was hit by Jacobsen seems to have been an isolated incident which never reoccurred. Jacobsen made no mention of it in his diary.

On a few occasions, the group had the opportunity to leave the zoo's enclosure. One such occasion described by Abraham was their visit to the wax museum:

One day in the evening, us wearing big coats and shoes, we went to see things (the wax works) exhibited in a large house,[65] we drove there (sitting) in a house.[66] When we arrived, we went in and saw many people gathered there, – but – they only looked like people (at the wax museum); they looked so much like real people that you did not notice anything. Yes indeed, some of them even took breath, and some were moving, and all that from the inside, indeed, to name all is impossible. We also saw Napoleon's wagon, it had been brutally snatched from him during the war. And all sorts of rifles, indeed, they really looked like humans, of great diversity. Nubians, Africans we have also seen, and Chinese and Indians and Americans and Californians. Yes indeed, the inhabitants of the earth, very many did we see in Berlin.

Fig. 28 Kaiser Gallery housing Castan's Panopticum, Berlin, 1900
(Wikimedia Commons)

---

[65] Abraham refers to Castan's Panopticum, the wax museum located in the Kaiser gallery at the corner of Friedrichstraße and Behrenstraße in Berlin.

[66] The French translation of Abraham's diary published in 1883 clarifies that this house was in fact a tramway. See Notes de voyages d'Abraham, l'Esquimau. (1883).

The *Eskimos'* presence in Berlin obviously attracted media attention and numerous articles were published in local newspapers which provide insight on their performances and daily life.

Norddeutsche Allgemeine Zeitung, October 18, 1880

The Eskimos started their show on Sunday in the Zoological Garden to massive applause from an audience of almost 7,000. The most interesting part of the show is probably the seal hunt. In it, Tobias plays the seal to be hunted, wrapped in furs. As soon as Tareganiak spots him, he drops to the ground imitating the sound of a seal, crawling towards him. Finally the animal is in firing range, the rifle thunders, the seal is hit and the hunter jumps up cheering, ties a leash he has brought with him around the body of the shot animal, and trails it to the hut where wife, kids, and friends await him. Tobias and Tareganiak play their roles with great enthusiasm, and Tobias patiently lets himself be trailed along the ground as the shot seal. The hunt on water is just as interesting. The kayaks of the Labrador Eskimos differ enormously in construction and handling from the Greenlandic boats. All Eskimos present here, especially Tobias and Tareganiak again, play in these harpoon hunts of seals, salmon, and seabirds; further they go on sledges pulled by dogs and show their talents at snowshoeing – all of which highly amuse the audience.

Norddeutsche Allgemeine Zeitung, October 21, 1880

A visitor of the Zoological Garden tells the 'K. J.' how fond of children the Eskimos already are after having been here for only two days: Among the curious people coming to the Eskimos on Monday were also very many children, who tried to communicate with the Eskimos by language and gestures. It was already getting dark and the spectators had left, and also the Eskimos[67] had gone into their huts. Only Tobias, the 21 years old, not absolutely unhandsome boy, sat outside leaning against a tree. He was surrounded by a group of boys and girls who joked with him and asked many things. A young, maybe 10 years old boy with a

---

[67] The German text actually says 'Greenlanders.' (Translator's note)

pretty always smiling face, found the special favour of the northern son, who petted and caressed the clever boy for every
comment. He might have touched the boy a little rough; the
boy pretended crying and Tobias jumped up at once, put the
boy's head on his chest, and covered him with kisses. When the
boy looked up again, laughing heartily, Tobias joined him laughing after a while and caressed and kissed the boy again. Almost
by force the Eskimo had to be separated from the cheerful children, and only after the leader of the group indicated that he
will see the children tomorrow again, he said goodbye to his
Berlin friends for the day and retreated into the hut.

Neue Preussische Zeitung, October 23, 1880

In the Zoological Garden, Abraham Paulus of the Eskimos especially draws the attention of the visitors. He is seen as the most
educated of his fellows. Shortly before his departure to Europe
he mapped the coastline of Labrador with its many bays and
courses of rivers upon his own journeys. The sketch of the map is
currently   in   the   hands   of   the   director   of   the   *Jardin
d'acclimatation* in Paris who wants to present it to the Geographic Society there. Abraham is also very skilled in drawing
figures. Among others he did his self-portrait in watercolors, an
achievement that, clumsy as it may seem, would nonetheless
satisfy higher expectations in regard of likeness. Abraham also
plays the violin, writes, and reads the language of his country.

Norddeutsche Allgemeine Zeitung, October 23, 1880

In general, the Eskimos have already settled here and especially
the young Tobias made many new friends, welcoming them with
a friendly *iltarnemek* (hello). *Kamutik suicksak* (sledge ride) gives
him the biggest pleasure. Very fast he follows the *Kingmiks* (dogs)
with his 20 foot long *Herautak* (whip), of which you can hear the
Schiknbuk (cracks) very far. Abraham prefers *Nankatorit* (boat-
ing) to the sledge rides. Tereganiak is not fond of work at all; he
prefers devoting himself to philosophical contemplation: "*schila-
lok obleme, kaugbot schilake, kangsabot Sonntag, innuit onuk-*

tut!"(Bad weather today, good weather tomorrow, the day after tomorrow Sunday, many people then!), he told his fellow yesterday; and even one not knowing the language could hear how the thought of the excitement caused by each Sunday terrified him. The language of the Eskimos from Labrador differs substantially from that of the Greenlanders. The Labrador Eskimos do not seem to have any songs from their native country; when singing they use German tunes which have been translated into their language,[68] like: *Jarit dreissig inkasat, atik ulikatigi vagit* (You are already 30 years old and have survived many storms.)

Charlottenburger Zeitung, October 24, 1880

From the Zoological Garden. The polar bear of the Zoological Garden, which usually is known for its contemplative calm, has been showing truly febrile excitement since the arrival of the Eskimos.

As soon as an Eskimo approaches its cage, it runs with a loud grunt to the bars [of the cage] and seems to want to break through them to attack his natural-born enemy, whom it recognized despite its long captivity. Also, the Eskimos cause a huge uproar in the building that houses beasts of prey, but they are hard to convince to enter that building because of their insurmountable fear of lions and tigers. In general, the Eskimos have already settled quite admirably.

---

[68] This observation is a reflection of the influence of the Moravian missionaries on the Labrador Inuit's life and culture. In 1880, Moravians had already been spreading Christianity through Labrador for more than a century. They had also been discouraging the Inuit from performing their traditional drum dances and songs as they considered them to be pagan rituals.

Fig. 29 Scenes from the Berlin zoo, 1880, Part 1
(Wikimedia Commons)

Fig. 30 Scenes from the Berlin zoo, 1880, Part 2
(Wikimedia Commons)

Norddeutsche Allgemeine Zeitung, October 26, 1880

The Eskimos from Labrador, who are now presented to us at the Zoological Garden, are relatives of a rapidly dying people. All missionary stations of the Herrnhuter are populated by only 1,100 Eskimos after the last census. The population of Hoffenthal [Hopedale] alone has decreased by 18 in the last six months. Only a few children survive to their 6th year. In Nakvak, hometown of the heathen Tereganiak , there are only 11 families – about 40 people – left altogether, another heathen settlement counts about 100, and a third one about 40–50 inhabitants. One can almost predict the year when the people of the Labrador Eskimos will be entirely gone from earth.

Fig. 31 Abraham and Tobias in their kayaks, 1880
(Museum für Völkerkunde Hamburg)

One Sunday in early November, more than 16,000 people benefited from the day's reduced rates to visit the *Eskimos*. The last Sunday of their stay in Berlin, a real seal hunt was organized on the pond. The event attracted thousands of spectators.

On November 9, upon hearing that a seal was to be hunted and killed by the *Eskimos*, Hagenbeck expressed his reluctance to Jacobsen:[69]

> I have just received a letter from Mr. Schoepf in which he writes that the seal is to be hunted, skinned and consumed by the Eskimos on Sunday. I urgently ask you to skip the first part of the program, for I do not want the animal to be harpooned in the pond, the seal is just to be slaughtered [...] I am happy to hear that the old Pängna is better.

Hagenbeck's request does not seem to have been heard since a hunt was conducted on the pond during which Abraham, Tobias and Tigianniak demonstrated their hunting skills.

The seal hunt performance[70]

The seal hunt, which attracted thousands of people to the Berlin Zoological Garden, proved to be a most interesting show. In the night to Sunday, the seal escaped from the pond next to the Eskimos' camp, originally intended as a hunting ground, and took refuge in adjacent waters. Shortly after two o'clock in the afternoon, the Eskimos' kayaks were launched and the chase began. First, Abraham and Tereganiak went in search of the fugitive. Shortly after, it was spotted and their aim became to wear it out by pursuing it so that they could get it more easily. It is for this purpose that Tobias joined the hunters with his kayak. The seal was clever: he remained mostly underwater and resurfaced briefly from time to time and never where we expected it. It was interesting to observe the hunters. While Tobias, in his youthful excessive zeal, from the beginning, naturally unsuccessfully, tried to harpoon the agile seal and while Abraham, a pretty impatient hunter, unmethodically travelled the pond with his kayak, old Tereganiak remained seated in his boat, leaning over and calmly on the lookout. Right from the start, connoisseurs knew that he alone would be the winner. After about three quarters of an hour, the seal resurfaced a few steps from Tereganiak's kayak; harpoon within reach and grasped nimbly, a quick throw and the seal received the deadly iron spike right in its back. Loud applause greeted the hunter. He pulled towards him the rope

---

[69] Thode-Arora, Hilke. (2002). p. 7.

[70] Charlottenburger Zeitung. (November 17, 1880).

tied to the tip of his harpoon with the seal that had rolled over, giving Abraham, who had immediately come closer, the opportunity to deal the animal the death blow in the chest with the solid tip of his harpoon. The hunt was over and the hunters, loaded with their catch, retreated to their camp where Ulrike had lit a fire in the summer tent in front of the orchestra. A fur was spread, the dead animal was laid on it and they opened its chest. Tereganiak began skinning the animal of its skin and thick layer of fat. While Mrs. Bägnu with the Eskimo's semicircular knife separated the fat, Tobias and Tereganiak emptied the animal and cut the ribs – the only parts consumed – in pieces the size of a hand. After superficially washing them, the woman Ulrike, threw them into the pot of boiling water. The only condiment used is salt. The offal was given to the dogs who, now that they are spoiled, did not take notice of what was once their favourite meal. After about an hour the meat was tender; it was removed from the broth, almost black and emanating a powerful smell, and placed on a plate. The Eskimos, crouched around the plate, grabbed a rib with their left hand, and holding the piece tight between their teeth, they cut the meat (whose taste resembles that of hare) with the knife they held in their right hand. They ate it with obvious pleasure, and with a certain pride, gave the public some to taste. The show lasted three hours.

The *Eskimos*' presence in Berlin was also talked about in London where the religious newspaper *Sunday at Home* published a description given by a Christian visitor:[71]

The Esquimaux

We have had in Europe of late years, Red Indians, Zulu Caffres, Laplanders, and other natives of remote regions exhibited in public. While the motive in bringing them has been merely that of commercial gain, opportunity has been given to 'stay-at-home travellers' to see the appearance and habits of strange people. None of these have more interest for readers of missionary reports or books of ordinary travel than these Esquimaux from the far North. A Christian friend, who saw them last year at Berlin, gave the following description of them.

---

[71] The Esquimaux. (1881, May 21).

Here are presented to our attention in the first place the huts of turf; tents of the skins of whales; a cabin, whence howl some dogs resembling wolves; a small pond, on which is seen a single boat (a kajak) like a canoe for one person, covered with a skin pierced by a hole, through which the Esquimaux passes his body; lastly, some tackle for the chase or for fishing – things that give to the public an idea of the encampment of the Esquimaux of the polar regions. Soon afterwards the Esquimaux themselves appear out of their huts and devote themselves to various exercises, intended to supply the chase and fishing, as practised in their country. [...]

But what a difference among these eight Esquimaux all coming from the same country! It does not fail to strike the most superficial observers; in Terrianiak and his companions, the hair in disorder, dirt, eyes without expression, a stupid and savage look; in Abraham and his family, an open expression, frank and sympathetic, a manner of living that contrasts singularly with that of the other family. Even the workmen at the Zoological Gardens find this difference, and one of them has rendered to Abraham this compliment: "What an honest and trustworthy man Abraham is!"

So far, the following is the sole article found in which the author is outraged that human beings are relegated to the role of an 'exhibition item' and shown in zoos. The author, J. K., chose to remain anonymous:

The Eskimos in the Zoological Gardens of Berlin[72]

As stated in the public announcements, the Eskimos from Labrador and Greenland began their 'presentations' last Sunday. But what are these curious, small and stunted human figures from the forbidding North presenting? Well, undoubtedly the first thing they have to offer is that which intrigues us 'middling sons of this earth' (daughters included, of course) the most – namely, themselves.

And thus we have arrived at a point which, however, does not reside within the field of anthropology proper – which has received so much attention recently, and which, of course, means

---

[72] Die Eskimos im Zoologischen Garten zu Berlin. (1880, October 21).

'knowledge about the human' in German – but which, seen from another angle, may well belong to this new field of knowledge after all.

Of course, we will most meticulously avoid taking issue in any way with these gentlemen belonging to the anthropological type. They must make their observations and conduct their measurements undisturbed; they must construct all thinkable and unthinkable lines and angles on the faces and skulls of Eskimos, and must assess in exact numbers the relationship among the former. Somewhere, in the filing cabinets of science, there must be a tiny compartment that has not yet been crammed quite full. One has to hurry up, therefore, to produce the necessary tabulations. But even for the filing cabinets of science there is a point in time when, as in the administration of the courts, the destruction of accumulated files is ordered, to make room for the new, which, in turn, and after a predetermined length of time, will be met by the same fate. If it continues following within the same ruts, the scholarly filing cabinet, section 'Anthropology,' will soon contain an alarming amount of stuff. Everything is recorded; each tiny fragment of a shard, each little peg of wood, each splintered piece of rock is kept. All of a sudden there is an 'anthropological museum,' and even a very 'interesting' one. Today, whenever something manages to establish itself as being 'interesting,' it has won the game. We are inclined to exclaim in the words of that profound Prince of Denmark: "To be interesting – that is the question!" This is the condition we have to reckon with the most seriously, because it is of such unconditional and unavoidable pertinence. Truly, the word of Dr. Faust is valid even in this matter: "Behold this sign, to which they bow, those black hordes." And the whites no less! 'It is interesting!' Against this fact there can be no logic, no objection, no questioning. It is interesting to be able to watch the stage-set life and the antics of these beings that have been brought from their home in the snowy drifts. Because, that's what it really is, and what it will remain forever. Just look at the little people a little more carefully, a little more in the proper sense of 'anthropological,' and you will realize immediately that there is a melancholy expression especially on the faces of the Eskimo women. They know fully well that they are being exhibited, exposed to the curious, prying glances of old and young. Who knows what these children of the roughest North may be thinking about their highly educated European fellow humans?

Too bad one has to be reminded of it! One could have almost forgotten it when faced with that 'interesting' anthropological play-act. And it would have been pardonable enough, since, not far away, the East-Indian pachyderms, the thick-skinned elephants, are romping about within their spacious and firmly built enclosure, where you can observe them in their natural existential expression (behaviour). And here you may likewise observe those northwestern bearers of thick furs in their natural existential expression (behaviour), romping peacefully, as it is their way, inside their huts that are only fenced off by a wooden wicket. And it is beyond telling how 'interesting' they are! Because those Northerners walk around just as we do. However, in their sealskin clothes they may seem a little clumsy to us, and a bit like bears. But who knows how we may appear to them? Yet, it is after all very interesting to see how the Eskimo mother carries her little child on her back in her hood. Maybe that is why the hood is cut in such a large and ungainly fashion. Maybe, it is only for the sake of the head of the mother, who may perhaps need the protection of the hood against the all too cutting cold. In -40° Reaumur[73] [-50°C] and more, even Eskimos will occasionally feel a little uncomfortable. And now for travelling on water in that narrowly pointed boat, in which the Eskimo sits, and knows how to propel his vessel with a rather primitive paddle. The boat even floats on the water. It is gigantically interesting! And whenever the Eskimo father wants to give the family the pleasure of a little voyage, he takes his little boy on his lap and lets his wife stretch out long on the narrow boat. As you have noticed, they are now all three in the boat, and again that is very interesting. And now for throwing the spear at the imagined fish-enemy – it is almost like going on manoeuvres, also against an imaginary foe. But the crown of all things interesting should be reserved for the sleigh-ride in a wooden chassis covered with reindeer skins and drawn by eight dogs.

Now we would maintain that nothing is gained by the most meticulous observation of all these 'interesting details,' even when see from the so-called anthropological point of view. Neither our education nor our knowledge have been expanded or deepened in any way. We cannot, however, and nor can many others, suppress a feeling of embarrassment about these recently proliferating 'human exhibitions,' and especially about 'human exhibitions' in zoological gardens! There is the species 'lion' in its different degrees, there is the family of pachyderms, there is the species 'monkey' in its countless variations. And now one is add-

---

[73] The Réaumur scale was designed in 1731 by French physicist and inventor René-Antoine Ferchault de Réaumur (1683–1757).

ing the 'species homo,' as they were recently called in a daily newspaper, in manifold degrees. We have already had opportunity to see Nubians, Negroes, Lapps, Patagonians, and, undoubtedly, other 'interesting peoples' will also send us their representatives. Or rather, our animal traders on their extensive travels will now and again be able to find some 'humans' who will suffer themselves to be persuaded to cooperate. And we do not want to interfere with anybody's 'trade.' While someone may travel the world in the company of tightrope walkers, with singers or virtuosi, others may travel with 'interesting foreign people.' Anybody may do as he pleases. But in our opinion one should not try to demonstrate the idea that there is only a gradual difference between all the species, in this graphic way of treating human beings like exhibitions pieces in zoological gardens! In our opinion this business in human exhibition pieces has something decisively repulsive. We cannot shake off the idea of the slave trade. Surely, this may not be the case at all. But to bring these 'Meschenkinder' (human children), these images of God, if we may say so, to bring them right into the middle of zoological gardens as exhibition pieces, seems to be absolutely incompatible with science and our knowledge about humans and the essential being of humanity.

We are totally prepared to have our opinion smiled at and ridiculed as sentimental by some. Nevertheless, we have wanted to express it here. If these 'interesting' human specimens need to be exhibited at all, a sense of 'racial ethics' should prevent us from displaying our equals in zoos. It should be easy to identify appropriate localities elsewhere.

J. K.
Berlin, October 20.

ABRAHAM'S FIRST LETTER TO BROTHER ELSNER

Before he started writing his diary, Abraham wrote a letter to Brother Augustus Ferdinand Elsner, a Moravian missionary who had been posted in Labrador from 1846 to 1878.[74] Abraham explained, among other things, the reasons that led him to decide to go to Europe with his family.

My dear teacher Elsner!

I write to you, because I'd like to tell you the following. We are greatly sad. When they brought me to Europe, I probably totally ignored it at first, but then I prayed to the Lord continuously that He might teach me, if it really was a mistake, because I believe in all His words. But because I was in deep misery, I often prayed to God to help me to free myself from this and to hear my sighs, because I even wasn't able anymore to take care of my relatives, which I was usually able to do, even when I did not believe in my Lord and Saviour yet who died for me. In different kinds of ways we have been lured, but even all this I didn't recognize. But as I was in doubt to pay all my and my late father's debts from kayaking,[75] I thought (at this chance) to collect some money for discharging them. I also believed that I might see you. Then I thought: Our way is destined by the Lord. We all cried a lot, my wife, I, and our relatives; but none of them wanted to hold us back.[76] This way we

---

[74] Rollmann, Hans-Josef. [n.d. b].

[75] Our interpretation is that Abraham refers to the revenue he gets from hunting and fishing, activities he practiced using a kayak.

[76] Note appearing in *Missionsblatt aus der Brüdergemeine*. (1880, December): By saying 'none of them' Abraham can only talk about his

took our decision before the Lord. Not that we would have been tired of our teachers, but due to the weight of my debts, of which I still have 100 shillings, I didn't want to act like a fool, but I remember to have wished to see Europe and some of the communities over there for a long time. But here I wait in vain for someone to talk about Jesus. Until now we only saw reckless people in our house.[77] We pray that the Lord may help us here and everywhere we will travel with our show.

I admonished my relatives that they above all do not forget Jesus. We didn't expect that! Such recklessness is not our pleasure. I thought we would see you very soon ... Once we have been to church, in a big community in Berlin.[78] (Because of that) we have been feeling happy until late night; yes indeed, we didn't want to go to sleep. The Lord seemed to be with us for a long time. Even as we went through the streets we sang praises and were astonished. And it became clear to us how well we were taken care of in our country, yes indeed, long and great are the blessings we receive, yes indeed.

The distance (between Labrador and Europe) is very big. We had lost hope of seeing land because, even though the wind was favourable, we spent 32 days at sea. The country we saw first was called Faul (?).[79] After no more land in sight until the 32 days were completed.

---

relatives; missionaries strongly advised against this trip and have tried their best to stop him.

[77] Note appearing in Missionsblatt aus der Brüdergemeine. (1880, December): This letter was obviously written before the visit of the Brothers of Berlin with Brothers Kern and von Dewitz.

[78] Note appearing in Missionsblatt aus der Brüdergemeine. (1880, December): This evocation of a visit to the church is not clear. The Eskimos Brothers and Sisters later came twice in our community hall.

[79] In his diary, Johan Adrian Jacobsen noted on September 16, 1880, that they sighted 'Fareloe, the most westerly island of the Shetland Islands.' Is he referring to the island of Foula (located forty kilometers southwest of the Shetland Islands) or to the Faroe Islands (an archipelago located halfway between Iceland and the Shetland Islands)?

Mr. Hagenbeck has done much good to us; he gave us beds and a violin and music to me. Now we will travel to different cities; therefore pray for us, especially when we are in Catholic countries.[80] We will suffer a lot from homesickness. We will go to Dresden, Paris, England, Herrnhut, Petersburg, and Vienna, if it's true what they say...[81]

I will have faith in God here in Europe that nothing bad will come across; that even the evil people, who surround us all the time, can't harm us.

The wife of the Northerner is sick, very sick indeed. We are very grateful that they have a home for themselves. We don't like their habits, both practice magic. I often ask them to convert, but it doesn't help. Again and again they catch a bad cold. They reject to take any medicine; they hope to get well by magic. We often suffer from colds, too, are often sick in Berlin and are very homesick and miss our land, our relatives, and our church. Yes indeed, we had to learn from our mistakes. I don't fear; I will be disadvantageous to our people (after our return). Far be it from me to do so. Already now I know better about many things, especially also that the commodities have to be brought to us on a long way, which in fact has to raise the prices,[82] and that the journey our teachers have to go on is very dangerous. Yes, we wonder that teachers long to come to us poor people, whereas we already had enough of one sea voyage!

---

[80] Note appearing in Missionsblatt aus der Brüdergemeine. (1880, December): It is naturally unlikely that their stay in catholic areas will be more dangerous than in protestant ones.

[81] Note appearing in Missionsblatt aus der Brüdergemeine. (1880, December): In case it is the truth, the cities mentioned will not be visited in that order.

[82] Note appearing in Missionsblatt aus der Brüdergemeine. (1880, December): This is probably the first time an Eskimo recognizes this fact. If he manages to have his countrymen accept this, the widespread discontent among them perhaps will somewhat be appeased.

The food here is no good. We don't lack dry bread; we also get some fish. Because of the fish we take some refreshment.

We thank you very much for writing to us. At this moment we probably don't lack anything physically.

We all send many greetings to you, your relatives, and all believers who surround you. We often see you both in mind and my wife sends her regards to your wife Bertha in the Lord. However we are, wherever we may be, we don't want to run away.

Abraham, Ulrike's husband

Brother Elsner received Abraham's letter on November 9, 1880, and hastened to write to Brother Reichel informing him that he was heading to Berlin without delay.[83]

Bremen, November 10, 1880

Dear Brother Reichel!

You will be surprised to get a letter from me again. But, as I think I already told you, I wrote to the Eskimos in the Zoological Garden in Berlin, gave them our serious warnings, but also many consoling words since I was certain they would be terribly homesick. After all, they are natives of Labrador! Finally, yesterday, I received the answer from Abraham, who used to be my pupil. I immediately translated it in order to send it to you.

Yesterday evening, I gave a short oral report about the Eskimos' situation to our local Christian Men's Association, based on the content of Abraham's letter.

The situation of these poor Eskimos moved the men of the Association very much. Many of them asked me whether I could travel to Berlin before they are taken to Saint-Petersburg or to Paris. The matter stayed undecided.

Once at home, I received a contribution of 40 marks to support the cost of the journey to Berlin. I could not help,

---

[83] Lutz, Hartmut et al. (2005). p. 20-27.

but see this journey as coming from the Lord.

However, since, according to today's report in the *Börsen-zeitung*,[84] this will be the last week of the Eskimos' stay in Berlin, the decision must not be delayed if this trip is to happen. I have therefore decided – it is God's wish – to depart for Berlin tomorrow morning, and I pray that the Lord may give His blessings to this journey. [...]

The local pastor really wants to include Abraham's letter in the local church paper. Until now, I have avoided the question, so that if the article is published, our papers will not print it after the others, since many religious and political papers often reprint the texts published in the *Bremer Kirchenblatt*. After my return from Berlin, however, I will not be able to avoid the inquiries any longer.

With heartfelt regards to you and please give my regards to the dear brothers of the UAC. I remain yours truly. [...]

Brother A. F. Elsner

The reunion of Brother Elsner with Abraham occurred on November 12. Abraham made mention of it in his diary:

Nov. 12. I saw Elsner who came (from Bremen) to see us. He came with (Emperor) Wilhelm's teacher (court preacher Stöcker[85]) and another one. They prayed because of us that we don't turn from the Lord and may not get lost. Also some religious women came to our hut and sang and led the prayers very greatly. Yes indeed, we have the believers here in Germany as our brothers and sisters, they even called us 'brothers' and 'sisters,' even cried in front of us that we might not get lost through Satan, they even knelled down in front of us reverentially, by greeting they often strengthen us greatly; many times they brought us good things to eat and thought that, by doing so, they would strengthen our souls.

---

[84] Financial newspaper.
[85] Adolf Stöcker (1835–1909) was a Lutheran theologian, politician and preacher at the court of Wilhelm I.

Fig. 32 Adolf Stöcker
(Wikimedia Commons)

MEETING WITH MORAVIAN
BROTHERS AND SISTERS IN BERLIN

This reunion with Brother Elsner was not the first occasion Abraham had to meet and pray with members of Berlin's Moravian community. The first occasion presented itself on October 22, 1880, when two missionaries, acquaintances of Gustav Adolf Hlawatscheck, stationed in Hebron since 1869,[86] came to visit them at the zoo.

> It was not until Oct. 22 that we heard that *The Harmony*[87] had arrived, when two acquaintances from Hlawatscheck came to us. They were two teachers (missionaries), and they were so happy when they saw us that they knew us immediately and called our names, told us to sing, and because we are not without knowing various things, they were very happy and even thanked us greatly and invited us to their house and their church. We really want to, but are not able to, as there are too many people. Indeed, going out by daytime is impossible because of all the people, because we are totally surrounded by them, by many very different faces.

The same day of October 22, Adolf Schoepf wrote to Jacobsen informing him that he was encountering difficulties to get the *Eskimos* to work: [88]

---

[86] Rollmann, Hans-Josef. [n.d. b].

[87] *The Harmony* was the ship used by the Moravian Church to maintain communications between Europe and its missions in Labrador (Hebron, Hopedale, Nain, Okak, Ramah and Zoar).

[88] Thode-Arora, Hilke. (2002). p. 6.

Having received your dear letter today, I will be glad when you will come here as the Messrs. Eskimos are not any longer the way we expected. Is it that they are already spoilt by the visitors or that they do not come out? In short, I have a hard time making them work; one always wants to pass it on to the other and they get down to work with obvious distaste. Hopefully, this will change when you are here as you know best what you have agreed on with the people.

On October 25, a group of eight Moravian brothers and sisters accessed the *Eskimos'* enclosure. Among them were Brother Carl Gotthelf Kern, a missionary Abraham had once known in Labrador,[89] and Brother August von Dewitz, director of the Moravian missions' school in Niesky, Germany.

Brother von Dewitz wrote an account of the meeting which was published in the December 1880 missions' journal (*Missionsblatt der Brüdergemeinde*). He wrote:[90]

It was a peculiar deeply moving after-celebration of the missionary feast in the Berlin Hall of Brethren, when we one day later – eight brothers and sisters in number – on Monday, in the morning of October 25, visited our 'brothers and sisters from Hebron' at the Zoological Garden in Berlin. Dr. Kern, known to the readers of the newsletter as former Labrador-missionary, and I went there on a special order of the mission-department.

Yes, there they came; Abraham in a hurried run when he saw his old teacher, then the young Tobias, then Ulrike, wife of the first mentioned, with her little, cute, only 11-month-old Martha [Maria] and the 4-year-old Sara; soon the heathen approached us: Terrieniak (fox) and his 50-year-old wife Paingu (homesickness); the daughter Nochavak [Nuggasak] (young caribou) appearing a little later, with long pendants of pearls in her ears like her mother. We shook hands in a friendly manner with all of them; with shining eyes our Christians especially welcomed Dr. Kern, to whom Abraham had already sent a letter a day before.

---

[89] Brother Kern was a missionary in Labrador from 1850 to 1874. See Rollmann, Hans-Josef. [n.d. b].
[90] Lutz, Hartmut *et al.* (2005). p. 29-41.

"The great teachers are sending us to you" – that is about how Dr. Kern turned to Abraham in their language – "They are very sad that you have been so foolish to come here. It will not do you any good, but now you are here, and so they send you their best regards as our brothers and sisters, admonish you to walk as Christians, and to remain faithful to the Saviour!" And they kept on talking to them in such a way. After the first joy, there was a look of embarrassment on Abraham's face; maybe he expected to hear a fiercer word of reproach. But what should be the use of it now? Now it was important to win their trust, and to show them that the love of the German brothers and sisters is with them. Soon the characteristically childish – and if I may say so – honest expression returned on his wide face, and he assured us that they already realized they had been foolish, and to tell the great teachers that they would not look at evil things crossing their ways, and that they would ask Jesus to let them keep their faith. For this moment it was meant seriously. We were so delighted to hear that Abraham faithfully performs his fatherly duties, and together with his family, prays daily in the morning and evening. The Eskimos have a hymnbook, a Bible and a Daily Textbook[91] with them. It was a moving moment when we eight brothers and sisters gathered with our Christian Eskimos in their housing, a reconstruction of their native huts; and when they sang in their language and we finally struck up together in both tongues the verse: *Die wir nun alle hier zusammen sind* (Now that we are all together here). We spent about three hours in their enclosure and managed to talk about more things, while they had to present their show several times in front of the audience: going by kayak, on a sledge and other things. We have to keep silent about other details. (...)

I think it is my duty, in order to correct possible misconceptions, to here acknowledge with gratitude that the physical and mental well-being of the Eskimos is cared for with great generosity and effort. We were lucky to meet Mr. Hagenbeck in person, who had just arrived this morning to see to these people's interest. Not only does he want to ensure that the Eskimos are given the appropriate food – regard-

---

[91] For over 284 years, the Moravian community has been publishing its annual *Moravian Textbook* or *Daily Watchword*. It is available in 52 languages and contains extracts of Bible verses and lay literary texts to be used as a guide for meditation and conduct.

less of the possibility of personal losses – but also that their moral well-being is taken care of. That is why the Christians and the heathen live in separate huts; alcoholic beverages are strictly kept away, and as far as possible, it is ensured that they are kept continuously busy by the preparation of food, by all kinds of sewing and wood carving activities and such things. An experienced and clever agent of Mr. Hagenbeck is around the Eskimos all the time for supervision, and he promised to inform our Dr. Kern in writing in case of necessity. In every respect we met only with the most endearing and most profound obligingness.

Fig. 33 Heinrich Bodinus
(Wikimedia Commons)

Much to our delight we heard from the director of the Zoological Garden, Dr. Bodinus[92] – who was also present – that we were given the permission to pick up our Eskimo brothers and sisters for a meeting in the Hall of Brethren the following evening. Abraham's eyes and those of his family members got shiny when they were informed about this. I would like to give a more detailed description of this missionary evening, but since it cannot take up too much space in the newsletter, there will be more about this in the Herrenhut. That evening the Eskimos did not wear their seal fur, but their white communion dress. Their joy at the idea of such a rich and special meal which they politely consumed in small groups; their moved faces after singing in German and after Dr. Kern preached in their tongue; the moment

---

[92] Heinrich Bodinus (1814–1884), director of the Berlin Zoo from 1869 to 1884.

when the whole community went down on their knees with them; the heartfelt final prayer with the Lord's Prayer in Es-kimo-language raising to the Lord who never stopped fol-lowing his foolish lambs all the way here; the joy on their faces when they heard the German choral song and the sounds of the trumpets of the Kirdorfer brass band; those are all unforgettable pictures for all those who witnessed this evening. For a moment we forgot – at least I did – the sorrow caused by Abraham's and Tobias' hasty decision and the consequences it could have without the excep-tional help from the Lord; at that moment we especially thanked the Lord for having souls among us that He has en-trusted to our brethren, they are weak children, but still children of the one Lord, who paid for them with His blood.

May the impression they give us remain the same when they visit us towards the end of March in the community of Herrnhut – that is what was promised to them and to us – after a long travel to Frankfurt am Main, Paris, Vienna and St. Petersburg via Dresden. We grew very fond of them. (...)

Brother V. Dewitz

In his diary, Abraham mentioned their October 26 visit to Berlin's Moravian Church.[93] The *Eskimos* prayed with their Berlin sisters and brothers. They visited the church a second time shortly be-fore leaving Berlin.

> Yesterday on the 26, we went to church, and prayed and sang together. We were all very greatly cheered (blessed), also all our *Kablunat*, very greatly we have been inspired. We people sang together in the church, *Jesu ging voran* (*Jesus Still Lead On*) and then recited the Lord's Prayer. The assembly was greatly inspired by our voices. And again, we were recommended plead-ingly to the Lord. And again, there was choir: *Wir stehen getrost auf Zion fest* (We rely confidently on Zion). Then we were at loss because of all the blessings, even the *Kablunat*, too. When the choir had finished, the man at the table called upwards, then the trumpets started

---

[93] Then located at 136 Wilhelmstraße.

playing; *Kommst du nun, Jesu, vom Himmel herunter auf Erden*[94] (Come Thou, Jesus, from Heaven to Earth) and other melodies. When we had finished, we were given an enthusiastic welcome, our hands were shaken greatly. Before the table we sat. After this event, the teachers often appeared in our house (in the zoo) and sang (and prayed); even women who came into our hut have joined in the singing and recommended us greatly to Jesus.

The religious journal *Sunday at Home* published the following text describing the reunions between the Eskimos and the Moravian community. It is through this text that we learned, among other things, that Abraham and Tobias gave gold and silver coins as offerings for the Moravian missions:[95]

Abraham's eyes gleam with joy. In one of these visitors he has recognized an old missionary of Labrador, who was formerly his pastor. Now, retired in Europe, and knowing the arrival of this Christian family of Esquimaux at the Zoological Gardens, he has come to speak with them in the language of their native country concerning the interest of their souls. Very soon Abraham's face became a little clouded by hearing the missionary tell him in his own language: "The chief men of the mission are very sorry to learn that you have been so unwise as to come here, where you cannot do any good, but they salute you cordially as brothers, and exhort you to conduct yourselves as Christians and to remain faithful to the Saviour." Abraham expected to hear some other reproofs, but no more were made to him. His conscience had spoken, and that was sufficient. [...]

During three hours, interrupted from time to time by the necessity in which the Esquimaux were placed of showing themselves in public, the visitors were able to converse with them; and in the hut, lighted by the glimmering flame of a small oil lamp, these natives of Labrador have been able to bend their knees together in prayer, to sing hymns and place themselves under the protection of the Good Shepard as sheep exposed to so many dangers.

[94] Written by Johann Sebastian Bach.
[95] *The Esquimaux.* (1881, May 21).

It was great comfort and enjoyment for these good Esquimaux to find in a foreign land friendly hearts testifying in different ways a brotherly interest. Many members of the Church of Berlin obtained permission to enter into the enclosure of the Esquimaux, and were able to assemble on many occasions with them in their hut. In considering only the exterior, what in common can there be between these civilized Europeans and these Esquimaux, short, beardless, broad-shouldered, with the head large, the face flat, projecting cheeks, the lower lip thick, small eyes, brown visage, and straight hair? And yet, there they are, these Christians, hand in hand, singing each one in his language, the same verses of hymns, united in the same sentiment of love the one for the other. One single word is equally understood by all, the name of Jesus, which Abraham repeats raising his hand towards heaven, and at this name a ray of celestial joy illumines his countenance. [...]

On two occasions, the one at the commencement, and the other at the end of their abode at Berlin, our Esquimaux Christians obtained permission to go to a Christian communion among the Moravian Brethren. [...] A numerous assembly is in expectation. At last the door opens, and introduced by the old missionary, Abraham, his wife Ulrike, carrying in her arms the little Sara, and Tobias make their entrance. The emotion is general; they silently and modestly take their places and with clasped hands and downcast heads seat themselves. When the assembly sings one of those same melodies which they have themselves so many times sung in their native country, a ray of joy illumines their faces. A choir had been arranged in honour of these guests. "It is almost as pleasant as at Hebron," said Abraham. After an exhortation, and a prayer, on their knees, which the old missionary made in their language, they said themselves the Lord's Prayer and sang several hymns.

At their second visit to the Moravian church, which was to be the last, on account of their approaching departure from Berlin, towards the end of the feast Abraham, with smiling eyes and profoundly happy mien, holds forth to the missionary and lays on the table a piece of gold, pronouncing with much emphasis the word: 'Missions.' Tobias in his turn following the example, searches in his pocket for some pieces of silver, and joyously places them by the side of the offering of Abraham, and repeats the same word. What an interesting spectacle; and what a testimony to the work of evangelising missions among the pagans; but also what a lesson for European Christians, for the poor not less than for the rich!

In a religious journal published in French in Switzerland, we find other pieces of information: namely, that Ulrike addressed the congregation and asked them to pray for her young child Sara:[96]

Tobias was found suffering from profound sadness and home-sickness seems to have gotten hold of all of them. Little Sara's illness was the last thing needed to fill the Eskimos' hut with pain and anguish. "Pray, pray," said Ulrike, the poor child's mother, shedding bitter tears. And someone said: "How can we now judge these brothers who got lost? How not to sympathize with their great misfortune?"

Brother Elsner was present when Abraham and his family went to the Moravian church for the second time. Hans-Josef Rollmann, Professor of Religious Studies at Memorial University in St. John's, Newfoundland-and-Labrador, who has also been researching Abraham's story for many years, recently published a text revealing that, during the evening, Abraham also addressed the congregation:[97]

[...] Abraham, impressed by the court preacher [Stöcker], took up his violin and played an impromptu *Heil Dir im Siegerkranz* (Hail to thee in victor's crown), the unofficial German national anthem, praising the Kaiser.

[...] For the apolitical Inuk, however, the highpoint of his European stay came during a second visit with fellow Moravians in Berlin, when the musical performances left a deep impression on him. He was promised that the choral piece *Jauchzet dem Herrn alle Welt* by Felix Mendelssohn-Bartholdy would be sent to Labrador.

[...] Before the visitors left their fellow Christians in Berlin, Abraham asked to address the congregation with Brother Elsner translating from Inuktitut into German.

[96] Les Esquimaux en Europe. (1881, March 6).
[97] Rollmann, Hans-Josef. (2013, November 7).

"I am here in Europe only as an exhibit," Abraham said, "but I have received here from all of you so much love that I want to say a few words of thanks. I have seen on my trip already very much and will see even more, but what I have experienced from you here and heard from you, Brother Elsner, I will never forget, and it will be the most excellent thing that I will be able to recount when I return to our country. We ask you to pray for us; we also will pray for all of you."

Professor Rollmann added that several years later, just as Abraham and Tobias had made a gift to the Moravian Church in Berlin, the Moravian community in Labrador raised funds for the benefit of the Berliners to help them rebuild their church from the rubble of World War II, including the destroyed building where Abraham and his family had been.

Fig. 34 Location of 136 Wilhelmstraße, Berlin
Location of the Moravian church where Abraham and his family came to pray in 1880. (© France Rivet, Polar Horizons, 2013)

W. A. Meyn lith.   Verlag von PAUL PAREY in Berlin.

Fig. 35 Illustrations of the eight *Eskimos*, 1880
See Virchow, Rudolf. (1880). p. 275.
Illustrations by W. A. Meyer based on the photographs taken by Jacob
Martin Jacobsen in Hamburg. (Courtesy of JSTOR)

THE *ESKIMOS* STUDIED BY RUDOLF VIRCHOW

In early November 1880, Dr. Rudolf Virchow, pathologist and co-founder of the *Berlin Society of Anthropology, Ethnology and Prehistory*, obtained permission to study the Labrador *Eskimos*. For him, their presence on European soil represented a golden opportunity to increase the scientific knowledge of these people. A session was organized during which Virchow studied the group's five adults and took a series of anthropometric measurements.[98]

Fig. 36 Rudolf Virchow
(Wikimedia Commons)

---

[98] Measurements of various parts of the human body.

His specific objective was to add to the existing scientific knowledge of *Eskimos* from Greenland to Siberia, demonstrate that they had a common geographical origin, examine their racial characteristics, and establish whether they were a race distinct from other North American native peoples. For this purpose, he conducted a detailed physical and cranial examination, asked questions about their food ways, their ability to count, and their colour perception in what constituted part of an anthropological deconstruction of their bodies, and compared their tools, clothes and tattoos. His findings, while compartmentalised into anthropology and ethnology, were far-ranging and extended beyond interpreting their skulls.[99]

An article published in the *Charlottenberger Zeitung*[100] tells us that the session was held on Thursday, October 28, 1880, and was more eventful than Virchow was expecting:

Sorcerer Virchow

On Thursday, Professor Virchow took the usual anthropological measurements on the Eskimos. The following psychologically interesting incident occurred.

The wild Pägnu, held in high esteem by her tribe as a sorceress, had from the beginning observed Virchow's examinations with obvious suspicion. When her turn came, it became clear to her that Virchow was nothing more than a sorcerer of the White men's God who had come to rob her, using his incomprehensible manipulations, of her own supernatural power.

In the middle of the measurement session, she suddenly jumped up, sat like a monkey on the tables and chairs emitting guttural sounds with her magical formulas designed to ward off the power of the 'dear colleague.'

Frightened, Professor Virchow and his two assistants stepped back and it was only after quite a while that they managed to calm Mrs. Pägnu.

---

[99] Baehre, Rainer. (2008). p. 20.
[100] *Charlottenberger Zeitung*. (1880, November 2).

Throughout this whole episode, Abraham's behavior was most interesting: even though he has been baptized, deep down in his heart he surely did not forget his ancestors' beliefs.

When he saw that Virchow, who must have seemed quite 'magical' to him, was timidly backing away from Pägnu, he became pale, watched the scene with eyes full of fear and muttered to himself in his mother tongue: "After all, my country's God is more powerful than the Christians' God." As for Pägnu, she came back to her own self, as she realized that the white men's magic could not harm her.

A few days later, on November 7, 1880, an extraordinary meeting of the *Berlin Society of Anthropology, Ethnology and Prehistory* was held at Berlin Zoological Garden in the presence of the *Eskimos*. Rudolf Virchow gave a lecture in which he shared the results of his study.

Early in his speech, Virchow clarified that the above article's author allowed himself to fantasize since no reporter was present during his examination:[101]

> I recently personally witnessed a little scene that was not correctly described in the papers. Some reporter allowed himself to include in his article some of his own fabrications. Since no reporter attended my study session, it was therefore not possible for him to make a personal account of it. In a general sense, the story's description is accurate, and I must say that I have never in my life seen natural passions explode in such a violent manner and at the same time as characteristic as in this episode.

Virchow described the scene as follows:[102]

> You will perhaps be interested to hear about the fit that I have recently observed with Mrs. Bairngo. You have now seen how shy the daughter is; she looks like a wild animal that has been trapped. The mother has not this squeamish nature, but she is extremely suspicious, so that one notices, with every step she takes in a place unfamiliar to her, how

---

101 Virchow, Rudolf. (1880). p. 253.
102 Virchow, Rudolf. (1880). p. 271-272.

much the new environment generates a great concern within her. It was very difficult to take her measurements, something that was rather easy for the others. I started with the simplest and tried to gradually convince her that it was nothing harmful, but each new attempt immediately aroused her apprehension, and when it was time to measure her body, she began to tremble and fell into the highest excitement. When I wanted to take her fathom length, as I was stretching out her arms horizontally, something that probably had never occurred in her life yet, she suddenly had the fit. She slipped underneath my arm and started 'carrying on all over' the room with such a fury and in such a way that I have never seen before, although, as a long-term physician in a prison, I have encountered the strangest fits of rage or spasms, whether they were simulated or real.

At first, I thought it would turn into a hysterical catatonic fit, but soon it became clear that there was absolutely no physical spasm, nothing somatic pathological occurred. It rather went on as a psychic cramp, comparable to what happens with people in a high state of rage. In these cases, people go around the room, smash everything they can get their hands on, and do the strangest things, which they do not remember anything of afterwards. Such was this case. She jumped around the room with both feet and in a slightly bent position, took chairs and tables and threw them in all directions. But while she was romping around the room, she didn't make the slightest attempt to escape out of the door or to attack those who were present. She jumped from one corner to the other screaming in a howling manner; her ugly face looked dark red, her eyes lit up, and there was a bit of foam at her mouth. To sum it up, it was a most disgusting sight. It was very surprising to see how her husband and daughter, who had been sitting the whole time in their chairs, did not show the slightest excitement or inclination to help her.

The attack lasted a good eight to ten minutes, and, all of a sudden, she stopped, put her head on the table, remained quiet for a few minutes in this position, then straightened up, and said in her language: "Now I'm good again." Of course, she was still trembling and I felt it was advisable not to make any more attempt to measure her.

I had the impression that this 'psychic cramp' was the exact same phenomena that happens when shamans perform their dances. As everybody knows, in the northeastern part of Asia, such excessive personal excitement, which mainly occur in shamanism, is being kept alive through a long tradition. However, unmistakable traces of it are also found in Greenland, where the shamans are called 'angakoks.[103]'

I have since learned from Mr. Jacobsen that the father Tiggianiak ('fox' in German), who is considered an 'angakok,' showed the same behaviour in a previous episode. As the boat that was bringing them to Europe approached the mouth of the Elbe River and a storm had risen, the Eskimo began to conjure. He went to the ship's bow, violently gesticulating with his hands and arms, yelled louder than the storm, and fell into the greatest excitement. After completing his incantations, he returned quietly on the lower deck in his cabin, promising they would soon have good wind. A few hours later when the storm subsided, he was pleased to say that it happened thanks to him. The point made by Mr. Jacobsen about Mrs. Bairngo in his little book (*Beiträge über Leben und der Treiben Eskimos in Labrador und Grönland.* Berlin. 1880, p. 17) seems particularly significant in explaining our case in the passage where he describes the conjuration scene: "Meanwhile Tiggianiak's wife, who also has the reputation of being a sorcerer among her compatriots, is sitting in her cabin and making the most curious movements and signs with her hands, but without making any noise." Obviously these people believe in their own magic, and when the inspiration arises, they get into a semi-artificial, semi-deliberate state of ecstasy that we must consider as the height of their inner excitement. Such was the case with our lady. Her mental excitement never ceased to grow as a result of the manipulations and the stress to which she was subjected to. She freed and threw herself as a frenzied in a seemingly senseless, but intentional rage. And after a while she was 'good again.' The rage had therefore been a means of inner liberation. For this reason, her relatives, who know her way of being, quietly let her be. From this point of view the whole scene is explainable. At the same time it sheds light on one aspect of this strange psychological manifestation that is shamanism.

---

[103] In Greenlandic, the plural form of *angakok* is actually *angákut*.

Before detailing the various measurements, Virchow introduced the two families and provided basic information on their place of origin and the aspects distinguishing one family from the other:[104]

> Although they all come from the same area of Labrador, which is located at almost the same latitude as the southern tip of Greenland, the Eskimos we are dealing with can be said to be comprised of two groups or families, even though, to use the same expression as in the North, a *Loskärl* [105] is also among them. They belong to coherent groups who differ not only in their religion, but show several differences in their outer appearance as well. One of them, namely the family of Abraham, consists of the husband, the wife, Ulrike, and two young children, along with the unmarried Tobias. They come from the mission of Hebron, founded by the Moravians in 1830, located at about 59° latitude North and 60° longitude west, south of Cape Chidley.

> This is one of six stations maintained by Moravians on this coast and the oldest, [106] Hopedale, goes back to 1770. According to the report of Mr. Jacobsen, who recruited these people and brought them back to Hamburg on his own boat, of approximately 2,000 Eskimos living in Labrador, 1,500 were converted to Christianity. The missionaries were able to support the education of these people to such an extent that they developed their intelligence to quite a degree and they are able to write with ease, to draw and to practice all kinds of skills of a civilized life. [...]

> The other family, consisting of the husband Tiggianiak (Tigganiak), his wife Paieng (Bairngo) [Paingu] and their daughter Noggasak, is still completely heathenish and, indeed, possesses features that are eminently fit for learning about the primitive nature of this population. [...]

> This family was hired by Mr. Jacobsen in Nachvak Fjord, a station of the Hudson's Bay Company located north of

---

[104] Virchow, Rudolf. (1880). p. 253-254.

[105] We have not been able to identify this regional word. Virchow may mean 'single,' or that a member of this family is a collateral relative. In any case, he must be referring to Tobias. (Translator's note)

[106] The oldest Moravian settlement in Labrador is actually the one in Nain which was founded in 1771. Hopedale was founded in 1782. See Rollmann, Hans-Josef. [n.d. a].

Hebron. It belongs to a small group of Eskimos little affected by European influences. In summer, the Eskimos here mainly spend their time hunting. Based on Mr. Jacobsen's narrative, there is still wood in this area, mainly pine and birch trees. Near Hebron only dwarf birch survives.[107] The people do not keep domesticated reindeer,[108] although there are numerous ones in the wild. They hunt using firearms. When fishing and hunting sea animals, they use their traditional tools. The Christians are concentrating more on salmon fishing. Dogs are kept in large numbers, they are mostly fed fish.

During his examination, Virchow had asked the five adults to write the names of different colours in their mother tongue. Attendees therefore were given the opportunity to look more closely at these lists[109] handwritten by each individual:

Later on, you will have the opportunity to look at the manuscripts written by these individuals, namely, the lists of colour names they wrote. Indeed, you know that for quite a while now we have gotten into the habit of determining the colour names used by our foreign guests. This is what has been done this time as well, with the peculiarity that they wrote

---

[107] Along the Labrador coast, the northernmost trees ('tree' being defined as a woody plant at least 2 m in height) are located at Napâttuk (or Napaktok) Bay (58° 01' 01" N), some 27 km south of Hebron (58° 12' 01" N). According to a 1979 study by Deborah Elliott and Susan K. Short, various studies conducted in the Hebron area have revealed no coniferous trees, but instead a dense shrubland of alder, various willow species, and dwarf birch was observed. Research following a 1957 report of a small clone of spruce in the Nachvak area did not yield any results. Jacobsen's statement that there were conifers in the Hebron area could therefore be misleading. The Elliott and Short report states: '...white spruce in a dwarf, shrub-form might at one time have existed somewhere in the Hebron area. This species has not been reported by other botanists working in this area since 1936. Therefore, the species may have been exterminated (either by the natives or a minor climatic cooling) or may be so local in extent that it has not been rediscovered.' See Elliott, Deborah L. and Susan K. Short (1979, September).

[108] In North America, reindeers are called caribou.

[109] Unfortunately, the *Berlin Society of Anthropology, Ethnology and Prehistory* was not able to find any trace of these manuscript documents in its archives. Email exchange dated January 19, 2014.

the words themselves, especially the husband and wife who wrote easily and in a very satisfactory manner.[110]

	Abraham	Ulrike	Tobias	Tiggianiak	Bairngo
schwarz	keinitak	kirnirtak	kirnitak	kernetak	kernetak
grau	kakortakasak	kakkuangajuk	kakuangujuk	kakoingajok	kernangajok
weiss	kakortak	kakurtak	kakurtak	kakyrtak	kakortak
roth	aupaluktak	auppaluktak	aupalutak	aupaluktak	aupaloktak
orange	kursuargujok	{aupalangajuk kuksuangajuk}	kursuangajuk	korsotak	songarpaluktak
gelb	korsutak	kuksutak	kursutak	songarpaluktak	songarpaluktak
grün	eviujak	iviujak	iviujak	tongujoangajok	tongojoktak
blau	tongujoktak	tungujurtak	tungnjutak	tongujoktak	tougujoktak
violett	tongujoingajok	kirnitangajuk	tungujuangajuk	kernaingajok	tongujoangajok
braun	tongulangajok	aupalangajuk	aupalângajuk	aupalangajok	kojoangajok

Fig. 37 Table of colour names
The identified colours are: black, gray, white, red, orange, yellow, green, blue, purple and brown. (Courtesy of JSTOR)

The lists presented are genuine, written mostly by them-selves (the Christians). They prove that these people know colours well; they can interpret the colour chart not only by differentiating the colours from one another, but also by designating them by name. They have encountered diffi-culties only for orange, yellow, purple and brown. There they used a variety of descriptive terms. Mr. Bessels[111] who met the same kind of difficulties with the *Itaner*[112] people on brown and blue, supposed that his people did not rec-ognize that they were different colours. Without further evi-dence I cannot see this as certain or conclude that their sense of colour is itself defective. It is well known, and here I would particularly like to address the purists in this field, that if we take our ordinary people, such as rural peasants, we also find that a lot of them cannot distinguish these colours with precision, they cannot name them, and they make similar combinations, as occur here, by nuancing the col-our blue and thus saying 'black-blue' or 'dark blue' or 'red-blue.' Altogether, the Eskimos that were interrogated indi-

---

[110] Virchow, Rudolf. (1880). p. 253.

[111] Dr. Emil Bessels (1846–1888), physician, naturalist and Arctic explorer.

[112] Name given by Emil Bessels (Die Amerikanische Nordpol-Expedition, 1879, p. 351) to the people native of Ita (Etah), on the north shore of Foulk Fjord in north-west Greenland. (Translator's note).

vidually exhibited such homogeneity in their answers that it cannot be disputed on linguistic congruence. They are obviously predisposed in this field and prove to not be of a lower, but of a relatively higher race, if we apply the once in vogue theory that the retina only develops with the culture.[113]

Also at the disposal of the audience were the artifacts collected by Jacobsen in Labrador graves. But, Jacobsen did not only collect objects. He also brought back skulls, one of which was given to Virchow by Hagenbeck:[114]

I can specify immediately that Mr. Jacobsen also brought back a series of objects from graves which he personally collected in the vicinity of Hebron. They are in the extraordinarily rich ethnographic exhibition taking place here and that is most likely representing the ancient culture of this population, since they were not recent graves, but probably one to two centuries old. There are few stone tools, same for tools made of bone; much of what has been collected is made of wood or iron. A series of objects clearly shows that contact with Europeans had already taken place.

Skulls from these graves were also brought back and provide the basis for a more rigorous methodical investigation. I have had only one at my disposal, but I can say on this basis that indeed a remarkable identity of shapes manifests itself in the whole extent of this Arctic region. We have had the opportunity, as you know, to see that type of skull from inaccessible places, when the German North Pole Expedition[115] reached the coast of Greenland in a location that had been isolated by ice for a long period.

Virchow proceeded with detailing the measurements obtained from the skull collected in Hebron by Jacobsen:[116]

---

[113] Ibid., p. 267.
[114] Ibid., p. 254.
[115] This is most likely the expedition of 1869–1870 during which the ship *Germania*, prevented from progressing by the pack ice, turned around and focused on exploring the fjords of the north-east coast of Greenland.
[116] Ibid., p. 263.

1. Measured Values

Volume	1,810 ccm[117]
Maximum length	201.0 mm
Maximum width	139.0 mm
Vertical height	151.0 mm
Ear height	127.5 mm
Horizontal circumference	550.0 mm
Vertical transverse circumference	335.0 mm
Longitudinal circumference	417.0 mm
Forehead width (bottom)	103.0 mm
Distance between the temporal bones (*plana temporalia*)[118]	130.0 mm
Facial height (from the root of the nose to the chin)	120.0 mm
Facial width (*Sut. Zyg. Maxill.*)[119]	103.0 mm
Distance between the jugal bones[120]	141.0 mm
Nasal bridge width[121]	23.0 mm
Nose height	54.0 mm
Nasal cavity width (*Apertura pyriformis*)	23.5 mm
Orbit width	44.0 mm
Orbit height	37.0 mm
Distance between the corners of the lower jaws	117.0 mm

2. Calculated Indices

Length-width index	69.3
Length-height index	75.1
Width-height index	108.6
Facial index	85.8
Orbital index	84.0
Nasal index	43.5

Virchow moved on to detailing his observations on various physical aspects of the five adults: the shape of their eyes, ears, nose, or skull; the colour of their skin, hair, etc.:[122]

---

[117] ccm means cm³ i.e. ml (milliliter). (Translator's note)

[118] The bones located in the temple region, on the side of the head. (Translator's note)

[119] Would this be the upper jaw joints? (Translator's note)

[120] The bones that form the cheekbones. (Translator's note)

[121] The upper, bony part of the nose, overlying the nasal bones.

[122] Ibid., p. 254-265.

Regarding the general anthropological assessment, let me first emphasize the fact that the observations I made and which you will now judge for yourselves, have shown in the most obvious way that their race is identical to the Greenland Eskimos who were once presented to us (March 16, 1878, Assembly Proceedings, p. 185). [...]

Thus, the deepening of our study is of great general interest. We will have to undertake various researches before being able to establish the ethnological relationship with absolute certainty.

But if you look very carefully at the people who are before you, and this even without really applying a scientific method of investigation, the conclusion, I think, will become more clearly than in the previous meeting, that they have a series of features which bring this population closer to some Asian populations, specifically the peoples of the Mongolian race. These characteristic features are this time much more pronounced in women than in men, whereas, strangely, last time with the Greenland Eskimos it was the opposite. In my report at the time, during the March 16, 1878, meeting, I formally noted that men showed these properties more acutely than women. This time it is the women, and above all those of the wild family (pagan). Unfortunately, the mother, who offered the greatest interest, is currently seriously ill, so you probably will not see her.

Besides, the daughter is also a prime specimen for observation. I have already stressed that the facial shape is Mongolian. What differs is the skull itself. If we imagine the head divided into two parts: the one that surrounds the brain, the skull itself, and the one that makes up the face, the facial features, we can say: the physiognomic portion is Mongolian, and the cervical part is distinctive, singular. You might see that the whole formation of the eye area reproduces exactly and even to a higher degree what I noted formerly. First of all it has a shape where the slanted eyes saliently stand out. The opening of the eyelid is narrow and straight, however it deviates outward more and more upward, so that especially with the wild family's young daughter, the eyes take an absolutely oblique position and are directed upwards and towards the temporal region. Added to this is the singular eyebrow height relative to the eye slit; they are a lot more distant from each other than usual. In addition, the eyes are wide apart, and finally, we observed in the eye's inner corner that particular bend in the shape of a half-moon which shows itself in certain individuals as a real bride. Our ophthalmologists consider it, when it appears among people of our race, as a pathological condition: epicanthus.[123] Everything indicates a singular formation of the orbit itself which is due to the different position of the cheekbone, protruding obliquely. Thus, the entire eye area seems to be exactly the same as the Mongols'. We recently had the opportunity, thanks to the increasing number of members of our Chinese delegation, to make comparisons about it and I can say that in my opinion this relationship is absolutely irrefutable.

Once this relationship is accepted and if one imagines that the Eskimos or, as they call themselves, the Inuit (singular Inuk), origin from a Mongolian branch which left for America and reached the east coast of Greenland, we would be forced to assume that they come from a not yet discovered variety of Mongolian origin with an elongated head, or that their skull's dolichocephalic[124] aspect only developed later due to specific local conditions in which these people have been living for who knows how long and which, it is true, should be strong enough to cause some changes in the skull's structure. I will only say here that their diet is certainly appropriate to bring fundamental changes in the structure of the face and skull. As you know, in this vast region, people almost never have the opportunity to obtain plant foods. Some plants, as we have said, grow in Labrador, but almost nothing that is actually edible. Greenlanders have even less, they are carnivores in the truest sense of the word, and since the meat and fat they eat are often consumed in the raw state, their masticatory muscles must spend a great deal of efforts to make use of this material.

---

[123] A skin fold of the upper eyelid, covering the eye's inner corner. It is at the origin of slanted eyes.

[124] Litterally means 'who has an elongated skull.' At the time, the cephalic index, the ratio between the skull's maximum width and its maximum length, was one of the indices used to establish the hierarchy of human races. A skull was considered dolichocephalic (long skull) if its cephalic index was less than 75, mesocephalic (intermediate skull) if the cephalic index was between 75 and 80, and brachycephalic (short skull) if the index was greater than 80.

They actually have remarkably strong masticatory apparatus; these muscles are enormously developed, a very prominent lower jaw, the points of insertion of the masticatory muscles on the side of the skull are strongly developed, and something that is particularly characteristic is that there is virtually no other human race in which these ties, called *lineae semicirculares temporum* normally found in us three fingers above the ear, go up so high that, as in the great apes, they get closer more and more to the middle of the skull. In several Eskimo skulls there is only a narrow area without muscles at the top of the skull. Thus, the skull is laterally covered by much more developed muscles, the muscles themselves reach a huge size, their anchor points are sometimes two times larger than that of an ordinary European who eats varied and well prepared foods and does not need a lot of chewing. I mean he has a lot to eat, but little to chew!

The strong development of the muscles going up the skull can certainly influence the shape of the head and it is permissible to think that after a thousand-year-old use, transmitted from generation to generation, a transformation of the cranial shape gradually ensued, such that a rounded head became an elongated head. This happens to be a typical characteristic of the race. Such a transformation would represent one of the most interesting cases of the theory called Transformism [or Transmutation of species], would inform us of the transition from one type to another, which, as you know, we have no really proven example. When asked how such a transition occurred and what external reasons caused it, we can obviously easily give a theoretical answer. But, while asking this question, I want to clarify right away that I am far from declaring this assumption as certainly demonstrable. [...]

The main objection is linguistic in nature. According to the prevailing linguistic point of view, Eskimos would form a language group with the people of northern Asia. [...]

I limit myself to mentioning that the little caravan's intelligent guide, Mr. Jacobsen, who gets along well with them, declared that the dialect of Labrador Eskimos slightly differs from that of the Greenlanders. [...]

I note here that the direct examination, which was limited to the 5 adults (3 men and 2 women), showed that this head shape is best developed in the Christianized woman (Ulrike). She has an index of only 68.2. If we consider that according to our criteria the number 75 is the upper limit of dolichocephaly, you will agree that this implies an unusual evolution of the narrow head. The others are regular dolichocephalic with 74.1, 74.9, 75.7 and only the Christianized bachelor Tobias finds himself in the mesocephalic category, with an index of 77.6. Ulrike can, to some extent, serve as a representative of the most developed type of this race. [...]

I will not go into all the details of these features. Something additional increases much more the uniqueness of this race: the colour of the skin as well as that of the hair and eyes.

Seeing these people who come from far north, you will find that the colour of their skin is so dark that it can quite compete, for example, with the skin of the Nubians we had here. If we use the Parisian table of colours,[125] the degree of colour appears so dark that one might believe, if we add faith to it, in some kind of relationship with Africans. It is deep reddish brown reaching the numbers 30 to 28 on the Parisian table of colours.

I must emphasize that this dark colour of the skin is not limited to the parts exposed to the air, face and hands, but the rest of the body, like the feet and legs, have the same intense dark colour. One could almost say that it is the opposite. Hands in particular are in some, for example in Mrs. Ulrike, so pale that one is surprised by the colour of the feet. It is absolutely impossible to explain this colouring by the effect of air.

I emphasize this because in the discussion on Transformism, it is said with an understandable regularity that the black colour, or at least that the dark colour is only the result of the temperature or of the effect of light. I am, of course, willing to admit that it is right to raise this question and, apparently, it is justified for Africa. But, I want to remind you that for tropical America, neither light nor temperature

---

[125] This is perhaps the table of skin and hair colour developped by Paul Broca as a method for classifying hair and skin colours. (Translator's note)

have the same strong influence. It is known that no native Negro race exists there. On the other hand, we find here in the Far North, in a region where the heat is almost totally lacking and the light is in short supply, a race so dark that you can actually put it in parallel with a number of tribes living in the equatorial zone. The dark colour of the skin, the absolutely black hair, which also by their thickness and stiffness is a reminiscence of the mane of horses, dark eyes well, they are not exactly black no doubt, but usually dark brown, allow for a new series of parallels with the tribes of the Mongolian race. You know, in fact, all members of the Mongolian race are relatively strongly coloured; the lightest ones are much more pigmented than in the case of the white race, and some members of the Mongolian race make up the transition with the lightest members of the black race. [...]

To our knowledge none of the outdoor conditions of the Eskimos' life provide an immediate explanation for the strong pigmentation of their skin. That is why, for the time being, we have to stick to heredity and include the Eskimos as part of a highly coloured race. This position seems also particularly justified by a fact to which I have already drawn your attention in my lectures, and for which my experience is totally different from that of the observers who have preceded me. I find the skin, in covered parts and not only among women, unusually tender, soft to the touch, fine, and with the particularly smooth texture that characterizes Africans. It is likely that we previously made do with considering their hands, roughened and calloused by hard work, and their face before anything else. Besides, the latter offers a relatively thick and rough skin, and curiously, it is the only part in all these people where a significant fat layer is developed. In the rest of the body, the hypoderm is relatively thin, which is very striking in the hands and feet. This difference is already evident among the children with big round and bright red cheeks. In most cases, the adults' cheeks are also quite red; it is only in the older man, the pagan Tiggianiak, that this feature is absent. It is most evident in the women, especially in the young 15-year-old girl. As her thick lips are also very red, her face shows a freshness we are not accustomed to see in coloured people.

On the whole, the skin colour is more uniform than what I observed in the Nubians. However, dark spots, like freckles, are visible on the face. These lentigines are particularly strong, of a black-brown colour in the woman Bairngo. However on covered parts, the neck, the forearms, and the legs, the colour is so uniform that even under tension we were unable to create the contrast between the upper and the lower colours that I reported in the Nubians. Brown, which is the basic colour for everyone, frequently turns, it is true, into yellowish brown and reddish brown so that the face often has a yellowish tint. But overall, we can speak of a dark brown. In this regard, I also note that the gums, especially in the lower jaw, are in most cases pigmented; the colour is leaden blue, sometimes with spots.

In addition, the pagan women have an artificial tattoo on the face and forearms. The Christians have abandoned this practice. From my research, this operation is performed, by men, among girls aged 15–16: pricks are made with a needle and coal is used to penetrate the skin. The old pagan has a series of blackish spots on the forehead, cheeks and lower lip which, on average, is more horizontal and slightly protruding; and on her forearms, she wears little more complex drawings arranged as follows (Fig. 1.):

Fig. 1.

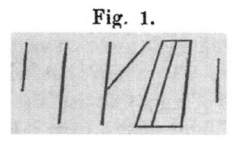

Fig. 38 Drawings on Paingu's forearm
(Courtesy of JSTOR)

These signs have an obvious resemblance with some ornaments (marks of ownership?) of their tools. (See Lubbock, *Prehistoric times*. 4th edition, p. 10, Fig. 3)

The hairiness of our Labrador people matches that of the people from Greenland in every respect. The colour of the hair is black without exception. Even the small children have very dark hair, only the eyebrows are rather brownish. The adult men's hair is relatively long so that it covers the neck and even the shoulders of the heathens. It is very thick, shiny black, like ebony, similar to a horse's mane, by no means curly or wavy, but very straight. For women, the hair has the same texture, but it is comparatively short and thus it rather gives the impression of certain sparseness. Mrs. Ulrike has hers simply parted and braided. In contrast, the pagan woman and her daughter have a knot at the neck and at both temples. The knots at the temples are covered with long pendants which are braided using reindeer hair and richly decorated with colourful (European) beads. The eyebrows of most of them are thick, only Mrs. Ulrike's are thinner. Even the men hardly ever have sideburns, whereas moustache and goatee are thicker, but the latter is restricted to the chin per se. A bit of a moustache is also found on Mrs. Ulrike. The rest of the body, as far as I had a look at it, chest, forearms, and lower legs are almost completely hairless.

About the eyes, I already said that for all of them the iris is brown. In Tobias and woman Bairngo, lighter brown, in the others, dark brown. I also noted in Ulrike a bluish discolouration of the sclera. In general, the eye is deep-set, the eyelid opening short and narrow so that the eyeball looks small, mainly because of the lower eyelid, while the top one seems all the more longer that, as I said, the eyebrows are highly placed. The fold in the inner corner of the eye that I mentioned above is particularly marked in Tobias and Mrs. Ulrike. In general, however, the inner corner of the eye is moved laterally and the distance between the eyes is larger – one of the most striking features of the Eskimo face. The distance between the inner corners of the eyes is 36.2 mm on average, the length of the opening of the eyelids, 59.7 [mm] (in Tiggianiak it is only 57.5 mm). The oblique position towards the outer top of the eyelids' opening, particularly strong in the pagan women is outlined in others; only Abraham has an eyelid opening that is perfectly horizontal. The orbit of the skull collected from a grave is large, but low, its index is 84 [mm].

Let's immediately add to the other features of the face, the ears which are generally large, especially heightwise. The vertical average is 65.2, with 70 for Tigganiak and 69 mm for Mrs. Bairngo. For most of them, the lobe is attached or barely separated from the cheek's skin. Mrs. Ulrike is the only one to have a small ear of only 60 mm in height, the lobe is also attached. We find ourselves in the presence of a feature that has often been and, probably wrongly attributed, to the Laplanders. The Eskimos' ear is also placed relatively low, as evidenced by the vertical 'height of the ear' measure. In the pagan woman only the distance between the earhole and the median line of the skull is low.

The shape of the nose is diverse. The index is, in general, average; it is on average 65.6 for the 5 individuals. That of the skull collected in the grave reaches only 43.5, so it is leptorhin.[126] I cannot draw conclusions from a comparison with bare skulls. It is only clear that significant differences exist. Abraham has a straight nose, with a shape that is quite European. In Tiggianiak, it is rather small and not very prominent, the edge is thin and the nostrils are just a little flat. In Tobias, it is very short and broad, more flattened right from the base, the shorter edge and the nostrils open forwardly. In women the flattening increases. Mrs. Ulrike's nose slightly exceeds the cheekbones line; overall it is not very prominent, and although the nostrils are narrower, the edge and tip move forward slightly. Herein it clearly resembles the nose of the Golden[127] and of the Gilyaks[128] I mentioned at the meeting of July 12, 1873 (Acts, p. 138). Although I then had to give my opinion against the identification of the Amur[129] tribes with the Eskimos, I was able to, at the Stockholm International Congress (International Congress 1874, Vol. I, p. 216), note some similarities between a skull from Greenland and a skull from the Amur region. This similarity is mainly based on the shape of the nose. Of all our people here, Mrs. Bairngo is the one who presents it most. Her nose is definitely not projecting, not even the tip, and the entire edge has a curved shape, flattened and almost simian. The nostrils, although small in themselves, are broad. Her nasal index is immediately after her husband's, the highest of the group.

---

[126] Having a long narrow nose with a nasal index of less than 47 on the skull or less than 70 on the living person. (Merriam-Webster Dictionnary).

[127] Old German name for the 'Nanai' people of Siberia, 'Hezhen' in China. See Brockhaus-Enzyklopedie. (Translator's note)

[128] Indigenous people of Russia, inhabiting the Amur River's estuary and Sakhalin Island. Now called the 'Nivkhes.'

[129] A river serving as a border between Russia and the People's Republic of China.

I have already said that the face is generally very broad. This width is mainly due to the strong prominence of the cheekbones. Besides, in men the forehead is also broad and rounded, which gives it something feminine. On the other hand, in women it is rather narrow and low at the same time, slightly receding. The lower jaw is rather strong, but in general the face thins down and the chin is generally narrow. The lips are large and relatively thick, especially the lower lip. This is all the more striking in the woman Bairngo since the upper lip is very flat. Overall the shape of the mouth, especially that of the women is very reminiscent of the mouth of anthropoids, namely chimpanzees. It moves forward more than required by the position of the teeth and alveoli. A true prognathism[130] is barely pronounced. Even in Tobias, whose mouth portion is the most prominent, the [lower] teeth coincide [with the upper ones].[131] These are worn very early because of the work on the tendons. The palate is deeply hollow; Tobias' shows at the back a median protuberance. The mouth often stays open.

Regarding the other features of the physical structure, I would like to highlight several facts which indicate a certain similarity with members of the Mongolian race. Namely the stature and the ratio between the body parts. You can see with your own eyes that this race is generally small. These people are without exception of small stature, 1,596 mm for men, 1,486 for women, an average of 1,552 mm. In relation to this small height, the head appears to be relatively big, the face above all very developed, moreover a long torso and the shoulders, in particular, remarkably broad. Consequently, their 'span' (the length of middle finger to the other) is, at least in the Christianized people, superior to their height, and often by 30 mm or more; it is smaller only among the pagans, but I remind you that I had to stop the woman Bairngo's examination because of her attack. However, the limbs are relatively short, especially the thighs. That is at least the impression that we get. Here are the results from the measurements that were

---

[130] The positional relationship of the upper or lower jaw to the skeletal base where either of the jaws protrudes.
[131] The words in braquets were added by the translator to ease the understanding. (Translator's note)

taken; I must clarify that for the limbs (excluding hands and feet) they were taken through the fur clothing:

Measurements	Abraham	Ulrike	Tobias	Tiggianiak	Bairngo
Upper arm length	307	280	300	284	-
Forearm length	247	217	226	217	-
Thigh length (femur epiphysis)	402	329	352	352	-
Lower leg length (internal ankle)	378	367	361	345	-
Foot length	245	237	233	236	210
Head Measures					
Maximum height	199	192	188	205	189
Maximum width	149	131	146	152	143
Ear height[132]	123	121	124	121	113
Facial height (~~root of the nose~~ hair edge to Chin)	194	192	198	191	177
Facial height B. (root of the nose to chin)	125	121	131	127	117
Facial width A. (cheek distance)	147	137	141	152	132
Facial width B. (distance of the upper jaw joints?)	107	94	95	106	94
Facial width C. (distance of the lower jaw corners)	116	117	123	136	116.5
Distance of the eyes A. (internal angle)	37	37	33.5	36,5	37
Distance of the eyes B. (lateral angle)	100	96.5	93	94	96
Nose A. height	59	53	57	60	51
Nose B. length	56	48	49	49	48
Nose C. width	37	32	38	42	35
Mouth width	57	51.5	50	57	55
Height of the ear[133]	62	60	65	70	69
Body Measures					

[132] We understand that 'Ear height' (Ohrhöhe) designates the vertical length of the ear itself. (Translator's note)

[133] We understand that 'Height of the ear' (Höhe des Ohrs) designates the height at which the ear is positionned on the skull. (Translator's note)

Measurements	Abraham	Ulrike	Tobias	Tiggianiak	Bairngo
Vertical height	1,635	1,524	1,550	1,605	1,448
Span	1,665	1,565	1,586	1,587	1,189
Shoulder width	358	347	366	378	-
Shoulder height	1,324	1,230	1,270	1,304	1,135
Elbow height	1,017	950	970	1,020	-
Wrist height	770	733	744	803	-
Middle finger's tip height	600	560	570	622	-
Extended arm length	694	660	679	645	-
Navel height	990	-	900	944	-
Femur epiphysis[134] height	850	755	780	775	-
Knee height	448	426	428	423	-
Ankle height	70	59	67	78	-
Foot length	245	237	233	236	210
Calculated Ratios:					
Body: foot (=1)	6.6	6.4	6.6	6.7	6.8
Leg: body (=100)	51.9	49.5	50.3	48.2	-
Arm: leg (=100)	81.6	87.4	87.0	83.0	-
Forearm: upper arm (=100)	80.4	77.5	75.3	76.4	-
Lower leg: thigh (=100)	94.0	111.5	102.5	98.0	-
Calculated Index-es					
Length/width index	74.9	68.2	77.6	74.1	75.7
Ear height index	61.8	63.0	66.0	59.0	59.8
Facial index A. jugal (a)	131.9	140.1	140.4	125.6	134.0
Facial index A. malar (b)	181.3	204.2	208.4	180.1	188.2
Facial index A. mandibular (c)	167.2	164.1	160.9	140.4	151.9
Facial index B. jugal (a)	85.0	88.3	92.9	83.5	88.6
Facial index B. malar (b)	116.8	128.7	137.8	119.8	124.4
Facial index B. mandibular(c)	107.7	103.4	106.5	93.3	100.4
Nasal index	62.7	60.3	66.6	70.0	68.6

---

[134] The epiphysis of the femur is where the muscles that make the thigh rotate are attached.

Note: For the calculation of the facial index A, we took into consideration the entire face height (hair edge to the chin), for the index B, the lower facial height (the root of the nose to the chin) (= 100).

First, this results in a fairly constant relationship between foot length and height, i.e. on average the height = 6.6 foot lengths. Among the pagans the foot is relatively bigger, among Christians smaller. Overall this corresponds to the usual ratios.

The ratio between the forearm and the upper arm, 77.4:100 on average, is considerably larger than in Europeans, as well as that between the lower leg and the thigh, which is 101.5 on average. If the latter figure is correct, it would show that the thigh is remarkably short; even if we assume an error in Tobias and Ulrike, it remains true that the lower leg's length is considerable.

The ratios between arm and leg, and leg and body height are relatively more constant. The first averages 84.7:100, the other 49.9:100.

These ratios have parallels in the Mongolian race. If you compare, for example, Japanese, you will find many individuals in whom these same features are found: large head, relatively long torso, short limbs. It is very interesting to see the smallness of the Eskimos' feet and hands, when they have to manually work so much and so hard that, from childhood on, a heavy physical workload falls on them on the land, and on the water. I took the contours of the hands and feet of these people and present you some examples (Fig. 2 to 5). They naturally show ratios that are a little larger than the actual ones. However they seem very small, although not disproportionate compared to the overall body measures. We know it is the same with the East Asian countries. Swords that come from these regions are characterized by their grip's smallness, just like the old bronze swords that are so often spoken about. Same thing for the feet, sometimes they are of an extraordinary narrowness and finesse. The ratio between width and length, the latter = 100, is noted.

The effect of hard and narrow shoe tips results, as for Europeans, in the compression of the toes; in Bairngo all her toes are gryphotic.[135] Overall, the second toe is the longest, only in Tiggianiak the first toe is. The foot's instep is generally high.

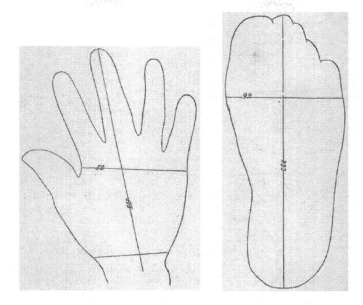

Fig. 39 Contour of Tobias' right hand and right foot (Fig. 2 and 3)
(Courtesy of JSTOR)

Abraham	40.8
Ulrike	37.1
Tobias	39.4
Tiggianiak	40.2
Bairngo	40.9
Average	39.6

[135] Abnormally thick or curved nails.

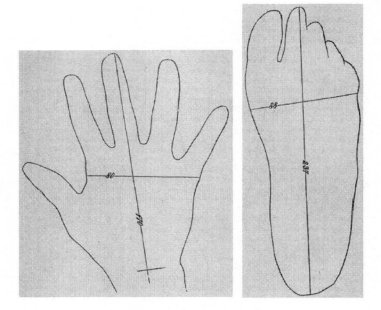

Fig. 40 Contour of Ulrike's right hand and right foot (Fig. 4 and 5)
(Courtesy of JSTOR)

Virchow continued his speech by discussing their intelligence and various aspects of their culture:[136]

> One also has to judge their intelligence in a similar way, I think. Nothing has ever more forcefully strengthened the impression that the Eskimos are part of a lower race than their clumsiness in the use of numbers. We find examples in Sir John Lubbock (*Prehistoric Times*, 4th edition. p. 525). Much more characteristic however is the observation by Mr. Jacobsen that the Christianized Labrador Eskimos make use in their language of the German words for numbers. This is obviously a strange phenomenon, but I lack documentation to analyze it. One can imagine that the necessity to count is very small in a population whose members live so scattered, own so few possessions and do not domesticate animals, except dogs. But yet, the large number of dogs they need for their sleighs indicates that they must have some sort of substitute for counting with words. In any case, the Christians prove that their brains, indeed, are able to develop, as is seen by numerous examples of artis-

---

[136] Virchow, Rudolf. (1880). p. 267-269.

tic achievements, even of the wild Eskimos. Especially Abraham, who seems to have enjoyed a complete education, proves to be one of the most educated and smart individuals one can see. Other than the map he drew of the area in question, we have here many of his drawings. First, the one he drew of himself. All the great painters do their self-portrait one day. Also a drawing of the mission of Hebron, etc.[137]

In addition to these absolutely modern performances, it is of great interest to see how, in the day-to-day technical works they produce for their local needs, they retain certain forms that obviously come from very ancient times. Here we must bear in mind the difficulties encountered in obtaining the most common tools in a country where almost nothing grows, where consequently the means provided by the vegetation is lacking. The wood they used was mainly driftwood rejected by the sea; fiber plants used for clothing did not exist, they only had furs, skins with bird plumage and seal intestines; to sew, nothing was found other than the tendons of animals which were shredded and made into thread. None of this has changed to a certain extent. Costumes that people make themselves come mainly from these materials. The most remarkable ones are those of women: a kind of tail coat with a basque[138] that extends to the calf level and within which patches of different colours are artistically interspersed. All this is sewn by women using thread from tendons which they chew with their teeth until they are sufficiently flexible and regular. They eat the leftovers since it is animal flesh. The whole technique is therefore based on the materials provided by nature. In this field, it is absolutely remarkable to see the level of perfection they managed to work the bones of northern animals, of seals, of walruses, and of whales and to draw objects from them, not only for domestic purposes, but also ornaments. If you would consider, in Mr. Hagenbeck's exhibition, the cords to which polished bones are clipped, you will be convinced by such delicate pieces, but you will also see that they

[137] Note added by Virchow: I note in passing that Mr. Jacobsen also brought back as an exhibition item a card of paper money samples. Since it seems that the international paper money will soon face a tunrning point, it could be taken as the basis for a future unification.
[138] A term of French origin that refers to the part of a waistcoat extending below the waist.

show a really surprising resemblance to the European Stone Age culture, especially that of southern Europe cavemen, represented by the troglodytic remains of southern France and northern Spain. You will also find that almost all the instruments used for fishing and hunting bear such a resemblance that one has the impression of being in a prehistory museum. The same applies to the strange stone tools they manufacture. It consists of a very convenient stone, a magnesite, easy to split and work; ancient cavemen also did not always use the hardest stones, but chose more convenient materials for certain types of usages.

While on one hand we find such parallelism of the greatest importance for the history of culture, on the other hand, a series of features rank Eskimos among the most inferior races of other continents. I would like to point out the extremely peculiar aspect of their spear-throwers.[139] I had already drawn your attention to the Greenland Eskimos' spear-throwers at the meeting of March 16, 1878. In today's collection of Eskimo instruments there are two kinds of spear-throwers: the ones used to hunt aquatic animals, the others are thrown at birds. For birds, one does not need javelins that are as big as those required for the stronger aquatic animals. The throwing itself is different.

To catch a low-flying aquatic bird that moves high enough above the water, the throw must be different from the one aiming to reach an animal that is at a respectable distance in the water. In the first case, they use a horizontal throw or at least one that is straight, more or less parallel to the sea's surface; in the other case, it is necessary to make a plunging throw so that the spear penetrates through the animal's top. For both these objectives, they not only have various spears and harpoons, but also various spear-throwers. Such a spear-thrower, called *nörsak*[140], serves to place the spear in the precise angle in which you want to project it. And the most remarkable fact is that for one of these devices, the bird spears of Labrador, the stick's shape is identical to the one Australians still use today across their continent and

---

[139] A device used to increase the initial speed and, by consequence, the reach or the penetration force of a projectile.
[140] Greenlandic word, also spelled *norsaq*. This type of propellant consists of a wooden board which had the effect of extending the arm of the person throwing it. Guigon, Gwénaële. (2006). p. 182.

for which we rarely find comparable ones elsewhere in the world: the spear-thrower, generally flat, hollow in the middle, lengthwise, and equipped on both sides with a lateral notch to ease the fingers' grip, has a seal tooth in its rear section which is fixed in a slot in the lance's back end.

Fig. 6.

Fig. 41 Labrador spear-thrower
(Courtesy of JSTOR)

On the other hand, the Greenlandic spear-thrower is built such that, at first, one does not understand how to use it. In two different locations, the lance has bone pegs pointing vertically or obliquely downwards, which are fixed into the spear-thrower's holes. The spear-thrower, also flat and slightly hollowed lengthwise, has in the middle two holes fairly distant from one another into which the lance pegs are inserted.

Fig. 7.

Fig. 42 Greenlandic spear-thrower
(Courtesy of JSTOR)

In this case, the lance extends past the propeller both at the front and back. One might think that in this device, holding the lance is restrictive; and yet they throw it with great ease and safety by projecting the spear by a shakeup. It results in a plunging throw. Both instruments here are made of wood; with the difference that, in the back portion of the Greenlandic spear-thrower, there is a plate made of bone which ends with a triangular extension (Fig. 7.) that serves to strengthen the wood.

In my opinion this is the most interesting of their achievements, as we very clearly see with what intelligence they, for the primary purpose of their existence, hunting, and with the simplest means, have invented an instrument which allows them to capture their preys with pinpoint accuracy and at a considerable distance.

It is not necessary that I speak about the Eskimo boats. They have already been sufficiently described and you see them here in action on the small lake. I will simply note that the wooden boats of the Labrador people, who have access to a certain amount of wood, are larger and more spacious than the Greenlanders' kayaks made largely of animal skins. On the other hand, the Labrador boats lack the watertight seal that unites the Greenlander's body to his kayak, giving him a great safety of movement on the sea and makes capsizing less dangerous.

Finally, Virchow ended his speech by asking permission to give his opinion on the article published in the *Magdeburger Zeitung* in which the author was indignant about the practice of exhibiting human beings in zoos:[141]

I will restrict myself to these remarks, but I would still like to ask you to allow me to briefly reject a strong attack that was published the other day in the *Magdeburger Zeitung* (N° 493, October 21). It takes aims, on the one hand, at any form of presentation of foreign races and, on the other hand, it argues against the use of zoological gardens for the exhibition of human beings. Since a newspaper is the organ of this attack, and since we live in a time when anything can obviously happen, even if it is deemed impossible, it seems necessary to me to categorically oppose to this first attack from a bewildered columnist.

In the article *The Eskimos in the Zoological Gardens of Berlin*, the author is not only content to declare that he is opposed to the exhibition of human beings, but he formally declares that, after consideration, we can rightfully expect the end of the exhibition of human beings in zoological gardens. I will briefly read his conclusion:

"We are totally prepared to have our opinion smiled at and ridiculed as sentimental by some. Nevertheless, we have wanted to express it here. If these 'interesting' human specimens need to be exhibited at all, a sense of 'racial eth-

---

[141] Virchow, Rudolf. (1880). p. 270.

ics'[142] should prevent us from displaying our equals in zoos. It should be easy to identify appropriate localities elsewhere."

The argumentation supporting this declaration is based on the idea – and that's actually what I particularly want to touch on – that there is no scientific interest, and that for the majority of people, there exists nothing more than sheer curiosity. The columnist says from time to time: "However, it is very interesting," as if that were a reproach. In this respect, it seems that this gentleman does not realize that the 'interest' itself can be diverse. Some things are merely interesting as curiosities, but those things we explore in the interest of science, like the progressing exploration of nature and human beings, are mainly brought home to us because they are interesting. Indeed, these theories about human beings are interesting for anyone who, to some degree, wants to be informed about the position mankind occupies in nature and about the human race's evolution.

Those who cannot understand that the most important and magnificent questions mankind can ask are driven by our curiosity about ourselves, seem least qualified to write feature articles. An editorial staff should at least think twice before including such comments in its papers.

That is the point I wanted to make. Furthermore, I testify that a positive scientific interest of the highest importance is linked with this presentation. Therefore, I do not want to pass up the opportunity to publicly express our special thanks to Mr. Hagenbeck and to ask him not to be deterred by such attacks and to continue, in the way he has done up to now, for the greatest benefit of anthropological science.

The only reaction to the lecture given by Rudolf Virchow that has been found so far is the one published in the religious journal *Sunday at Home*:[143]

A celebrated professor of Berlin, Mr. Virchow, gave a public conference to which he caused all these Esquimaux to come, and in

---

[142] The word 'Rassenanstand' is within quotes in Virchow's text. (Translator's note)
[143] The Esquimaux. (1881, May 21). p. 328.

exhibiting Abraham and his group, he exclaimed: "See, gentle-men, what civilization can do for the most degraded people." This learned man has not given the right word. What has civilized these Esquimaux is the Gospel of Jesus Christ, announced to them by the Moravian missionaries, and which they have re-ceived into their hearts by faith. Abraham and his people have become Christians after being pagans; the other father and his wife remain pagans. By this, and not by anything else, comes all the difference between them.

Ah! They, who think that evangelistic missions among pagan people are of no use, have here by a palpable fact, a proof, that the Gospel, which is the power of God for the salvation of every man that believes, is also the most powerful agent of civili-zation.

THE STAY IN PRAGUE

The group departed from Berlin on November 15 at 8 a.m. That same day, an ad appeared in the *Bohemia,* a Prague newspaper, informing the public of the arrival of the Labrador *Eskimos* at the Kaufmann Menagerie. The site was to be closed for the next two days to allow its reorganization. The public was invited to come and meet them from November 17 until the 28.

Fig. 43 Advertisement, *Bohemia*, November 15, 1880
See the transcript on the next page.
(Czech Republic National Library)

Carl Hagenbeck's Labrador Eskimo families

A first in Europe
Arrive here from Berlin today and are staying at
C. Kaufmann's Menagerie
Due to internal rearrangements
Today and tomorrow, closed.

Wednesday, 17 November at 11 o'clock
First presentation by the Eskimos
With their 'ice dogs,' summer and winter huts,
equipment for hunting and fishing and
an interesting ethnographic collection

From Wednesday 17 to Sunday 28 of the month
Four daily performances:
11 in the morning, 4 and 6 in the afternoon and 8 in the evening

At 4 in the afternoon and 8 in the evening
also appearance of all animal trainers
At 11 in the morning and 6 in the afternoon
with the Elephants performance
The Eskimos remain in Prague for 12 days
and then leave for Paris

The details collected so far on their stay in Prague come from Abraham's diary:

Nov. 26. I am writing in Prague here far away, in Austria, in the country of Catholics, in a big city. We are here for two weeks, inside a big long house. To go out is impossible, so that we may not be caught by the Catholics. Yes indeed, we are highly regarded and have a house in the big house. It also has a seal, coming from Holland for us to eat, but it only is allowed to be stabbed with the seal harpoon. But until now I still have seen few believers, those, which are not from us. They sang with little voice because of their fear of the Catholics.

We too with a little voice can sing and pray to get help from the Lord, so that nothing happens to us through the Catholics, because they are always asking if we are believers; we are unable to deny and we claim it constantly while we wonder if they will do us harm. Yes, indeed, because everything is to be feared here, we feel that we need a lot of help.

One day in the afternoon at 4 o'clock, countless soldiers came; the big ways were totally filled. They carried fire[144] as well as lanterns with a handle; the horses had fire as well. But they have also made beautiful voice (music), most delightful to hear, with the trumpets.

Nov. 27. Have caught a seal (netsek) in Prague in a pond, while there were enormously many people, yes indeed countless. When I harpooned it with the seal harpoon, everybody clapped their hands greatly like the eider ducks. When I was done with it (when I killed it), the voice makers sang greatly with violins, drums, trumpets, and flutes. Yes indeed, to talk to each other was impossible because of the many voices.

Fig. 44 Advertisement, *Bohemia*, November 19, 1880
(Czech Republic National Library)

---

[144] The French translation of Abraham's diary published in 1883 specifies that these were torches. See Notes de voyages d'Abraham, l'Esquimau. (1883).

On November 29, they all packed up and the caravan set off for Frankfurt.

Kaufmann's Menagerie also departed to travel to Munich, so we travelled together as far as Schwandorf, where we separated and continued our journey to **Frankfurt**, where we arrived on the 30th. On the 31st we sat up our exhibit and prepared everything. (J. A. Jacobsen's diary, November 29, 1880)

The Stay in Frankfurt

In Frankfurt, the *Eskimos* were exhibited at the local zoo. Each family's hut was erected by the pond on either side of the music pavilion.

Fig. 45 Frankfurt Zoo, 1878
The music pavilion appears on the left, overlooking the pond. The tower housed the aquarium. (Courtesy of Frankfurt Zoo Archives).

Jacobsen's diary is silent concerning their stay in Frankfurt except for a note about the weather being continually unfavourable, with permanent rain and fog, which influenced the number of visitors. Meanwhile, Abraham seemed to find that, here too, there were a lot of visitors.

From Prague, we left for Frankfurt, where it has many people. There we had two houses in the open in an enclosure. In our whole village grove, we were guarded day and night by soldiers, who took turns. There are many Jews there; the Catholics are very greatly despised there. But there we very often paddled the kayak even on a pond.

Fig. 46 Map of the Frankfurt Zoo, 1875
(Courtesy of Frankfurt Zoo Archives)

The local newspapers provided most of the information regarding the exhibition in Frankfurt.

Wöchentliche Anzeigen, December 3, 1880

Despite the weather becoming cooler, two Eskimo families from Labrador ventured with their huts, dogs, boats and all their rigging from Berlin to Frankfurt am Main, staying there for two weeks outdoors at the zoo. They find the climate of central Germany quite enjoyable and are even required to participate in the general census on December 1, even though, as foreigners with temporary residence permit, they cannot be counted as members of the German population.

Frankfurter Nachrichten, December 3, 1880

In the night from Nov. 30 to Dec. 1, our city received a rare as well as interesting increase in population, namely two Eskimo families, eight heads altogether. The high ladies and gentlemen, or rather the ladies and gentlemen coming from high up north arrived just in time to be included in the census. Mr. Carl Hagenbeck from Hamburg, the one who in the past had introduced us to the children of the south, the Nubians, has also brought us these guests from the northernmost populated areas. And they are children, just as they are; because even if the so-called culture has already greatly influenced them, for us, there still remain enough interesting and natural things about them to observe and maybe also to admire.

As we already know, we distinguish two tribes among these inhabitants of northern polar countries, who are quite different in their particularities: namely, the Greenlandic people, and those tribes who live on the Labrador coastline, meaning the American continent. Our guests belong to the latter category: strictly speaking, they are under the head sovereignty of England. But England does not seem to care much for 'Her Majesty's subjects,' at least there are no English officials in that region, so that these children of nature, still very naive in spite of civilization's efforts, are completely left into the hands of the Hudson's Bay Company, or more precisely, of the Herrnhut colony. Looking at Mr. J. A. Jacobsen's personal messages, one could almost doubt if this is to their advantage. This man, who had been sent out on the instruction of Hagenbeck to go to the Eskimos in their home country and to induce them into a 'voyage' to the European continent, talks inexhaustibly about how they are dependant on the ones named above. Not only can the Eskimos obtain the things they need only through their mediation, they are also so personally dependent on them that none of them would, for example, try to even temporarily leave the country without their permission. But the Danish government in Greenland as well as the Herrnhuters in Labrador have their own fairly important reasons for keeping their subjects cut off, if possible, from the outside world. They especially and firmly oppose their visit to Europe, because they fear that they could, on that occasion, get to learn some unpleasant things about the real value of the products derived from hunting they barter, as well as about the real price of the materials they receive in exchange.

After long wanderings between the west coast of Greenland, Cumberland and Labrador, Mr. Jacobsen finally managed to find only two Eskimo families who, in spite of everything, felt independent enough to take part in such a tempting journey to Europe. Since this journey was really tempting to all of them, and had it been possible, all the Eskimos living in Labrador, who are only about 2,000 heads, would have liked to all move together to Europe. Stories were told to them by three Inuit fellow (from Greenland), the first ones to come to Europe three years ago. They related their travelling experiences and how they earned quite considerable amounts of money. These stories have stirred the wish in the whole population to become rich in the same easy and pleasant way. Therefore, Mr. Jacobsen can consider himself lucky to have recruited these two families for his undertaking, and after they were shown in Berlin and Prague, they arrived here, as we said before, late in the evening of the last day of November.

In the Zoological Garden people had already set up two earth huts for them on the right and left sides of the music pavilion. These huts are, even if not built by the Eskimos themselves, yet created in accordance with a model of the dwellings in their home country. The so-called wild Eskimos, i.e. the ones that could preserve their freedom to a certain extent and kept themselves independent from the missionaries, live in tents during the summer, but in earth huts in the winter, which are similar to those we can see built in the Zoological Garden.

They are dug into the earth as a shelter from the cold and consist of a wooden shed which is covered, on the outside, with piled up earth, here with grass. The real ice huts are only built by those who live so far north that they cannot find any soil or driftwood. A tunnel, several yards long, and which always faces south, leads to the door of these huts. The inside, as far as we can see it here in the Zoological Garden, is neatly covered with boards, but as Mr. Jacobsen asserts, the huts in Labrador also enjoy this luxury. There are even hinges and door locks on the small huts, approximately 15 to 20 feet wide; the Herrnhuters' stores have made these and many other luxury articles indispensable for these inhabitants who were originally undemanding. The only thing that does not seem to be influenced by European culture is the semi-transparent window made of seal intestines, which is installed on the roof of each hut. The shared sleeping area faces the entrance, about half a meter above the ground. It is richly provided with furs, but here again, mattresses looking very civilized remind us of the European culture.

The Christian Eskimo family dwells in the left hut, west of the music pavilion. They come from the Nakkwak colony [sic], which is quite far up north and consists of Abraham, the head of the family, his wife Ulrike, and their two daughters Sara and Marie, as well as their companion Tobias. Abraham is 35 years old; he is the most intelligent of all of them, even though he is not the most handsome or, to be more precise, the least ugly one of the group. He acts as the interpreter, is able to read and write, is also said to be musical and tries his hand at drawing, but because of the move into his new dwelling and of the unpacking of all his possessions, the Northern whiz did not yet have time, and was not yet at leisure, to demonstrate all of his talents. His wife Ulrike, even if she is not really a Venus, has a fair appearance. She is 24 years old and has the two chubby-cheeked children named earlier, the oldest of whom is 3 years old and the youngest not even one year old. Tobias, the companion, is at the happy age of 21, and being neither worried by the military service, nor probably by any other awkwardness linked to a culture that is totally unknown to him, he gives the impression of a full-moon-face perpetually smiling and shiny from fish oil. We probably do not need to go into details about the looks of all of the ladies and gentlemen here, because these looks are already known too well through pictures and texts, and the Eskimos present here do in general live up to the expectations we are used to have of them. All of them have a short, stocky physique and, even if they are not of the same dwarfish size as their namesakes from Greenland, they still do rarely reach the medium size. Because of their clothes made of seal-furs they seem to be even stockier and plumper than they really are. In addition, when we imagine the black hair growing quite thick, long and straggly, the leathery yellow complexion, the slanted deep-set eyes, and the wide mouth, we get a picture that pleasantly brings together ugliness, kindness, and comic. The comic aspect, especially, becomes obvious in the women because of their peculiar clothing. Besides the obligatory seal-boots and trousers they wear a tail-like upper dress, the appendage of which dangles behind them like a beaver tail. A big hood completes this un-Parisianlike promenading dress, and Mrs. Ulrike, married to Abraham, simply uses the hood, now back in fashion among our women, to put her child Marie in. These women's seal-tails appear even funnier when it is cold and a second, a third, or even a fourth layer is put on. One is actually quite mistaken to believe that the Eskimos are tough and, to a high degree, insensitive to cold. In fact, it is quite the opposite, and they can only protect themselves against the harsh effects of the cold with the help of their extremely warm clothing, and experience shows that we as Europeans can stand the harshness of the Nordic climate much more easily than the native people. Thus yesterday morning, with the temperature well above zero, we could see the women running around with two tail-coats, one on top of the other. By the way, this whole 'national costume,' at least in the family converted to Christianity, seems to be disappearing very quickly, and the women at the mission are even already ashamed of it and particularly like to follow European fashion and to wear wool skirts. It was with a lot of reluctance that the members of Abraham's family agreed to return to their forefathers' custom during their stay in Europe. But this did not happen unconditionally either, because we can see European vests and shirts peeking out from under the seal furs the men wear, while 4-year-old Sara protects her head with a crocheted woolen hood, although she already possesses a beaver tail with hood. By the way, the dresses made from seal furs, in spite of their awkward shape, do not lack a certain elegance, because the makers knew how to get good variations by combining different types of furs.

The second hut, east of the music pavilion, accommodates the second family who is not yet converted to Christianity. It consists of Tigganick, about 40 years old, his wife Paeing [Paingu], probably 10 years older, and their 15-year-old daughter Noggasack. The family is more interesting than the previous one, in so far as culture has not smudged too much of their naturalness. In their home country, they are happy to live together with three other families, cut off from the whole world, without any knowledge of 'authorities' and everything that ensues from it. The survival instinct controls their whole life; they do not know any task other than to supply their stomach with fat and their lamp with fish oil, a task which, under the prevailing circumstances, certainly seems big enough to fill a whole human life. Besides that, Tigganick also acts as a magician, in which he is faithfully supported by his better half. Madam Paeing is the complete model of female ugliness, however, she is said to be a lady with considerable natural wit, in contrast with Miss Noggasack, her daughter, who is said to be of great stupidity. Besides, these so-called wild Eskimos, too, have very quickly got used to culture's blessings, at least with regard to food, because even if in the first days of their stay in Europe they demanded and received their national drink, fish-liver oil, they do not long for it anymore and are content with fish and meat.

The Eskimos do, of course, have their entire household and fishing gear with them; furthermore, they also brought a pack of the famous, half-wild dogs with them, which they use to pull their sleds. These animals are remarkably strong, comparable to wolves, and, according to the declarations of their masters, are dumb, disobedient, and voracious, so that their masters can only manage to keep them in order with the help of a colossal whip. The grey animals belong to the Greenlandic race, while the black ones live in Labrador. In the morning of the day before yesterday, when we had the opportunity to observe our foreigners, they could not yet show us their ability to drive the dog-sled, nor their boat, the famous kayak, but they will well make up for it in the coming days. Besides, Mr. Hagenbeck has also brought a large collection of Greenlandic antiquities and native tools, an exhibition which was put up yesterday.

Fig. 47 Frankfurt Zoo's Pond
(© France Rivet, Polar Horizons, 2013)

Ten days later, a shorter version of the above article was published in a different paper:

Wöchentliche Anzeigen, December 14, 1880

In Frankfurt, the Eskimos were, for twelve days, the zoo's main attraction for all friends of natural sciences and of ethnology as well as for many teachers and students from near and far. These two families of Eskimo origin, which are considerably different in character and religion, live on the Labrador coast of the American mainland's far north, under British rule, but independently of English officials, under the sole authority of the Hudson's Bay Company and of the Moravian colony. It is through them that they get, at excessively high prices, most materials (iron, door locks, guns) that they need for the daily seal hunt which is essential to their survival. In summer, they live in small tents; in the winter, they live in sod huts, like the ones built at the zoo. So that people are protected from the cold, these huts are dug in the ground and consist of a wooden construction of 15 or 20 feet in length covered with earth or sod. A single window, made of seal intestines, provides from the roof's top a low light into the hut where a common sleeping place, half a meter high, is well equipped with skins. One can see next to it a pot for cooking on stones.

The Christian family occupied the hut in the foreground, to the left of the music pavilion. The hut that accommodated the heathen Eskimo family was in the back. From the Nachvak [sic] colony, the Christian family consists of the head of the house, Abraham, aged 35, a sealer by profession, and his wife Ulrike, aged 24, two chubby-cheeked daughters, Sara and Maria, aged 3½ and 1 respectively, and Tobias, a family friend, who — untroubled by any military service, professional choice or family — shows always a smiling full-moon face, shiny from seal blubber. Their stockier body appearance is, by the way, larger than that of their Greenland cousins [and] makes them even more rotund in their sealskin clothes than they actually are. Their hair is long, thick and strong with black locks covering their yellow leather-like face, almond-shaped eyes, and big mouth. Despite the ugliness of their facial features, they display a sense of kindness and humor. Also the women wear pants and boots made from sealskin, over which they wear a tail-coat-like garment (2 or 3 when it is very cold) with, at the back, an oval whitish addition made of sealskin with a red border resembling a beaver tail. Also the little

4-year-old girl walks around with a little beaver tail and collects all kinds of coins for the parents. Totally separated from the Christians, the non-Christian Eskimo family lives with eight wolf-dogs, dog sleds, and boats. It consists of Tigganick, the father aged 40, his older wife of 50 years, Mrs. Paceng [Paingu], and their 15-year-old daughter Roggasack [Nuggasak]. The latter is the perfect embodiment of stupidity and ugliness; her mother, cunning and funny, practices with her serious, tall husband the side-business of magic. They treat their stomach to bacon, their lamp with oil, and their dogs with seal meat. They smoke in turn the same short earthen pipe and only take care of their very simple fishing gear and utensils. Their culture is much less advanced than that of Nubians, who, under the influence of warmer sun, exhibit agility, artistic ability and intelligence. When given a doll, Mrs. Paceng, the Eskimo mother aged 50, seemed already amazed beyond measure and demonstrated a naive and child-like delight. On December 13, the Nordic visitors, which were already in Prague and Berlin, left for the south.

Fig. 48 Nuggasak, 1880
Photo by Jacob Martin Jacobsen.
(Moravian Archives, Herrnhut)

THE STAY IN DARMSTADT AND
NUGGASAK'S DEATH

On December 12, the day of their departure from Frankfurt, young Nuggasak fell ill. The group left for Darmstadt[145] accompanied by Mrs. Jacobsen. "From there, we went away again in a sleigh with wheels and horses in the night, all of us, to Darmstadt," wrote Abraham.

In Darmstadt, the group was exhibited at the Orpheum, a rotunda with an indoor skating rink which was built for Princess Alice, the youngest daughter of Queen Victoria and wife of Louis IV, Grand Duke of Hesse. Located in Washington Square, at the intersection of Spessartring and Alfred Messel-We,[146] the Orpheum was said to be the Mecca of entertainment for the local population. Around 1895, it was transformed into a theater and vaudeville.

Abraham described his temporary home as follows:

> In Darmstadt, we had a beautiful house in a beautiful big round house, which is a playground for ice-skating on wheels. There we often sleighed round and round inside the house, all of us sitting on it. There one of us, Terrianiak's daughter, Nochasak, stopped living (died) very fast and suffered terribly greatly.

Indeed, it is in Darmstadt that the group was first struck by the death of one of their own. In the afternoon of December 13, young Nuggasak's state had worsened and she was refusing to take medication.

---

145 Located approximately 25 km from Frankfurt.
146 The building was destroyed by an air raid on the night of August 25 to 26, 1944.

On the morning of December 14, 1880, stupor struck:

> At 8 o'clock in the morning we awoke to the shout "Nog-gasak is dead!" You may well imagine our shock. The physician diagnosed a rapid stomach ulcer as having caused the death. The poor parents did not stop crying from morning until evening. Of course it also had a very depressing effect on the others and on us as well. (J. A. Jacobsen's diary, December 14, 1880)

On December 15, local newspapers were not yet aware of the girl's death when they published a short text on the *Eskimos'* presence in their city:[147]

> The demonstrations [exhibitions] of two Eskimo families in the skating rink are evoking much interest among the visitors because of the highly peculiar northern scene that is being shown. It is quite unfortunate that such unfavourable weather will prevent many from experiencing these unusual impressions. The people, though very small, appear healthy, happy, and well-kept and they try, by using their sleds (pulled vigorously by six strong sled dogs), [and by] advancing stealthily towards seals and others, to convey to the audience somewhat of a notion of life in the Arctic. The shows are ending today, Wednesday.

But, no later than the next day, on December 16, the two local daily newspapers announced Nuggasak's death. One pretended that the mild climate had been fatal to the young girl. It is likely through this newspaper that the hundreds of onlookers who attended the funeral took note of the time and place of the ceremony:[148]

> *Darmstädter Tagblatt.* One of the two Eskimo families, namely the heathen one, who were shown here at the local skating rink for a few days, has experienced a terrible loss through the sudden death of their 15-year-old daughter. In any case, it appears that this winter's mild weather had a baleful influence on the

---

[147] *Darmstädter Tagblatt*, (1880, December 15).
[148] *Darmstädter Tagblatt*, (1880, December 16) and *Darmstädter Zeitung*, (1880, December 16).

young Eskimo, in that she died the day before yesterday, after having shortly before experienced strong stomach cramps. According to our information, the funeral will take place this afternoon at the local cemetery at 3 o'clock; whether it follows their country's customs we do not know.

Darmstädter Zeitung. Darmstadt. December 15. Of the Eskimos that were recently exhibited here at the Skating Rink, the 15-year-old Eskimo girl Nagasak died yesterday. The deceased is the daughter of the Eskimo chieftain Teggianiack (called the tracking fox) and his wife Beango [Paingu] (called the fleeing stag). The family's hometown is Nachvak in Labrador, they are heathen.

Jacobsen wrote the following concerning the burial:

Schoepf had meanwhile departed for Crefeld[149] and Mr. Walter had been sent by Hagenbeck to attend the burial, which took place at 4 o'clock in the afternoon. It had been advertised among the public by the registrar's office, and on our arrival at the cemetery, we therefore found several thousands of curious people, who had come to see the burial. I had the parents and Abraham in a hackney carriage which I had driven up to the grave to avoid the throng. I led the parents to the grave. But since the mother broke out in loud crying, I let them board the hackney coach again and drove them home. (J. A. Jacobsen's diary, December 16, 1880)

Nuggasak's death was recorded in Darmstadt's vital records on December 14 by the Orpheum's owner, Mr. Kranich.

The teenager was buried in section II-J, row 3, grave 16 of the old cemetery.[150]

---

[149] Until 1929, Crefeld was spelled with a 'C,' since then, it is spelled with a 'K.'

[150] Darmstadt's cemetery and archives were heavily damaged during World War II. The section of the cemetery where Nuggasak was buried is still there, but her grave no longer is.

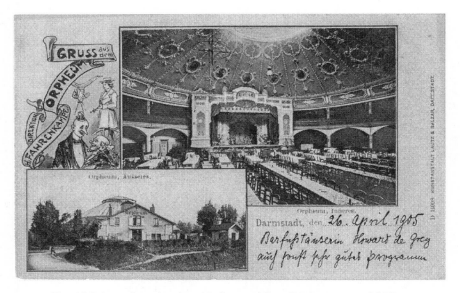

Fig. 49 Internal and external views of the Orpheum, ca 1905
(Courtesy of Stadtarchiv Darmstadt – ST 53 Fotosammlung)

Fig. 50 Section II-J, Darmstadt cemetery
(© France Rivet, Polar Horizons, 2013)

THE STAY IN BOCKUM AND
THE DEATHS OF PAINGU AND MARIA

In the morning of December 17, the group left Darmstadt and headed to Bockum, a suburb of Crefeld, where it was to be exhibited at the local zoo until December 30.

> Departure for Crefeld in the morning at 8 o'clock. The parents were quite composed and even became talkative while we were travelling the beautiful route from Mainz to Crefeld. I showed them the vineyards. The Rhine was very choppy because it ran very high, and at several places it had caused damage (by flooding). Arrived at **Crefeld** at 7 o'clock in the evening. We were welcomed by Mr. Schoepf and the director of the garden, Mr. Stickmann.[151] (J. A. Jacobsen's diary, December 17, 1880)

The Bockum Zoo was an oasis delimited by the following streets: Uerdinger (called Crefelderstraße at the time), Schönwasserstraße, Grenzstraße, and Glockenspitzstraße (called Oppumerstraße at the time). Tiergartenstraße ran through the middle of the park from east to west.[152] The park, developed by the banker Gustav Molenaar in the 1860s, was covered by a network of winding paths that bore a variety of trees (chestnut, beech, maple) and lush beds of roses. The park's northern part was purchased in 1879 by Carl Müller-Kuchler who turned it into a recreation center with a restaurant and animal pens. He also offered

---

[151] Jacobsen is actually referring to Hermann Stechmann, the Bockum Zoo director.
[152] The area where the Bockum Zoo was located in 1880 is now a residential area. All buildings were destroyed and the pond was filled. Today's zoo, the Krefeld Zoo, was opened in 1938 a few blocks east of the original location.

boat rides on the pond, concerts of famous musicians, pony rides, and ice skating.[153]

Fig. 51 Bockum Zoo's Pond, 1906
(Polar Horizons Collection)

It is here that the Eskimos celebrated Christmas 1880. But, a few days before the celebrations, Abraham, Tobias, and Tigianniak went into the city to meet the population:[154]

Recently, in the evening, dressed in European clothes and accompanied by their guide, the three male members of the Eskimo families visited two restaurants in the city. While the oldest, the heathen Terrianjack with his stoic composure, but quietly enjoying it, consumed the offered delicacies available to him, Abraham and Tobias, aged 21, were in the most exuberant mood; the latter showed a promising gift for delicate gallantry. Their simple cheerfulness, their efforts to join the conversation by saying a few words in German and English, the willingness with which they gave examples of their writing and drawing, and the satisfaction of seeing their art recognized, clearly showed how at ease they felt. On Christmas Eve which young and old anticipate with joy, the Eskimos, who will be familiar from the Christian family at their mission colony, will also celebrate in their family's intima-

[153] Kremers, Elisabeth. (2002). p. 91-92.
[154] *Crefelder Zeitung*, (1880, December 24).

cy with a Christmas tree and gift distribution. Immediately after Christmas they will leave Crefeld and go directly to Paris.

Had an order from Mr. Hagenbeck to buy varied Christmas presents for the Eskimos. The ballroom of the restaurant had been made available to us, and there we prepared a beautiful Christmas tree. After everything was ready, we let the Eskimos come in. They were quite heartily delighted, both at the tree as well as the gifts. (These consisted of underpants, vests, etc., and for Abraham a violin, and for Tobias a guitar. In addition, each family received a large group picture that had been photographed in Prague). We ordered wine and were together until 11 o'clock at night, not knowing which cruel blows fate had in store for us. (J. A. Jacobsen's diary, December 24, 1880)

CREFELD.
Partie aus dem
Tiergarten.

Fig. 52 Concert hall where Christmas was celebrated, Bockum
The Kaiseraal (the Emperor's Hall) opened in 1879.
(Polar Horizons Collection)

In the evening of December 25, Paingu suddenly fell ill with the same symptoms as Nuggasak. Doctors were called in and they reassured the group that it was rheumatism; there was no need to worry. The doctors' next visit reached the same conclusion:

rheumatism. At the same time, young Sara started showing the first signs of illness. She complained of being cold and vomited.

On December 27, tragedy struck again:

> The woman is seriously ill, and may it not go with her as with her daughter. Sara is also ill. How will it all end? We were supposed to depart tonight, but cannot travel under these circumstances.
>
> Tonight at 7 o'clock the old Paingo died. We all stood next to her. Ten minutes earlier the physician had examined her and gave us the assurance that it was not dangerous. We all then went down to the coach, where we stood talking about the patient, when Mrs. Jacobsen approached and told us to come immediately, because the woman was lying dying. She died one minute after we had returned. Peace be with her. She was a good old woman. The husband is very sad, of course, and expressed his wish to be able to accompany his wife and daughter soon. (J. A. Jacobsen's diary, December 27, 1880)

Later, Jacobsen added:

> On margin: It is still a puzzle to me that none of the many physicians could recognize such a disease as dreadful as smallpox. Neither do I understand why none of us Europeans became infected, who after all, had been with the people constantly. (J. A. Jacobsen's diary, December 27, 1880)

An autopsy was performed on December 28 and Paingu was buried that evening:

> Today the woman was dissected by three physicians, Dr. Jacobi, Dr. Zimmermann (junior doctor at the hospital), and an additional older sensible physician, whose name unfortunately I have forgotten – nothing was found however that allowed diagnosing a specific disease. She was buried in Bockum[155] in the evening, attracting a large

---

[155] Bockum is now a district of Krefeld (in the north-east section).

> number of people. Her husband and Tobias attended. It is
> a dreadful time for us. I feel directly responsible for the people. (J. A. Jacobsen's
> diary, December 28, 1880)

Fig. 53 Paingu, 1880
Photo by Jacob Martin Jacobsen. (Moravian Archives, Herrnhut)

Jacobsen attended Paingu's autopsy, a procedure during which physicians removed her skullcap to expose her brain. Jacobsen took the skullcap, wrapped it in paper and, for the coming weeks, carried it in his luggage among his clothes!

Paingu's death was recorded in Bockum's vital records on December 28 by the zoo director, Hermann Stechmann. It reads as follows:[156]

> Before the undersigned registrar appeared today, the person of Director of the animal park Hermann Stechmann, residing at Bockum N° 270, who indicated that (unemployed/not earning income) Baengnu the wife of Teggianiak, 50 years old, (heathen) religion, place of residence

---

[156] Stadtarchiv Krefeld, December 27, 1880 (Standesamt Bockum C N° 148/1880).

Nachvak (Labrador), born in Nachvak, (daughter of two parents unknown to us) died in Bockum in the animal garden on December 27 of the year one thousand eight hundred eighty at 7 o'clock in the evening.

The city of Krefeld's death records also include a notice to the effect that Paingu would have died from pulmonary edema.[157]

According to the 1894 map of Bockum, the cemetery was located on Verbergerstraße north of Uerdinger street on the right-hand side. The site has since been converted into a park and hosts a daycare. Near the playground at the back of the park, a memorial to soldiers killed during the Franco-Prussian War of 1870–1871 is the sole monument left to remind us that the site was once a cemetery.

Fig. 54 Site of Bockum's cemetery where Paingu was buried
(© France Rivet, Polar Horizons, 2013)

The *Crefelder Zeitung* reported Paingu's death and attributed it to old age:[158]

Yesterday, after being sick for only 2.5 days, died a member of the Eskimo troop that is presently staying at the local zoo, by the name of 'Bängnu,' the wife of the heathen Eskimo 'Täggianjak,' preceded 14 days ago, during the troop's tour in Darmstadt, by her 15-year-old daughter 'Nogosak.' Mrs. Bängnu was treated by two local doctors and, after her death, autopsied by three. The autopsy's result was negative and the cause of death is proba-

---

[157] Stadtarchiv Krefeld, December 27, 1880 (StadtA KR 6/290, Bl. 7).
[158] *Crefelder Zeitung*, (1880, December 29).

bly old age. The woman had already reached an age between 50 and 55 years, which has to be called a respectable age since the age of Eskimos generally does not exceed 60 years in their Northern homeland. 'Täggianjak,' Bängnu's husband, who loved his wife very much, was very calm.

On December 29, doctors noticed that young Sara showed symptoms of smallpox. Her admission to the hospital was most urgent. Despite her parents' dismay, Sara was admitted to the hospital that evening.

Fig. 55 Alexianer hospital, Crefeld, 1883
(Courtesy of Alexianer Hospital, Krefeld)

The collection was packed and in the evening, everything was loaded (at the train station). Today the physicians diagnosed that little Sara is suffering from **smallpox**, and a transfer to the hospital is absolutely necessary, which was achieved the same evening – I first had a hard fight with the parents, who did not want to part from their child. Had to seek help from Schoepf. Eventually, Abraham let himself be persuaded to hand over the child to the hospital; he followed her there himself, prayed with the child and parted in tears. Mrs. Jacobsen stays with the child as a nurse. (J. A. Jacobsen's diary, December 29, 1880)

The general practitioner Jacobi immediately informed the Crefeld burgomaster's office on the situation. He wrote: "The child

Sara Paulus, daughter of Abraham Paulus, Labrador Eskimo who resides in the zoo in Crefeld is sick with smallpox."[159]

This disease with fatal consequences resulted in the zoo being officially closed for a few days.[160]

At 8 o'clock in the morning of December 30, the group headed to Crefeld's train station. The train departed sixty minutes later.

> I was almost surprised at the calm shown by the Eskimos. We travelled via Aachen, Erquelinnes, Namur and Saint-Quentin. At the French border, the coaches were filled to the brim with soldiers on leave. We sat so tightly packed like herrings in a barrel. (J. A. Jacobsen's diary, December 30, 1880)

> Arrived finally at Paris at 5 o'clock in the morning. I must admit, it was the most tiring journey I ever did on a train [...] At 11 o'clock, Mr. Schoepf received a telegram from Hagenbeck which announced the death of little Sara. I must admit that it had a devastating effect on all of us. In the first moment I was totally at a loss because one thing had now become certain: smallpox was among the unfortunate Eskimos, and it became clear to me at last that the two others had also died of smallpox — only that they did not break in a rash — the more dangerous. The final hour of the old year was also to end in a bad news. It was a sad year for me. May the new one be better, but the prospects are truly not very promising. The first thing we will do tomorrow is to have the people be vaccinated, because none of them were vaccinated in their old homeland, because there are no physicians there. Thus ended the old year.
>
> On margin: Upon arrival in Hamburg, none of us had thought of having the people vaccinated. In 1877, I had the Greenlanders vaccinated in Greenland, but this time, it was forgotten. It probably had to do with my being sickly all summer, as reported before, and that upon our

---

[159] Stadtarchiv Krefeld, StadtA KR 6/290, page 7.
[160] Stadtarchiv Krefeld, StadtA KR 6/290, Events section.

arrival in Hamburg, I had to go to the hospital myself.
(J. A. Jacobsen's diary, December 31, 1880)

In his diary, Abraham recounts the death of Paingu and Sara as follows:

[...] in another country, in Krefeld, her mother also died, greatly suffering as well. After her, also little Sara stopped living, peacefully, with a great rash and swellings, because she was swollen all over. After two days of being sick, she died in Krefeld.

While she was still alive, she was brought to hospital, where I went with her. She still had her mind, while I was there. She still prayed the song *Ich bin ein kleines kindelein* (I am a little child, you see). When I wanted to leave, she sent her greetings to her mother and little sister. When I left her, she slept; from then on, she did not wake up anymore. For this we both had reason to be thankful. While she was still alive we went to Paris and travelled the whole day and the whole night through.

Abraham's diary ends on this last sentence.

Sara's death was recorded in Bockum's vital records on December 28 by an employee of the hospital and reads as follows:[161]

Before the undersigned registrar appeared today, the person of (hospital office servant) Philippe Hoffmann, residing in Crefeld, who indicated that Sara Paulus 3 years and (six months??) old, (catholic) religion, residing in Labrador, born in Labrador, (daughter of the now residing in Paris Eskimo parents whose names are unknown to the signed officials) died in Crefeld in (municipal hospital) on December 31 of the year one thousand eight hundred and eighty (before noon) at 10 o'clock.

What a shock Abraham would have had to see that his daughter was identified as Catholic!

---

[161] Krefeld Archives, December 31, 1880 (Standesamt Krefeld C No. 2037/1880).

Sara was buried on January 1, 1881 in section D, row 30, grave 19 of the 'old cemetery' on Martinstraße Street. The *Crefelder Zeitung* announced her death four days later:[162]

Sarah Paulus, the 3½ years old Eskimo child who suffered from smallpox, succumbed on the second day in the hospital's epidemiological section, namely this Friday, December 31 at 10:30 in the morning and has been buried here on Saturday afternoon in Crefeld's cemetery [Old cemetery, Crefeld]. After her clothes and effects were thoroughly disinfected and partly burned, the child's nurse, Mrs. Jacobsen, left for Paris on Friday night.

---

[162] *Crefelder Zeitung*, (1881, January 4).

The Arrival at the
Jardin d'Acclimatation in Paris

Having left Crefeld at 9 a.m. on the morning of December 30, the railroad trip to Paris required more than 20 hours and multiple stops:

Aachen (Germany)	12 h 30
Verviers (Belgium)	14 h 25
Pépinster	14 h 39
Liège	15 h 15
Namur	17 h 38
Maubeuge (France)	20 h 45
Aulnoye	21 h 23
Busigny	22 h 40
Saint-Quentin	23 h 40
Ternier	12 h 45
Noyon	1 h 36
Compiègne	2 h 23
Creil	3 h 30
Paris (*Gare du Nord*)	4 h 45

Extracted from the Railway North schedule, September 1880.
(Archives historiques de la SCNF)

A few hours before the group's departure, at 6:10 on the morning of December 30, the Crefeld burgomaster, Mr. Schuiler, sent the following telegram to the Prefecture of Police de la Seine:[163]

> Five Eskimos with their suite will be arriving in Paris on December 31 at 4:45 in the morning, from Liège. After their departure, smallpox was diagnosed by doctors in a sick child left here and who was part of the group.

---

[163] Colin, Léon. (1881a). p. 7.

The Prefect of Paris immediately forwarded the dispatch to the Prefecture of Police who contacted Albert Geoffroy Saint-Hilaire,[164] director of the *Jardin d'acclimatation*, the bois de Boulogne's zoological garden where the *Eskimos* were to be exhibited while in Paris. The latter assured the authorities that the group would be vaccinated upon arrival. That said, was it a voluntary decision or was the vaccination "imposed by the Prefecture of Police" as a certain Mr. Girard claimed during the January 26, 1881, meeting of the *Société de médecine publique et d'hygiène professionnelle* (Society of public medicine and occupational health)? The question hasn't been resolved yet.

An article published in the *Revue d'hygiène et de police sanitaire* informs us of another incident that would have occurred at the Franco-Belgian border and would have resulted in a second dispatch being sent to the Prefecture of Police in Paris, this time by the Prefecture of the North:[165]

> [...] Several members of the caravan were suffering from the most severe forms of smallpox and died within a few days.[166] But others, offering doubtful signs of an eruption[167], showed up at the border to go from Belgium into France to continue their journey to Paris. The prefect of the *Département du Nord* wisely thought it was dangerous to let individuals potentially infected by smallpox circulate on the railway system and in wagons; uncertain of what to do, he asked for instructions from the upper administration in Paris. The latter decided that the individuals would be intercepted at their final destination; they would be isolated and given the necessary care. All persons still valid and part of the small tribe were to be immediately vaccinated.

It is therefore possible that the group was welcomed by the health authorities upon arriving at the *Gare du Nord,* but neither Abraham nor Jacobsen mentioned it in their diaries. No trace of the incident was found so far in the archives of the *Département du Nord* or in the Archives of the Prefecture of Police in Paris.

---

[164] Albert Geoffroy Saint-Hilaire (1836–1919) was the director of the *Jardin d'acclimatation* from 1865 to 1893.

[165] Vallin, E. (1881a).

[166] The author is referring to the deaths of Nuggasak, Paingu and Sara.

[167] Signs of smallpox, such as pustulation.

557. PARIS (10ᵉ arrt) — La Gare du Nord   C. M.

Fig. 56 Gare du Nord, ca 1921
(Polar Horizons Collection)

In any case, the day after their arrival in Paris, on January 1, 1881, at 2 p.m., the five survivors were vaccinated by the *Jardin d'acclimatation*'s physician, Dr. Panneval, "with animal vaccine kept in tubes. The same operation was repeated five days later, given the failure of the first inoculation."[168]

From January 1 to 6, the group presented its show at the *Jardin d'acclimatation*, and according to Jacobsen, everything seemed fine.

A small brochure entitled *Les Esquimaux du Jardin d'acclimatation*,[169] prepared by the Jardin's administration for the benefit of its visitors, informs us that the group was put up by the pond on the 'big lawn'[170] facing the main stables.

This brochure was obviously written in mid-December 1880 as it announced the arrival of seven individuals. The authors therefore took Nuggasak's death into consideration, without making mention of it, while Paingu and Sara were identified as members of the group expected at the Jardin. The text read as follows:

---

[168] Colin, Léon. (1881a). p. 11.
[169] *Les Esquimaux du Jardin d'acclimatation*. (1881).
[170] At the time, that lawn was used to let the large ruminants graze. Today, it is a playground for children.

Of the seven Eskimos brought to Europe by the *Eisbär* chartered specially for this expedition by renowned Hamburg importer, Hagenbeck, five: — a single man, Tobias (twenty-one); a married man, Abraham (twenty-eight); a woman, Ulrika (twenty-three); a little girl, Sara (three and a half); a small girl, Marie (10 months); — are Christians.

The other two: Tiggianiak (Ice fox), forty years; his wife, Paieng (plunging otter), fifty-five; have not received baptism.

Both families will be housed on the big lawn of the *Jardin d'acclimatation* in huts made of sod and built with the most scrupulous accuracy on the model of the homes characteristic of each tribe. That of the Christians will be similar in every respect to the one erected in 1877 for the first convoy, but the hut for the idolaters will not quite look the same.

These Eskimos bring with them the dogs needed to pull their sleds, their kayaks (canoes) used for hunting, and all their arsenal of harpoons, spears, floating bladders, in a word, all tools without which life would be impossible in the Polar Regions. In preparation for their arrival, seals were released into the *Jardin d'acclimatation*'s pond, and the hunting of these animals, practiced according to the rule book, will not be one of the least interesting episodes of the Eskimos' stay at the bois de Boulogne. Also to be seen will be an important collection of antiquities found in excavations made recently by the sailors of the *Eisbär* under the direction of their brave captain and interpreter Jacobsen. Prehistoric objects found in these excavations and all household utensils of the Eskimos, and the products of their primitive industries, will undoubtedly generate great interest among the *Jardin d'acclimatation*'s visitors.

Interestingly, the *Jardin d'acclimatation*'s authorities who wanted to reproduce the authenticity of the huts used by the Labrador Inuit in their homeland, opted to build them according to the Greenland model, one that was not in use in Labrador.

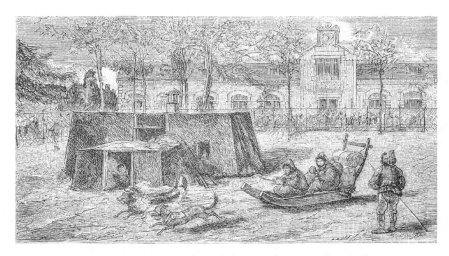

Fig. 57 1877 Greenlanders at the *Jardin d'acclimatation*
The hut for Abraham's family was built identical to this one.
(*Bibliothèque historique de la ville de Paris* / Roger-Viollet)

Fig. 58 Inuit sod house in Hebron
(Moravian Archives, Herrnhut, collection *Labrador Inuit Through Moravian Eyes*)

BOIS DE BOULOGNE. — Le Jardin d'acclimatation.

Fig. 59 The 'big lawn' and the stables, *Jardin d'acclimatation*
(*Bibliothèque historique de la ville de Paris* / Roger-Viollet)

An article published in Paris newspapers *La Presse*[171] and *Le XIXe siècle*[172] claims that the visitors from Labrador were most happy at the *Jardin d'acclimatation*:

If the newly fallen snow was for most Parisians an unpleasant surprise, it was quite the opposite for the Eskimos currently camped at the *Jardin d'acclimatation*.

[171] *La Presse*. (1881, January 8).
[172] Faits divers. *Le XIXe siècle*. (1881, January 10).

For the first time since leaving Labrador, these good people found themselves in their element.

They couldn't have been happier! They would finally be able to go full speed on their fast sleds.

The Eskimos seem very happy at the *Jardin d'acclimatation*. Already they have been able to eat seal, and they will certainly have the satisfaction of hunting even more of these amphibians, as sealers from Crotoy[173] were asked to send all captured animals to the bois de Boulogne.

Upon their arrival, the seals are dropped in the *Jardin d'acclimatation*'s lake. For a few weeks, the lake becomes a fish pond of a new kind, allowing the Eskimo's harpoon to pick the victim.

Ten days later, an article was published in at least two United Kingdom newspapers claiming that the group was in Paris for Christmas dinner [they actually were in Crefeld] and was offered seal as the main course:[174]

The Esquimaux in Paris. The Esquimaux or Esquimo at the Zoological Gardens, in the bois de Boulogne were enraptured at the sight of the first snow. They felt themselves quite at home, and brought forth their sledges, but the ground was not sufficiently carpeted for their exercise. The directors regaled them with a fine seal for their Christmas dinner; the blubber appeared to be highly relished by them. The phoca is one of the few animals which we had no opportunity of tasting during the siege,[175] but even the strong gusto of the Esquimo for this viand inspires us with no envy. – Paris Correspondent.

[173] A port city in the Bay of Somme in Picardy.
[174] The Esquimaux in Paris. (1881, January 17) and The Esquimaux in Paris. (1881, January 18).
[175] In 1870–1871 during the Franco-Prussian War when Paris was besieged, animals from the *Jardin d'acclimatation* were sacrificed to feed the population. Wolf, antelope, bear, kangaroo, giraffe, camel, python, peacock,... were featured on some restaurants' menus. See *Menus extravagants et bizarreries culinaires*. [n.d.].

It appears that the posters that were put up throughout Paris to announce the *Eskimos'* presence yielded results. Visitors were indeed coming to the *Jardin d'acclimatation* since in its 1881 annual report we find the following statement: "expenses incurred for the *Eskimos* totaled 7,680.20 francs. During their stay, the average revenue was 1,028 francs a day; an unprecedented result!"[176]

---

[176] Situation financière du Jardin [d'acclimatation]. (1882).

ABRAHAM'S LAST LETTER TO BROTHER ELSNER

On January 8, 1881, Abraham wrote what was to be his last letter. He addressed it to Brother Elsner in Bremen, Germany.

Paris, January 8, 1881

My dear teacher Elsner!

I write to you in a very despondent mood and I am even very distressed, due to my relatives; because our child, who I loved so much, is also not living anymore; she died of the evil smallpox; four days after the outbreak of her sickness, she passed away. My wife and I will be very soon reminded through the death of the child that we also have to die. She died in Krefeld, although she had many doctors. They indeed could not do anything; as our doctor, we more than anyone else wanted to have Jesus, who died for us. My dear teacher Elsner! We kneel down in front of him every day, bent because of our presence here and ask him that he forgives our aberration; we also do not doubt that the Lord will hear us. Every day we cry together, for our sins to be taken away by Jesus Christ. Even Terrianiak, who is now alone, when I tell him that he should convert, desires to become a property of Jesus, sincerely, as it seems. He has been assiduously taking part in our prayers until now, so does my child Maria. But even her life is doubtful, because her face is so swollen, Tobias is also sick, and although many doctors come they cannot help. I remember very well that only He can help when our death time comes, yes indeed! He is everywhere where we are. I really wish I could tell my relatives, who are over there, how friendly God is; indeed, my wife also sheds tears easily because of our sins. Our superior does buy a lot of medicine, no doubt, but all this still does not help; but I trust in God that He will hear my prayers and will collect all my tears, every day. I do not long for earthly possessions, but this is what I long for: to see my relatives again, who are over there, to talk to them of the name of God for as long as I live. I hadn't grasped this before, now I understand. I shed tears easily, but the words uttered by Him console us very much again and again. My dear teacher Elsner, pray for us to the Lord that the evil sickness will stop if it is His will; but may God's will be fulfilled. I am a poor man who's dust.

In Paris also it is cold, in fact very cold; but our superior is very kind to all of us now. I'll write again soon. I send you my regards, and my wife sends hers as well to everyone in the unity of Bremen.

I am Abraham, Ulrike's husband

If you write to the great teachers, tell them that we send our greetings to them.

The Lord be with you all! Amen.

THE *ESKIMOS'* DEATH IN PARIS

In early January, everything seemed fine and Jacobsen dared think that their misfortunes were things of the past. But, as Abraham said in his January 8 letter, the harsh reality struck again when the signs of smallpox appeared on little Maria and Tobias.

> Today our little Maria fell ill and, indeed, with smallpox. Had the physician here three times. They were all vaccinated again with a fresh vaccine, because the first vaccination (on January 1st) had produced no results with any of them. Beautiful prospects, that! (J. A. Jacobsen's diary, January 7, 1881)
>
> Today Tobias and Terrianiak fell ill, and most certainly of smallpox. Preparations were made to transfer them all to the hospital. I also feel unwell myself. It is probably an attack of fever, because I am freezing most terribly. (J. A. Jacobsen's diary, January 8, 1881)

In the morning of January 9, the *Eskimos* as well as Johan Adrian Jacobsen were admitted to *Hôpital Saint-Louis*.

> Today Abraham also became ill. All Eskimos were transferred to *Hôpital Saint-Louis* – and I was also given a room in the same shack for the epidemically ill – and I was rather ill, even without this terrible upset – because according to my own perception, not one of us will ever leave this hospital. The physicians saw us at 10 o'clock and confirmed smallpox in all four of them, but with me until now cold fever. The wife of Abraham has been spared until now, but cannot be moved away from her child. They all seem to suffer terrible pains. There are also a lot of French here with smallpox. In the afternoon we had a visit by Mr. Schoepf.

> On margin: In spite of my miserable condition, I went to each of my poor [and sick] people and tried to console them. But here the sickness was obvious. The face was very red, the eyelid swollen as were the lips. They all [suffered] great pain. In short, it was terrible. (J. A. Jacobsen's diary, January 9, 1881)

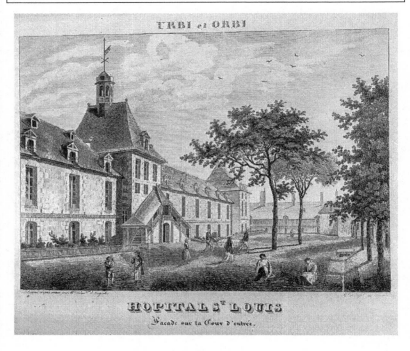

Fig. 60 *Hôpital Saint-Louis*, front of the courtyard entrance (Courtesy of BIU Santé)

In order to get the message out to the population that it should no longer come to the *Jardin d'acclimatation* to see the *Eskimos*, and to do so without raising any cause for concern, a small ad was published in various Parisian newspapers pretending that the *Eskimos* had decided to head back to Labrador: [177]

---

[177] Départ des Esquimaux. (1881, January 9). Départ des Esquimaux. (1881, January 10).

DÉPART DES ESQUIMAUX

Les Esquimaux du Jardin d'acclimatation ont quitté Paris, hier soir samedi. Pris du mal du pays, ces habitants des régions hyperboréennes regagnent le Labrador.

Fig. 61 *The Eskimo's Departure*
(Gallica, Bibliothèque nationale de France)

THE ESKIMOS' DEPARTURE

The Eskimos of the *Jardin d'acclimatation* left Paris, yesterday evening, Saturday. Homesick, these inhabitants of hyperborean regions are on their way back to Labrador.

The *Eskimos* were definitely not en route to Labrador! They had been admitted to the 'smallpox Pavilion,' a wooden barrack located outside *Hôpital Saint-Louis'* main walls. The barrack contained sixty beds: two large rooms with 24 beds each (one for men, one for women), a room of twelve beds reserved for the gender with the most people in need, and two rooms each with a single bed.[178]

The list of materials written in 1879, in preparation for the smallpox pavilion's opening, provides interesting details:[179] the sixty patients had access to, among other things: 10 'servants,' one bathroom with 4 bathtubs, 6 bedpans, 30 spittoons, 100 tea pots, 3 bleeding bowls, 8 carafes, 40 wine vials for men, and 20 for women. Each mattress was 18 inches wide.

Dr. Émile Landrieux, in charge of the smallpox unit, examined the *Eskimos* upon their arrival at his unit. The admission logbook shows that he diagnosed their illness as: confluent hemorrhagic smallpox[180] for Abraham, Tobias, and Ulrike, confluent smallpox[181]

---

[178] Archives de l'AP-HP, Cote 9L 141 – Service des varioleux, 1887.

[179] Archives de l'AP-HP, Cote 9L 141 – Service des varioleux, 1879.

[180] Hemorrhagic smallpox is a severe form that is accompanied by extensive bleeding into the skin, mucous membranes and gastrointestinal tract. In hemorrhagic smallpox the skin does not blister, but remains smooth. Instead, bleeding occurs under the skin, making it look charred and black, hence this form of the disease is also known as black pox. (Wikipedia)

for Maria and simply smallpox for Tigianniak. As for Jacobsen, he was diagnosed with intermittent fever.

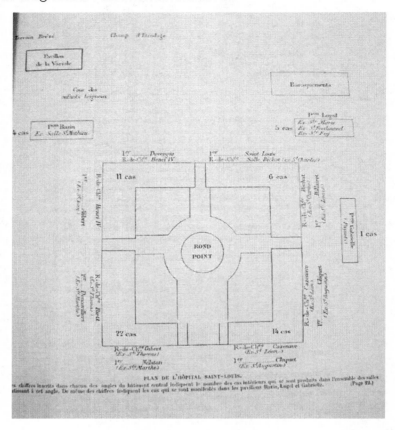

Fig. 62 Hôpital Saint-Louis Plan
The *'Pavilion de la Variole'* (smallpox pavilion) appears in the upper left corner. (*Archives de l'Assistance publique – Hôpitaux de Paris*, 9 L 12)

Ulrike and her daughter Maria were assigned bed N° 1. Tigianniak, Abraham, and Tobias occupied beds N° 34, 35, and 36 respectively. Jacobsen was in bed N° 50. Their profession was recorded as 'travellers,' the *Jardin d'acclimatation* in the bois de Boulogne was listed as their place of residence, and Hebron

---

[181] Confluent smallpox is a severe form in which the lesions run into each other, forming large suppurating areas. (Medical Dictionnary – The Free Dictionary)

(America), or Nakvak (America), was identified as their birthplace.

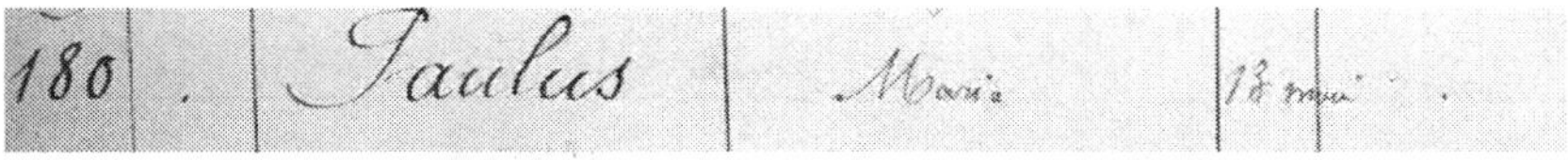

180	Paulus	Maria	18 mois

Fig. 63 *Hôpital Saint-Louis*' admission logbook for Maria. (*Archives de l'Assistance publique – Hôpitaux de Paris.* 9 L 141 – IQ2/169)

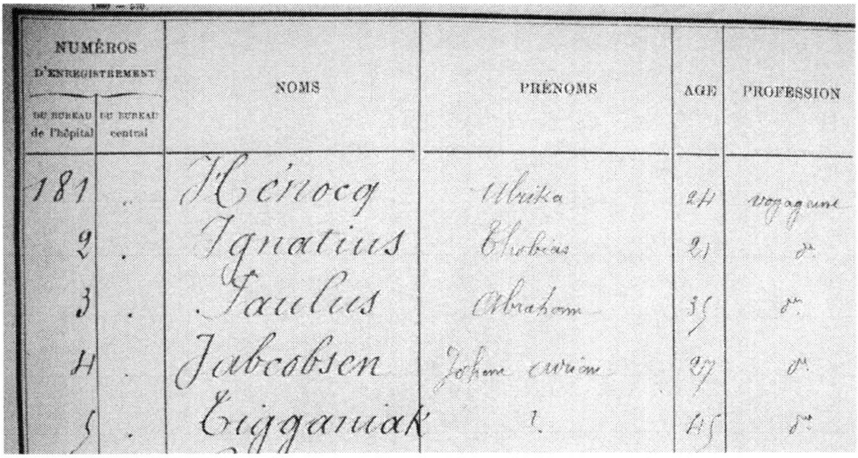

NUMÉROS D'ENREGISTREMENT DU BUREAU de l'hôpital	DU BUREAU central	NOMS	PRÉNOMS	AGE	PROFESSION
181	.	Nenocq	Ulrika	24	voyageuse
2	.	Ignatius	Tobias	21	d°
3	.	Paulus	Abraham	35	d°
4	.	Jacobsen	Johann Adrian	27	d°
5	.	Tiggavíak	1.	45	d°

Fig. 64 *Hôpital Saint-Louis*' admission logbook for the five adults (*Archives de l'Assistance publique – Hôpitaux de Paris.* 9 L 141 – IQ2/169)

The first to succumb was Maria, the day after their admission.

> This morning at 11 o'clock little Marie died. She was everybody's darling. It looks terrible here. We are surrounded by sick and dying people. A man of about 40 years died in the room next to mine. Because all walls here are made only of thin boards, you can hear every moan and every sound. Although I am sick myself, I am not too sick to support, as best I can, the poor Eskimos, who have to suffer intolerable pains. And I have to admire the nurses,[182] as well as the nurses' aides, who spare no pain to help

182 The German word 'Schwester' may mean a nurse or a nun. In France, until the end of the 19th century, the patients' care in hospitals was reserved to 'consecrated women,' i.e. nuns. (Translator's note)

> those afflicted. But with the Eskimos, it is more difficult, since they do not understand a word of French. Poor Tigianniak is asking for a rope to strangle himself because he is suffering terrible agonies. In this sickness death is hard indeed. (J. A. Jacobsen's diary, January 10, 1881)

Maria's was the 13th death to occur at *Hôpital Saint-Louis* in 1881. The hospital's death register read as follows:

The named Paulus, Maria, aged about 13 months, daughter of Abraham and Ulrika Henocq, native of Hebron, Department of America, usually residing in Boulogne, Seine Department, at the *Jardin d'acclimatation,*

Entered this establishment on January 9, 1881,

And died here today January tenth one thousand eight hundred eighty-one at two o'clock in the evening. This death was reported to the Officer of the Registry Office of the 10th arrondissement, by me, the undersigned Director, pursuant to Article 80 of the Napoleonic Code, and within the prescribed period.

The margin reads: Isolation 1bis – confluent smallpox.

Fig. 65 *Hôpital Saint-Louis* Death Records – Maria's death record
(*Archives de l'Assistance publique – Hôpitaux de Paris,* 3Q2/39)

The next day, on January 11, Maria's death was recorded in the 10th arrondissement's vital records[183] under number 164. It reads:

In the year eighteen hundred and eighty-one, on January 11 at noon: Death certificate: Maria Paulus, aged thir-

---

[183] Kept at the *Archives de Paris.*

teen months, born in Hebron (North America) died at 40 Bichat street last night at two o'clock, domiciled in Neuilly (Seine) *Jardin d'acclimatation*, daughter of Abraham Paulus and Ulrika Henocq, his wife, without further information. Compiled by us, Julien Lyon, Deputy Mayor, officer of the Registry Office of the 10th arrondissement of Paris, on the declaration of Eugene Gay, aged fifty-eight and René Lubineau, aged sixty-three, employees at 40 Bichat Street, who signed with us after reading.

Tigianniak was the second person of the group to be freed from his suffering. He succumbed on January 11 at 6 p.m. in bed N° 34 of the isolation section. His was the 14th death to occur at *Hôpital Saint-Louis* in 1881 and was recorded in the city's vital records at 1 a.m. the next day.

Fig. 66 Tigianniak, 1880
Photo by Jacob Martin Jacobsen. (Moravian Archives, Herrnhut)

Today the old Terrianiak was relieved of his sufferings. The bodies are immediately removed to the morgue by the gravediggers and are buried the next morning. Most of the sick are lying in one hall, and the beds are only a few feet apart. Of course, the sexes are segregated. The women have a different hall. Tobias lay next to Terrianiak, and right after he [Tigianniak] died, he [Tobias] got up and covered the corpse with a bed sheet, despite being so sick himself that he could die at any moment.

On margin: I too stood by, but without being able to render any help, apart from perhaps giving the dying a last glass of water. Death is terrible, especially if people die in such huge numbers as here all around me. (J. A. Jacobsen's diary, January 11, 1881)

On January 13, both Tobias and Abraham passed away. The death register of *Hôpital Saint-Louis* shows that Tobias died at 2 a.m. in bed N° 35 of the isolation section. His was the 17th death to occur at *Hôpital Saint-Louis* in 1881, and was recorded at noon in the 10th arrondissement's vital records.

As for Abraham, the death register indicates that he died at 6 p.m. in the bed N° 36 of the isolation section. His was the 20th death to occur at *Hôpital Saint-Louis* in 1881 and was recorded the next day at 2 p.m. in the 10th arrondissement's vital records.

This morning at 2 o'clock, Tobias died after having suffered terribly. He was brought into the room next to mine yesterday, but the poor guy came into my room again and again. He could no longer speak in the end, because his tongue was so swollen. His face was frightfully distorted, his shirt was bloody all over (they all spat blood in the most horrible way). Since he was much stronger than the others, he had to endure much more than the others.

On margin: It seemed as if Tobias was always seeking help from me, because when the death struggle came, he threw himself upon me, who was lying sick in bed myself, though not with smallpox. With the nurses' aid we then managed to put the corpse back into the bed of his own.

Right after he was gone, a seriously ill Frenchman was brought into the same room. That poor man also wrestled hard with death. He tore up his sheets and could hardly be restrained. His neck was closed up so that he could not breathe. They virtually suffocate. It is an uncomfortable feeling to be looking at death eye to eye, especially if death is as agonizing as with these unfortunate ones.

On margin: When the death struggle came for the Frenchman, he stretched so violently, that the bedstead tore apart, and the corpse with the mattress came to lie on the floor.

Ulrike has fallen ill, but does not want to be separated from her husband. We partly had to force her to go to bed in a small room.

On margin: All this I was forced to see and hear. It was enough to make a healthy person sick. Only the nurses remained always their same selves.

Tonight at 9 o'clock our dear Abraham died. I can hardly say what I feel. He and Tobias have given me the errand to deliver their assets to their relatives in Labrador. Hagenbeck has faithfully executed this testament and added miscellaneous. (J. A. Jacobsen's diary, January 13, 1881)

Finally, the *Hôpital Saint-Louis* death records show that the last survivor, Ulrike, passed away on January 16 at 3 a.m. in the bed N° 2bis of the isolation section. Hers was the 25th death to occur at *Hôpital Saint-Louis* in 1881 and was recorded at 1 p.m. in the 10th arrondissement's vital records.

Ulrike died this morning at 2 o'clock – the last of the eight – horrible. Should I be indirectly responsible for their death? Did I just have to lead these poor honest people from their home to find their graves here on foreign soil? Oh, how everything became so totally different than I had thought. Everything went so well in the beginning. We had only now gotten to know each other and begun to hold each other dear. [...]

On margin: When I saw to Ulrike shortly after midnight, I noticed that she too would end her struggle soon. I tried to comfort her, but she waved me off with her hand, as if she did not want to see me at all. That was no surprise, because she knew that all the others had gone before her. I felt guilty to a certain degree for the death of these unfortunate people, even if unintentionally. Had I not come to Labrador, they would still be alive like all their relatives. (J. A. Jacobsen's diary, January 16, 1881)

All five deaths are recorded in the 10th arrondissement of Paris' vital records as having occurred at 40 Bichat Street, the address of the hospital's main entrance at the time. All entries are signed by Julien Lyon, Eugene Gay and René Lubineau.

In the vital records, Tigianniak's death bears N° 183; Tobias' bears N° 194; Abraham's bears N° 212 and Ulrike's bears N° 214.

It should be noted that when they recorded Tigianniak's death in the vital records, a mistake was made: he was identified as being a woman. This error was passed on to all documents and records that ensued. Tigianniak's death record reads as follows:

> In the year eighteen hundred and eighty one, on January 12 at one o'clock in the evening: Death certificate of Tigganiak aged forty-five, born in Nakvak (America) died yesterday evening at six o'clock, 40 Bichat Street, domiciliated in Neuilly (Seine) at the *Jardin d'acclimatation*; daughter of... widow of Pengu, without other information. [...]

The five bodies were buried in a common grave in section 17 of the Parisian cemetery of Saint-Ouen on the northern outskirts of Paris. Each of the bodies carried a plate bearing the number it was assigned in the cities' vital records. They were buried either the next day or two days after their deaths.[184]

- Maria was buried on January 12, 1881.
- Tigianniak was buried on January 13, 1881.
- Tobias was buried on January 14, 1881.
- Abraham was buried on January 15, 1881.
- Ulrike was buried on January 17, 1881.

On January 16, when the news of the death of all *Eskimos* reached him, Carl Hagenbeck sent the following message to Jacobsen:[185]

> Dear Jacobsen. I have received your sad letter. You can well imagine how I feel. ... Just see to it that all the Eskimo things are burned, and as far as the collection is concerned, I do not want to have it brought to Hamburg for I do not want to see anything more of Eskimo things. I do not

---

[184] The dates were obtained from the curator of the Saint-Ouen cemetery.

[185] Thode-Arora, Hilke. (2002). p. 11.

care what will be paid for it, only away with it, and I mean everything without exception.

Jacobsen was discharged from *Hôpital Saint-Louis* on January 17. On leaving, he paid 65.75 francs to cover the costs of the care he and the *Eskimos* received.[186] Accompanied by Adolf Schoepf and Mrs. Jacobsen, he moved into a hotel near the hospital. Together they went to the *Jardin d'acclimatation* to care for the dogs.

On January 20, the three of them were brought to the train station by a man named Martinet. They left Paris for Germany. Mrs. Jacobsen returned to Hamburg. Schoepf probably headed to Dresden.[187] As for Jacobsen, he stopped for some time in Aachen to cure his intermittent fever, before returning to Hamburg.

---

[186] Registre des entrées de l'hôpital Saint-Louis. Archives de l'AP-HP. Cote 1Q 2/169.

[187] In 1881, Adolf Schoepf succeeded his father, Albin Schoepf, as the Dresden Zoo director and held this position until 1909.

Fig. 67 Paingu, Tigianniak and Nuggasak, 1880
(*Museum für Völkerkunde Hamburg*)

The Autopsies Results

On Friday, January 14, 1881, at a meeting of the *Société médicale des hôpitaux de Paris* (Medical Society of Paris Hospitals), Dr. Émile Landrieux presented the results of his diagnoses following the *Eskimos'* admission to his smallpox unit as well as the results of the autopsies performed. That morning, Dr. Landrieux visited Ulrike, the last survivor. That evening, he told the audience she was very ill and had probably succumbed in the course of the day.[188] Here is the text of Dr. Landrieux's presentation:[189]

Fig. 68 Dr. Émile Landrieux
(Courtesy of BIU Santé)

On January 2, 1881, several Eskimos arrived at the *Jardin d'acclimatation*: having left their native Labrador, they ar-

[188] Petit, André. (1881, January 21). p. 41.
[189] Landrieux, Dr. (1881, January 14).

rived in Hamburg on September 27, 1880; and from there toured many German cities, such as: Berlin, Prague, Frankfurt, Darmstadt and Crefeld. From the latter, they came directly made their way to Paris. But, at this point in their tour, they had already lost three of their companions; the first one succumbed in Darmstadt, twelve days after their departure from Prague; she was a 16-year-old girl, who died without showing any eruption; then, in Crefeld, a 40-year-old woman passed away without exhibiting any eruption, and a young child died on the second day of a variolic eruption.

Four or five days after their arrival at the *Jardin d'acclimatation*, they were vaccinated, on January 5 [sic] and January 7. Since all these poor souls greatly suffered, and the young 14-month-old child already having an eruption, all five were sent to *Hôpital Saint-Louis*, where an isolation pavilion designed specifically for smallpox sufferers exists.

They were admitted to the hospital on January 9, and I could, that same day, examine them carefully: the child, aged 14 months, had confluent smallpox, to which she succumbed on the third day of the eruption.

Another patient, aged 22, was admitted on the second day of the eruption. He deceased on the sixth day of the eruption, that is to say, on January 13.

A third patient, aged 44, suffering predominantly from rachialgia [pain in the spine], headaches and bronchorrhagia [pulmonary haemorrhage], succumbed on January 11, the fourth day of the invasion period.

Finally, the husband and wife were the last two to succumb to the disease: one on January 13, on the fourth day of the eruption, and one on January 16, on the fifth day of the eruption.[190]

---

[190] How could Dr. Landrieux report on January 14 that Ulrike's death occured on January 16? The assumption is that the *Société médicale des hôpitaux de Paris* (SMHP) modified the text of Dr. Landrieux's speech before publishing it.

All of these miserable unvaccinated people were victims of smallpox. The progression, shape and appearance of this disease presented some peculiarities that I think I must report.

Of the eight individuals, three succumbed during the invasion period (smallpox without smallpox) and presented two main symptoms: rachialgia and most severe headaches.

For the other four individuals who passed away during the eruption period, the sight of these poor people was most dreadful: all were suffering from continuous bronchorrhagia and their urine was made of almost pure blood. The evolution of the eruption progressed very slowly, the pustules were outstretched by blood, some resembled pemphigus[191] blisters.

The characteristics of the pulse did not offer anything special; the auxiliary temperature hovered between 39 and 40° 5; all had a huge proportion of albumin in the urine. In none of these patients, I observed a rash; death occurred without delirium, by septicemia[192] or asphyxia.

Not finding in these Eskimos, who were young, vigorous, robust, and not addicted to alcohol, the explanation of such a terrible and so constantly fatal end, I looked for the cause in the anatomo-pathological disorders.

I could autopsy four[193] Eskimos, and I will give here a brief overview. I will not mention the many and profuse hemorrhages that filled, for example, the calyx, the pelvis, infiltrating the adipose capsule of the kidneys, after the rupture of the fibrous envelope of these organs, the hematorrhachis, the microscopic changes in the blood whose crenellated

---

[191] Pemphigus is a group of rare skin disorders that cause blisters of your skin or mucous membranes. (Mayo Clinic)

[192] 'Invasion of the bloodstream by virulent microorganisms and especially bacteria along with their toxins from a local seat of infection accompanied especially by chills, fever, and prostration.' (Webster-Merriam)

[193] Some publications state that Dr. Landrieux reported doing three autopsies, not four. As for the date of Ulrike's death, we presume that the SMHP altered the text of Dr Landrieux's presentation before publishing it: the three autopsies performed as of January 14 therefore became four following Ulrike's death.

hematites no longer piled up and were separated due to the presence of many leukocytes [white blood cells], to achieve more significant alterations.

The liver, in these four Eskimos, was enormously developed, weighing from 2 to 3 kilos, yellowish, discoloured, could easily be depressed, offering, in one word, all the macro-scopic characteristics of a fatty liver. There was, in one word, a steatosis that could simultaneously be designated as physiological, since it does not impair health in any way, and pathological, as it destroys any vital resistance when the body must fight against toxemia such as smallpox.

The mesenteric ganglions were themselves very large, and yet there was no concomitant alteration of the intestinal mucosa.

On the other hand, the spleen had its normal volume, but the kidneys were extremely large; the heart had excess fat on the surface, and the myocardium [cardiac muscle] was discoloured, with the colour of dead leaves.

Here is now the summary of the microscopic examination that I owe to the kindness of M. A. Siderey, an intern.

The liver has a remarkable congestion, characterized by the dilation of blood vessels, which are filled with blood cells. We see on all the preparations, a large number of fat droplets highly coloured in black by osmic acid and irregu-larly distributed in the lobe. [...]

In the kidneys, there is a widespread and intense conges-tion, intracapsular and intra-tubular bleedings. Some tu-bules of the kidney are invaded by a granulomatous fatty degeneration.

The heart's muscle fibers are absolutely clear; there is no al-teration other than a considerable fat infiltration in the in-ter-muscular spaces.

The therapeutic efforts were powerless to fight against this form of disease: despite the jaborandi, the eruption did not progress; despite subcutaneous injections of ergotinine, the bleeding persisted; the tonics themselves remained without result.

All these Eskimos who had arrived in Europe in September 1880, disappeared, swept away by confluent hemorrhagic smallpox.

I think that the extreme gravity of this epidemic has been mainly attributed to the liver steatosis [fatty liver], a consequence of this population's eating habits where they eat almost exclusively oils, fat, and fish.

Moreover, smallpox, which is sometimes brought to these climates by European and American vessels, results there in similar ravages, the process of vaccination being almost completely unknown.

These unfortunate people, who were not overworked or alcoholics (they never use alcohol), have therefore succumbed due to their lack of resistance to toxic diseases, consequences of the steatosis of some of their organs.

In the minutes of the November 18, 1881, meeting of the *Société anatomique de Paris*, we discover a few more details regarding Ulrike's autopsy. Indeed, although he did not name her, the intern M. A. Siderey, who conducted the microscopic studies on the corpses, mentions the case of Ulrike as an example contradicting an accepted theory involving women who breastfeed. It reads:[194]

> [...] The scholarly research by Mr. de Sinéty has long established that the hepatic lobule's central regions were undergoing fatty degeneration in lactating females. And classical authors today agree that the degeneration of alcoholic or cachectic origin begins in the lobule's periphery, leaving the monopoly of central degeneration to the state of lactation.

> However, when analyzing my observations, I found six cases that are inconsistent with this theory; three relate to women who succumbed in full lactation, and whose liver showed no trace of fat around the central vein. [...] In one of them, who died of hemorrhagic smallpox, fat was almost exclusively localized in the endothelial cells of the intralobular capillaries. And in this case, the rarity of the fat was all the stranger that she was an Eskimo woman, accus-

---

[194] Siderey, M.A. (1881). p. 637.

tomed to a diet where fat held an important place. It is true that these three women had stopped breastfeeding 24, 36, and even 48 hours before death. Is this period sufficient for the complete modification of the primitively degenerated elements?

Various texts published in newspapers and other publications provide interesting facts and statistics about the smallpox epidemic which prevailed in Paris and, in particular, in *Hôpital Saint-Louis'* smallpox pavilion.

Fig. 69 Ulrike and Maria, 1880
Photo by Jacob Martin Jacobsen.
(Moravian Archives, Herrnhut)

From January 3 to 9, 1881, 36 persons suffering from smallpox were admitted to Paris hospitals, and from January 7 to 13, there were 18 deaths from smallpox.[195] The following week, the number

---

[195] Bulletin hebdomadaire de statistiques. (1881, January 16).

of deaths had increased to 25, due to the *Eskimos:*[196]

Smallpox ended in death 25 times instead of 18. According to Mr. Dr. Landrieux, head of the smallpox unit at St. Louis, this increase is due mainly to the Eskimos who brought to the *Jardin d'acclimatation* the smallpox they contracted in Germany, where many of them died. Already, he said, five of those who arrived in France died in St. Louis from hemorrhagic smallpox, a form which is inevitably fatal. Poor Eskimos!

The following short text from an epidemiological bulletin also mentions the *Eskimos* and tells us that smallpox was also raging in London and Vienna:[197]

Smallpox – Paris, 120 deaths. An increase of 20 over the previous month and 18 on average. The epidemic does not stop. It should be noted that this number includes the deaths of five Eskimos, which are discussed in this issue. The Paris garrison, entirely revaccinated, continues to be free from this disease. In London and Vienna, smallpox has been raging ceaselessly with enough vigour for the last two months.

In the minutes of the May 13, 1881, meeting of the *Société médicale des hôpitaux de Paris*, Ernest Besnier compares the death statistics for the first three months of 1881 with those of the same period the previous year. We learn, among other things, that the *Eskimos* were not the only foreigners to have died in Paris in January 1881, but they were the only non-Europeans:[198]

While undergoing its seasonal increase, and its normal peak in mortality, smallpox has declined significantly in its multi-annual curve; instead of 798 deaths caused by it during the first quarter of 1880, it has caused 356 in the first quarter of 1881 (less than

---

[196] La santé publique. (1881, January 26).

[197] Bulletin épidémiologique. (1881).

[198] Besnier, Ernest. (1881). p. 160-161.

half).[199] [...]

Of the 18 subjects, certainly unvaccinated, treated by Mr. Landrieux, at *Hôpital Saint-Louis*, during the first quarter of this year, there were nine foreigners: 5 Eskimos, 2 Belgians, 1 Italian and 1 Austrian. [...]

Ernest Besnier's report also includes a summary written by Dr. Landrieux and an intern, Mr. Bourdel, giving details on the patients treated at the smallpox pavilion of *Hôpital Saint-Louis* during the winter of 1881:[200]

The first quarter of 1881 was marked by a resurgence of the epidemic. Instead of the 167 patients admitted in the last quarter of 1880, there are 237 cases of smallpox (152 men, 85 women) that are distributed as follows: hemorrhagic smallpox, 16; confluent s., 57; coherent s., 48; discrete s., 38; varioloid 78.

We still notice this important fact: it is the newcomers to Paris and the foreigners who provide the greatest number of our patients.

Living in Paris for less than a year, 63; for one year 15; [...]. In this number are many foreigners; several of them, overworked by excessive work, eating poorly, suffered from severe forms, and died. [...]

Confluent smallpox includes 57 cases, 40 ended in death.

Age:
Under 1 year, men, 2, death 2; women, 1, death 1. –
Under 10 years, m. 0, d. 0; w. 1, d. 1. –
From 15 to 20 years, m. 2, d. 1; w. 2, d. 0. –
From 20 to 25 years, m. 7, d. 6; w. 5, d. 4. –
From 25 to 30 years, m. 8, d. 4; w. 1, d. 1. –
From 30 to 35 years, m. 8, d. 5; w. 2, d. 1. –
From 35 to 40 years, m. 7, d. 3; w. 4, d. 3. –
From 40 to 45 years, m. 6, d. 6; w. 0, d. 0. –
From 45 to 50 years, m. 2, d. 2; w. 1, d. 1. –
Total: m. 40, d. 28; w. 17, d. 12

[199] For the month of January alone, the report shows that the number of deaths from smallpox went down from 286 in 1880 to 110 in 1881.
[200] Besnier, Ernest (1881). p. 167-169.

Of these 40 deaths, death occurred 23 times by toxemia; in one case, before the eruption's onset (it was one of the Eskimos);[201]
[...]

While in the last quarter of 1880, of 167 patients, there were 21 deaths, i.e. a mortality rate of one eighth, we find in the current quarter, of 237 patients, 58 deaths i.e. a mortality rate nearing a quarter.

From this table, we notice that during the first quarter of 1881: Maria was the only child from 1 to 10 years old to be admitted to the *Hôpital Saint-Louis* and to succumb of confluent smallpox. For Tobias' and Ulrike's age group (20 to 25 years), six of the seven men and four of the five women died. For Tigianniak's age group (40 to 45 years), all 6 men admitted passed away.

---

[201] According to Dr. Landrieux's January 14 presentation, this person would be Tigianniak since he is the only one to have died during the invasion period, not during the eruption period.

Fig. 70 Tobias, Abraham, Ulrike, Sara, and Maria, 1880
(Moravian Archives, Herrnhut)

THE *ESKIMOS'* DEATH IN THE PRESS

To date, the first newspaper found to report the group's death is the *Nikolsburger Wochenschrift* (Prague) in its January 29, 1881, issue:[202]

> None of the eight members of the Eskimo group, which introduced itself in Vienna [sic] some time ago and recently travelled through Germany, has survived. In Germany, two women and one child died quickly, the latter of smallpox, while the cause of death of the two women could not be clearly determined; the Paris police authority, where the people had last been taken, insisted that they be vaccinated.
>
> Vaccination was given twice without success. Nevertheless, the people fell ill and died a few hours later. Finally, a few days ago, Abraham's wife, and indeed all of them, as diagnosed by Parisian doctors, died of a form of smallpox without any external outbreak. The disease of the people who died last and their rapid demise occurred with the same symptoms as among the non-Christian women who died in Germany. We can therefore assume that they also died of smallpox.
>
> From this sad example we can see how exceedingly fast primitive people can be exterminated, as soon as one of our epidemics seizes them. In Hamburg, Mr. Hagenbeck, who in recent years and with such paternal solicitude, brought us closer to primitive people from north, south, east and west, was so shaken by this sad case that, as he announced, he is committed to give up entirely the presentation of such ethnological shows.

---

[202] *Nikolsburger Wochenschrift.* (1881, January 29).

In Paris, it seems that it wasn't until February 8, 1881, that the news was made public through the *Gil Blas*, a humoristic newspaper. Did the paper intend on making a bad taste joke when it falsely claimed that employees of the *Jardin d'acclimatation* died of smallpox after being infected by the *Eskimos*? And what is the source of their statement pretending that the *Eskimos* were travelling with bears?:[203]

An extra-medical drama recently happened here at home, which was not covered sufficiently by the press. At the beginning of January, picture posters announced the impending arrival of an Eskimo family. Naturally, these children of the North were headed for the *Jardin d'acclimatation*, Parisians' beloved walking place.

Shortly after New Year's Day, the Eskimos indeed arrived, and were handed over to Mr. Geoffroy Saint-Hilaire, the Honourable Director of the zoological establishment of the bois de Boulogne. In all, there were eight of various ages, six men and two women. There were also bears.

But in the early hours of their arrival, it was realized that there was no way the travellers could appear in a public exhibition. When setting foot in Europe, the Eskimos brought with them the germs of a terrible epidemic of black smallpox. This evil, almost invincible, was communicated to their guardians and other junior staff of the Jardin. All succumbed.

Neuilly, which is in the vicinity, complaining, Geoffroy Saint-Hilaire sent the eight Eskimo patients to the *Hôpital Saint-Louis*, the place in Paris where skin diseases are best treated. It was in vain. All eight died in turn, and they died regretting, it seems to have left their country of snow. As for the bears they brought, they are doing well.

The next day, on February 9, 1881, a very brief text is published stating that the *Eskimos* simply could not acclimatize themselves:[204]

---

[203] Nouvelles & Échos. (1881, February 8).
[204] *Les On-Dit*. (1881, February 9).

An Eskimo family, who had left its Northern ice to show itself to the eyes of Parisians eager for novelties, could not acclimatize, even to our winter.

The eight individuals, men, women and children who made up this family which arrived in January, have been successively infected with black pox, which has taken them.

To come so far to die!

Also on February 9, 1881, the news of their death crossed the English Channel. For the next four days, it appeared in various UK newspapers under the title *Sad Faith of the Eskimos*:[205]

Sad Faith of the Eskimos

The troop of luckless Eskimos which Mr. Hagenbeck has been lending about Central Europe for some time past, for the entertainment of sightseers in the great cities of Germany, Austria, and Switzerland, is now utter extinct. After their very successful performance in Berlin, where Professor Virchow and other scientists made them the subject of study and writing, they were carried off to Darmstadt, the capital of the Duchy of Hesse. Here an attractive young girl belonging to the troop died. They were moved next to the manufacturing districts of Westphalia where they lost a woman and a little child; the latter died from smallpox. At Crefeld, they ended their service in Germany, and their 'proprietor'(?) resolved to carry them into France. The survivors – now only five in numbers – arrived in Paris. Mr. Hagenbeck was waited upon by the sanitary officials, who informed him that he could not be allowed to open his performance until all the members of this company had been duly vaccinated. The astounded and terrified Esquimaux had to submit twice to this painful ordeal. In spite of the double precaution the experiment failed utterly. The five Esquimaux sickened of the smallpox in spite of this more than scrupulous and careful vaccination – the anti-vaccinationists will perhaps say because of it. They died after a

[205] Sad faith of Esquimaux (1881, February 9); Sad faith of Esquimaux (1881, February 10); Sad faith of Esquimaux (1881, February 11); Sad faith of Esquimaux (1881, February 12); Vaccinated to death. (1881, January).

few hours of suffering, so that no single member of this poor company of strangers will return to his own land to give his kinsfolk an account of the marvels of the civilized south.

On March 6, 1881, a Swiss French-language religious paper, la *Feuille religieuse du Canton de Vaud*, announced the group's death to its readers in the following terms:[206]

In northern Canada, bathed by the waters of the Hudson Bay and those of the Atlantic, extends northward the large Labrador Peninsula, inhabited by poor tribes of Eskimos. The elevation of its mountains and the constant mist make it an icy country. Rum freezes when kept outdoors, spirit condenses as oil. This miserable country, which doesn't offer much more than a pile of rocks interspersed with lakes and rivers, yet produces some trees and a bit of grass for the animals. It is along its northern coast that the Moravian Brethren founded, from 1769, the missions of Hoffenthal[207] [Hopedale], Zoar, Nain, Okak, and Hebron among the wretched inhabitants of these desertlike regions. The Lord has given his blessing to this work of devotion; today, many Eskimos profess the Christian faith and make up churches, that are more or less important and lively, that have their own pastors.

A few months ago, Eskimos from this country, including several members of the Church of Hebron, were tempted by the offers of an exhibiter of curiosities to visit Europe. Despite the missionaries' advice, they persisted in their intention; embarked and never again saw their homes. Newspapers have recently told us that they had all succumbed to homesickness or disease caused by a change of life. The last five died in Paris.

On April 30, 1881, the Portsmouth's *The Evening News* reported the death of not 8, but 12 individuals:[208]

---

[206] Les Esquimaux en Europe. (1881, March 6). p. 104.

[207] As noted previously, the first Moravian settlement was established in Labrador in 1771.

[208] The Spread of Small-pox. (1881, April 30).

The Spread of Small-pox

[...] not a single man had escaped out of twelve unvaccinated Esquimaux, who caught the disease, and who died in turn in one of the Paris hospitals. There is now further evidence of the value of vaccination, and of the danger which is incurred by those who neglect to submit themselves to the simple operation. [...]

In May 1881, the religious paper *Sunday at Home*, reported that the huts and property of the Eskimos were still visible at the *Jardin d'acclimatation*:[209]

[...] We are sorry to learn from the latest *Periodical Accounts* of the Moravian missions, that all these poor Esquimaux are dead, the last dying in the *Jardin d'acclimatation* in Paris, where their huts and property may still be seen; a melancholy memorial. [...]

Finally, in September 1881, the *Vaccination Enquirer* reproduced the text published in March by a German magazine:[210]

The *Vereins-Blatt* for March contains an account of the death of Abraham Paulus, a native of Greenland [sic], occupied in the construction of a map of the Labrador coast. The account states that some time since Paulus, with his family, eight persons in all, arrived in Germany, where three of them died, the remaining five going to Paris to reside there. It does not appear whether they were vaccinated in Germany, but on arriving in Paris the authorities insisted on their undergoing the operation, which, proving abortive, they were re-vaccinated, and this time with such results that the whole five died in a few hours. – *Dulce est pro scientiâ mori*. (It is sweet to die for science)

---

[209] The Esquimaux. (1881, May 21). p. 330.
[210] The Vaccination Inquirer and Health Review. (1881, September).

Fig. 71 Tobias, Abraham, Ulrike, Sara, and Maria, 1880
(Moravian Archives, Herrnhut)

The Commission of Inquiry on the Eskimos' Death

On January 21, 1881, five days after the death of all *Eskimos*, the *Conseil d'hygiène publique et de salubrité* (Council for Public Health and Safety) appointed Dr. Léon Colin, a medical officer and epidemiologist for the army, to study the causes of the *Eskimos'* death. Dr. Colin had been, among other things, the chief physician of the smallpox ward at *Hôpital Bicêtre* during the Franco-Prussian War of 1870–1871; had published, in 1873, the book *La variole au point de vue épidémiologique et prophylactique* (Smallpox from an epidemiological and prophylactically point of view), and had been elected to the *Académie nationale de médecine* in 1879–1880 in forensic medicine and hygiene.

Fig. 72 Dr. Léon Colin
(Courtesy of *Bibliothèque Académie nationale de médecine*, Paris)

Dr. Colin's mandate was three-fold:

1. Identify the nature of the disorder;
2. Determine where the infection occurred;
3. Describe the measures that could have been taken to avert the death of the victims, and identify the steps that have been taken, or are to be taken, to prevent the spread of the germs that have affected them and which, in turn, they have multiplied.

Dr. Colin presented his report[211] to the Council on February 4, 1881. The main highlights for each of the three components are:

1° Nature of the disorder

It was thought that the disorder from which these patients have died differed from the smallpox of temperate climates, if not by its nature, at least by some of its clinical features; like the absence of an eruption in two cases; by its distinguished gravity; by the steatosis of the viscera; to support the arguments, testimonies were quoted from travellers who confirmed that it was indeed the special kind of smallpox observed in Labrador; and, in a letter he kindly sent us, Mr. Director of the Jardin d'acclimatation gave us a proof of the commonplace belief in the greater malignancy of the virulent germs affecting people of this country: "A German missionary, who spent 30 years in Labrador, was invited to Paris to receive the last wishes of our Eskimos. He replied that he knew the Eskimos' smallpox as most dreadful, and he did not want to, at his age, expose himself to contagion."[212]

---

[211] Colin, Léon. (1881a).

[212] Interestingly: in a letter dated January 13, 1881, Brother Elsner wrote that he had put an end to his plans to go to Paris, the probability being that he would not be allowed to see the *Eskimos* because of the infection and, had he obtained permission, he would have been kept out as long as it had been proven that no infection had occurred. Obviously, the invitation made by the Director of the *Jardin d'acclimatation* seems to not have reached him or a middleman misinformed him. Similarly, one of the middleman would have made up a false response coming from Elsner. Why? In whose interest? Another interesting fact to note: On January 12, 1881, Hagenbeck's records show that he sent a sum of 100 marks to Brother Elsner. Was it to cover

If the people who have accepted the opinion that Labrador's smallpox is of an unusual severity had extended the scope of their research, we are confident that they would have concluded to this form of the disease being, in general, found in all countries where there is neither of the two main conditions of its attenuation under our climates: 1° the practice of vaccination; 2° chance of a previous smallpox contagion. Indeed, smallpox epidemics are of an equally exceptional severity in wild tribes of intertropical regions than they are among the peoples of the North; when penetrating Mexico, with Christopher Columbus, smallpox destroyed half of the population in a single epidemic period; and, to mention only modern facts, I can point out the wars of the British against the Ashantees of Guinea's coast, where smallpox germs transmitted by European troops, were sufficient to annihilate the enemy's army! That's because here, as in Labrador, vaccine is unknown. In addition, the scarcity of communications and the low population density allow the contagious germs to die out permanently while here, under our climate, they are constantly renewed by the agglomeration of people and the ease of contact; so that any new import finds, in general, in those distant countries, a virgin population, having no immunity either by vaccination or by an earlier epidemic.

And yet, it is not necessary to go that far to find forms of smallpox comparable to the Eskimos'; we also notice them here, although less frequently than before Jenner's discovery, but still too commonly, mostly for the past few years, and particularly since the great upsurge of smallpox in 1869.

Not only do we observe secondary hemorrhagic smallpox in our population, i.e. the form where the body is already covered with smallpox pustules, but also the even more frightening form, if such thing is possible, where the hemorrhage does not wait for the eruption, but precedes it, and in which, as in several of these Eskimos, the evil kills before wearing his characteristic physiognomy. [...]

---

the costs of his trip to Paris? Elsner returned the money to Hagenbeck a month later, on February 23, 1881.

What is especially important to note is that the same vari-olic germ, whether it stems from a very serious case, as the ones above, or from a benign one, may give rise, depend-ing on the receptivity conditions of the subject, to either a confluent black smallpox; to the mitigated forms of the af-fection, its mild forms: discrete smallpox, or even abortive; varioloids.

It therefore remains established that the Eskimos' epidemic is in no way a strange, exotic disease; it represents one of the usual manifestations of a common disorder in Europe; it does not result from an especially malignant virus; nor, in turn, does it have the power to generate germs that are more dangerous than those that arise so frequently around us by the daily impairments of the Aboriginal population.

Let us just add that besides their greater predisposition to severe forms, as newcomers, the Eskimos perhaps offered an anatomical condition associated to this predisposition; the hypertrophic steatosis of major viscera, which was largely the result of their diet made up mainly of oil and fat, may have contributed to more easily place them on the path of the anatomical alterations caused by severe smallpox, where fatty degeneration of these organs, espe-cially that of the liver, is also observed.

2°   Determine where the infection occurred

The first fact to emerge from our study is that the Eskimos' disease is not of a Parisian or French origin; the information provided to us, first by Dr. Panneval, physician for the *Jardin d'acclimatation*, who cared for the patients until they were admitted to *Hôpital Saint-Louis*, second, by Mr. Dr. Land-rieux, show that the first morbid accidents observed on the Eskimos in Paris, began on January 5 and 6; on the 5th, a child (Maria Paulus) and her father (Abraham Paulus) showed the symptoms of an invasion: fever, stiffness, vomit-ing; on the 6th, the same symptoms in two men (Tobias Ig-natius and Tigganiak); the woman who was the last to suc-cumb (Ulrike Paulus) was taken only on the 8th, the eve of the admission of all patients to the hospital.

From these facts, one could already conclude that, on the one hand, the impregnation of the disease had to have occurred almost simultaneous; secondly, according to smallpox's usual average incubation period, which is from eight to twelve days, one could set the beginning, especially for four patients, to a date between December 25 and 28, 1880, i.e. prior to the entrance of the caravan on French territory.

Meanwhile the attached dispatch arrived from Crefeld, on December 30, 1880, addressed to the Prefect of the Seine, and by him transmitted to the Prefect of Police:

"Five Eskimos with their suite will be arriving in Paris on December 31 at 4:45 in the morning, from Liège. After their departure, smallpox was diagnosed by doctors in a sick child left here and who was part of the group.

> Superior Burgomaster
> Schuiler"

This document was given to me on Friday, January 21, when the Council gave me the mission which I have now the honor to report on. I contacted immediately Mr. Director of the *Jardin d'Acclimatation* and the burgomaster of Crefeld. They both sent me, with the greatest eagerness, the following information on the Labrador Eskimos' route, and the losses suffered by the group before coming to the *Jardin d'Acclimatation*.

The eight Eskimos landed in Hamburg on September 26, 1880. They stayed:

In Berlin, from October 18 to November 19;

In Prague, from November 20 to November 30;

In Frankfurt, from December 1 to December 11;

In Darmstadt, from December 13 to 18;

In Crefeld from December 18 to 30.

And, as we have said, they arrived in Paris on December 31, 1880. They had lost three persons along the way:

1st In Darmstadt, on December 14, died a girl (Nogasak), who no doubt died of smallpox; the eruption was visible;

2nd In Crefeld, on December 27, died a woman (Baignu), in whom the eruption was not visible, but had all the other symptoms of hemorrhagic smallpox; she was the wife of one of Eskimos (Tigganiak), who was to die at St. Louis, also without an eruption;

3rd Finally, we report the death, in Crefeld, the day after the burgomaster's dispatch was sent, of young Sarah, who was the subject of this dispatch; here the diagnosis was fully confirmed by the outbreak of the characteristic eruption on the day of death, December 31.

This historical background seems to indicate that the first morbid impregnation, that of the victim who succumbed in Darmstadt, on December 14 (Nogasak), occurred in Prague, where smallpox reigned with gravity during the stay of our travellers, from November 20 to 30, i.e. from 15 to 25 days prior to her death; it is there, in Prague, that the initial contamination of the caravan took place.

It seems likely that the first victim passed it on to the second (Baingu), who died in Crefeld, thirteen days later, on December 27, and probably to the third (Sara), who succumbed on the 31st of the same month.

Finally, it is to these two second-hand patients, but above all to the last one, young Sara, that we feel duty to link the simultaneous infection of the five survivors who came to Paris; after living at her side from the beginning of her illness, they parted from her on December 30, the day before her death, and six days before they were hit themselves, leaving her at the Crefeld hospital, and probably lavishing on her their care and expressions of sympathy until the time of separation and their departure for Paris.

Obviously, we can also suspect the contaminating influence of the common effects to the whole caravan and soiled by the first patients. But it seems to me that the simultaneous contamination of the last five victims seems to point to a danger suffered during a narrower time period, which corresponds precisely to the period of the young girl's disease.

What is important to remember from this historical background and from this discussion is that Germany, probably Prague, was the source of the infection; that the Eskimos, having reached Paris, arrived during smallpox's incubation period, and had they gone to any other destination, they would have died anyway, because their fate was set before leaving Crefeld.

3° Prophylactic measures taken towards the Eskimos and the populations threatened by the contagion of their disorder.

The first prophylactic act accomplished was the dispatch from the Crefeld Burgomaster, advising the Prefect of the Seine of the suspicious nature of the caravan expected at the *Jardin d'acclimatation* on December 31, 1880.

Needless to emphasize the value and merit of such a warning, as we have been repeatedly calling for its application by the authorities and doctors in charge of public health management.

However, to fairly appreciate its degree of usefulness in the current circumstances, it was important to know if the warning could not have been sent earlier; even if, before leaving Crefeld, the group had not given sufficient proof of its morbid impregnation to justify sequestration, or at least to forbid him from travelling on main communications routes. We tended toward this opinion more so that our information, as we saw, told us of the death of the second victim, also in Crefeld, on December 27.

The Crefeld Burgomaster answered our questions in the most emphatic and satisfactory manner. It was not in Crefeld, but in a zoological garden located in its vicinity, near the village of Bockum, that the caravan stayed for ten days. It is in this garden that the woman Baignu succumbed, as we said, she died without any eruption and, therefore, without attracting the attention of the health authorities; the Eskimos visited Crefeld only at the time of their departure for Paris; and nearly a month after their departure from the German city, on January 24, 1881, date of Mr. Burgomaster's letter, no cases of smallpox had appeared in the resident population. The first case reported to him was therefore the one which he warned the French authorities about: the admission to the Crefeld hospital of the young patient who had been left there at the time of their departure, on December 30.

When he received this dispatch, Mr. Director of the *Jardin d'Acclimatation* immediately took the actions that were corollaries; and on January 1, at 2 o'clock, the day after their arrival, the five Eskimos were vaccinated by Dr. Panneval with animal vaccine kept in tubes. The same operation was repeated five days later, given the failure of the first inoculation.

We will not fall on the value of the vaccine used, certainly inferior to an infant vaccine inoculated arm-to-arm; nor, in revenge, on the difficulty that arouse to immediately get more, on January 1, especially, the day where even we were not able to bring to Val-de-Grâce a number of vaccinifer children, ready for the revaccination of the garrison.

We must recognize that the administration of the *Jardin d'acclimatation* has done everything in its power to meet the urgent necessity to act promptly; but would its vaccine have been better, it was too late, and the operation was to almost inevitably fail. These poor survivors were already into the incubation period during which the failure of the vaccine inoculations is the rule; [...]

It is not France that it was appropriate to proceed with the vaccination of these poor expatriates; it was in Hamburg, at the time of landing; it was at the time they were taken to Prague, home to an epidemic known for its seriousness; it was in Darmstadt when the first victim succumbed, her eruption providing the evidence of the danger hanging over all the others. It was then that the vaccine would have taken on them, as wonderfully, if it is allowed to use such a term, as was to do its terrible antagonist, smallpox.

We hope that the *Conseil d'hygiène* will allow us, in our conclusions, to hint to the share of responsibility that may lie with the individuals who, under the title of interpreters and, perhaps with the disinterest of the American Barnum, followed these unfortunate people, step by step, from Hamburg to Paris; staying for three months in a country, Germany, where vaccination is legally binding; not seizing this opportunity to prevent dangers, for the Eskimos themselves, and for the onlookers that would be attracted, by this travelling exhibition through so many cities where smallpox is almost endemic.

It is fair to recognize that during the last twenty days of their existence, that is to say, during the period when contact with them could cause the most significant amount of dangers, these dangers have been reduced by the special conditions of their past residences; on the one hand, in Crefeld, they lived in a zoo distant from the city; on the other hand, in Paris, where not only were they set up remotely from the urban area, but they occupied in the *Jardin d'acclimatation*, a special pavilion offering nearly the conditions we would have tried to achieve, had we wished to put them in quarantine.

Before assessing the value of the measures that have already been applied, or that are yet to be taken on the sources of dangers that survived the poor victims, including their hut and the objects they have infected, your delegate considers that it is necessary to assess calmly, and to its fair value, the whole of this danger.

As we mentioned earlier, it is not a question of contagion from one of these exotic diseases such as plague or cholera, against which our sanitary regulations provide us with special weapons, because they only arrive here through importation, thus justifying our right to ban anything that comes from infected countries, and if need be, to destroy the sources.

It is an endemic disease in Europe, whose transmission is also to be feared whatever the nationality of those who give it, whatever the severity of the cases who breed the germs. The housing infected by the Eskimos at the *Jardin d'acclimatation*, a housing which is not really one, since it is a hut and nobody will lie there for a long time to come, seems less dangerous than all the city's dwellings where people die every day from smallpox, and which, after a short period of disinfection and ventilation, are often made available, day and night, to other occupants.

As for their belongings, they were used only by individuals incubating the disease, that is to say, at a time when the morbid germs are not yet regenerated by the body; are they more dreadful than the masses of bedding objects soiled every day, directly in Paris, either in hospitals or in private houses, by patients who undergo all the phases of their disease, including eruption, suppuration, drying, these three periods of acuity and expansion of the contagion?

Not a single employee of the *Jardin d'acclimatation* has been suffering from the sickness imported there, more than a month ago, by the Eskimos.

It seems wise to bring things to their true proportion, considering that the health practices deserve to be sanctioned by their degree of usefulness, and must be shielded from the exaggerations of some alarming demonstrations.

But far from us the thought to state that there is little or nothing to do here; we even think that some caution should be added to the series of wise measures already taken, by order of Mr. Director of the *Jardin d'acclimatation* [Albert Geoffroy Saint-Hilaire], including the three times repeated disinfection of the Eskimos' hut by chlorine vapors, in accordance with the instructions of the Prefecture of Police, and vaccination by means of a heifer, of all staff of the Jardin.

In an institution where the public is attracted, the sanitary conditions cannot be too widely guaranteed. Therefore, we believe that the disinfection of the hut should be conducted, even if this complement were to be superfluous, using a method that proved itself on board ships and which was recently used successfully in several military barracks. In earthen vases, light an amount of sulfur representing about 50 grams per cubic meter of the capacity of the area to be purified; immediately close all openings for 24 hours, then ventilate widely and extensively, keeping open all day and night for a month. As for the personal effects left by the Eskimos, we recommend to destroy by combustion all those of minimal value, sanitize the others by immersing them in boiling water, or in a sterilizer heated to 100°.

Finally, we would like, despite its immunity to this day, and despite the success of the animal vaccine on some employees, that the staff of the Jardin be subjected to the inoculation of an arm-to-arm child vaccine. This involves an expense of barely thirty francs for two children to carry the vaccination through, which would be more than sufficient for all of the staff.

Finally, the *Conseil*'s delegate has the honor to propose the adoption of the following conclusions:

1° Send an official thank you letter to the Crefeld Burgo-master for the telegram notice sent to the Prefecture of the Seine, and for the documents provided to your delegate.

2° Approve all the preventive measures applied by the Director of the *Jardin d'acclimatation* and invite him to complete them;

 A. By the revaccination of the Jardin's personnel, using arm-to-arm child vaccine;

 B. By the disinfection, using sulphurous vapors, of the premises occupied by the Eskimos from January 1 to 8, 1881;

 C. By the purification, using a sterilizer or boiling water, of the victims' belongings that are of value, and the combustion of all other objects from the same source.

3° Forward a copy of this report to the Minister of Foreign Affairs, with a plea to assess the opportunity to report the facts therein contained to Germany's public health authorities;

4° Bring out to the attention of the French government the importance of this fact from the point of view of the application of international hygiene rules. The landing of Eskimos at any port of the European coastline can be as prejudicial to them as their landing in Hamburg. It seems worthy of the *Conseil de salubrité de la Seine* to take advantage of such an example: not only to demand from the competent authorities, to the extent possible, the immediate vaccination, in our ports, of individuals from countries where neither vaccine or previous smallpox have attenuated their responsiveness; but above all to seek penetration in these countries of the benefits of preventive health care. To introduce there the vaccine is not only ensuring a few individuals against the dangers of a trip to Europe, it is to protect the general population against the dangers of smallpox germs imported through navigation, and which, at intervals have, on-site, cruelly decimated these unfortunate people;

5° These facts demonstrate once again the merits of projects aimed at creating public disinfection chambers, and devoting specialized vehicles for the transport of patients with contagious disease conditions to the hospital.

The Conseil believes it needs to take this opportunity to emphasize the need to complete, in proportion to the total population, the number of specialized vehicles whose construction is planned.

Please accept, Mr. Prefect, the assurances of my highest consideration.

Léon Colin

THE DEBATE ON COMPULSORY VACCINATION

In 1881, the debate on the vaccination for smallpox was a major concern for both the medical and public health authorities, and for politicians.

A few days before Dr. Colin handed over his report, the *Eskimos'* death was the subject of a discussion at the January 26, 1881, meeting of the *Société de médecine publique et d'hygiène professionnelle* (Society of public medicine and occupational health). They discussed the importance of compulsory vaccination and voiced their opposition to the upcoming sale of the Eskimos' furs. The text contains some factual errors namely nine "Eskimos" instead of eight, four of which would have died in Hamburg:[213]

> Dr. Laborde: For several months, posters plastered on walls all over Paris announced the arrival of an Eskimo family that was to be exhibited at the *Jardin d'acclimatation*. These Eskimos, nine in total when they left their country, lost four persons before they arrived in France; they died in Hamburg from smallpox contracted during the voyage; the five survivors just succumbed to the same disease in its most severe form at *Hôpital Saint-Louis*. This event represents yet another reason, it seems to me, to emphasize the need for vaccination, as the Société has been seeking, and as our colleague, Dr. Henri Liouville, demands it to Parliament through the law he has tabled. It is for this reason that I think I must report these facts; should we not vaccinate all foreigners who come to Paris in these conditions? It even seems that the furs worn by these individuals will soon be

---

[213] Laborde, Dr. (1881, January 26).

auctioned. I request that the Société takes steps to prevent this sale. [214]

Dr. Brouardel: If the Society wants it, because of my personal relationship with Mr. Director of the *Jardin d'acclimatation*, I will pass on to him, our colleague's legitimate demand. I would add that it should be noted that these Eskimos died as it happens in severe smallpox, even before appearance of pustules; smallpox was probably already in a state of incubation when they arrived in France, since they had already had to leave behind five of their sick companions.

The *Journal officiel de la République française* (Official Journal of the French Republic) also argued in favor of vaccination of foreigners arriving on French soil and mentioned the case of the Labrador *Eskimos*. Here as well, the text contains a few factual errors on the number of *Eskimos* and their place of death: [215]

Among communicable diseases, smallpox is one of those that still appear to be the most dreadful; but what are its ravages today compared to those that produced the great epidemics that preceded the inoculation of smallpox and especially Jenner's[216] discovery! Pockmarked individuals, to mention only survivors, are no longer in the majority, as in the eighteenth century; now they are the exceptions.

However the number of people affected by smallpox is still far too high, especially if one thinks, as Professor Brouardel rightly stated last September at Turin's International Congress of Hygiene, that the day will come when we measure the degree of

[214] No information has yet been found confirming the fate of the group's furs but Gwénaële Guigon, specialist of Arctic collections in French museums, is of the opinion that "because the Inuit had smallpox, it is likely that their clothes were burned. It is noted that very few furs have survived till today because the storage conditions of the time did not allow optimal preservation. Through the inventories of different museums, we discover fur anoraks marked with the mention 'destroyed by moths.' It was not until the postwar that conservation techniques were more appropriate."

[215] Martin, A.-J. (1881, February 9).
[216] Edward Jenner (1749–1823), an English physician known as the first physician to have used the smallpox vaccine.

civilization of a country by the number of smallpox patients it generates. Indeed, smallpox is, among contagious diseases, perhaps the easiest to combat and prevent, for science has completely determined the various means specific to this purpose, among which, top-ranked, vaccination and revaccination, which a proposed law tabled by Dr. Henri Liouville, soon to be discussed in the *Chambre des députés*, aims to make compulsory.

But if we must guard ourselves against the spread of smallpox among the inhabitants of our country, is it not also necessary to try to prevent the import from foreign countries? A recent event shows its full interest. A few days ago, all Parisians noticed the walls covered with posters announcing the arrival of an Eskimo family at the *Jardin d'acclimatation*. The public's curiosity, usually very eager for exhibitions of this kind, could not be satisfied because they all died of smallpox a few days after their arrival. Having left Labrador, the nine individuals probably contracted smallpox on the ship during the voyage, as three of them died in Hamburg, soon after landing; the others went to Antwerp, where one of them stayed also suffering from smallpox, and the five survivors left for Paris. The Prefecture of Police had been notified by telegram by the mayor of Antwerp, and had them immediately vaccinated on January 1, and revaccinated on the 7th as an additional precaution.

On the 9th, said Dr. Landrieux before the *Société médicale des hôpitaux*, they entered his service at *Hôpital Saint-Louis* and they soon succumbed with all the symptoms of a most serious hemorrhagic smallpox, even before the appearance of pustules, as usually happens in such cases.

These Eskimos, who had never been vaccinated in their home country, therefore arrived in Paris in possession of smallpox and one may wonder whether it would not be appropriate, as suggested Dr. Laborde at the last meeting of the *Société de médecine publique*, to vaccinate at the border all foreigners who arrive in these conditions. In all such cases should we, as was mentioned, force a sort of land quarantine similar to maritime quarantines?

In Labrador, the vaccine is unknown; also when a foreign ship imports smallpox, this disease depopulates whole villages. In all unvaccinated countries, it is the same, and it is still the deadliest epidemics in Central Africa, in India, in the kingdom of Burma among others. It is therefore of utmost importance to provide all these people with the means to protect themselves from it.

Our Navy's health force, whose usual zeal and devotion do not back off from any difficulty, has introduced the regular practice of vaccination in Cochinchina, since our occupation. Its scholarly Director, Dr. Jules Rochard learned, from the discussion raised by the death of the Eskimos, that in 1878, the Navy physicians vaccinated 13,248 natives, in 1879, 26,939 and 43,045 for the first quarter of 1880, that's a total of 83,332 [83,232] in 30 months. From this number, we could verify the results on 44,843 subjects and found 35,880 successes, that is to say 80 percent.

[…] It seems that the means employed in this distant country to spread vaccination could find an equally easy implementation in France. […]

A.-J. Martin

In the 17th edition of his *Dictionnaire annuel des progrès des sciences et institutions médicales* (Annual Dictionary of Scientific Progress and Medical Institutions) covering the year 1881, M. P. Garnier refers to the efforts of Dr. Léon Colin who's demanding international vaccine. He also holds up the case of the *Eskimos* as an example:[217]

The death from hemorrhagic smallpox of the Labrador Eskimos who landed in Hamburg and came to the *Jardin d'acclimatation* in Paris, from where they soon went to *Hôpital Saint-Louis* to die, seems to have been the decisive motive for this measure [international vaccine].

In addition, since 1880, Dr. Henri Liouville, physician, professor of medicine at *Université de Paris* and deputy of the Meuse department (1876–1887), had been trying to pass a bill to make vaccination and revaccination compulsory.

At the March 7, 1881, session of the Chamber of Deputies, during the debates surrounding this bill, the case of the *Eskimos* held up once again as an example. The *rapporteur parlementaire*[218]

---

[217] Garnier, M.P. (1882).

[218] Member appointed within a commission to study a project or a proposal and present in his name, in a public session, his observations and amendments. (Lexicon – National Assembly, France)

encouraged his colleagues to adopt the bill in the first deliberation. His speech contained the same factual errors as those published in the *Journal officiel de la République française*:[219]

> [...] Please allow me, gentlemen, to make a short observation. Smallpox is a highly contagious disease. Of all contagious diseases, it may be the deadliest. In the last year, in 1880, smallpox made 2,258 victims in Paris alone. Those who witnessed the siege of Paris[220] were able to see how intense it prevailed at that time, on an agglomerated and starving population.
>
> To give a more recent example, I remind you that Eskimos, nine in number, left Labrador at the end of last fall to come to Paris. Three died in Hamburg, soon after landing; a fourth died in Antwerp, and the last five came to die in Paris, at *Hôpital Saint-Louis*, with all the symptoms of hemorrhagic smallpox, also known as black pox. These are the actions of smallpox. In the presence of a real public danger, it is the duty of the legislature to address this general hygiene issue head on. The bill proposed by Mr. Liouville is essentially a social act, and it is for this reason that I have come to ask you to kindly pass it in the first deliberation.

In 1881, opinions were still divided and the pressures of anti-vaccination leagues delayed the adoption of the bill. It was not until 1902, 21 years later, that such a law passed in France.

---

[219] *Annales de la chambre des députés – Débats parlementaires*, (1881).
[220] From September 19, 1870, to January 28, 1871, during the Franco-Prussian War.

Fig. 73 Dr. Henri Liouville
(Wikimedia Commons)

THE *ESKIMOS'* BELONGINGS
RETURN TO LABRADOR

On January 18, 1881, Brother Elsner, informed by Carl Hagenbeck, wrote a letter to Brother Reichel to bring him the news of the tragedy that had taken place in Paris:[221]

Bremen, January 18, 1881

Dear Brother Reichel!

Today, I have to bring you news that deeply move us all, and tell you that all the Eskimos in Paris have been called home by the Lord. I believe that in my last lines to you, which I noted on the letter's envelope, I told you that the second child of Abraham and Ulrike had passed away. That news had also reached me through Mr. Hagenbeck. A short while later (two or three days after) Mr. H. told me in response to my inquiry, and presumably in reaction to my wire telegram, "that I would not be admitted to see the Eskimos who were suffering from smallpox in Paris."

Thus it became easier for me to decide to abstain from the trip to Paris for the time being until he Lord would smooth the path of a journey which has been so full of serious obstacles until now; but this does not mean at all that I had given up the journey altogether.

But then, tonight, we were overwhelmed by the sad news of their departure from life, which had also affected Mr. Hagenbeck very profoundly. The news from Paris seems to be based on a wire telegram, and there are no further details. Mr. Hagenbeck adds the following: "My managers will

---

[221] Lutz, Hartmut *et al.* (2005). p. 42-45.

stay in Paris for another 14 days and on the return trip will come to see you."

It is a great consolation in this very sad story that the Eskimos were so thoroughly prepared for their passing, yes, they were ready. They brought no shame upon the Lord or upon the Mission: wherever they went, and even without words – because they could not be understood – they were a testimony to the fact that the belief in which they lived, that of redemption through the Saviour's suffering, gives us a new heart and a new essence. They were free of the concerns of this earth except for their single wish: to see their relatives once again, but even in this, they surrendered to the Lord's will.

Brother Elsner

At the end of May 1881, Johan Adrian Jacobsen met Brother Elsner in Bremen.[222] Jacobsen was not the only one to have paid him a visit. As Brother Elsner reported to Brother Shaw in England, Carl Hagenbeck and Adolf Schoepf, both appalled and in tears because of the death of the *Eskimos*, had come to see him.[223]

The group's personal belongings that were decontaminated were sent from Paris to the Moravian Church in London through Carl Hagenbeck. The leaders of the Moravian Church preferred to sell these goods on behalf of the bereaved to avoid any risk of contagion in Labrador. Brother Elsner did not wish to assume this task. It was therefore performed under the responsibility of the *Society for the Furtherance of the Gospel* (the commercial branch of the Moravian Church).[224]

Brother Elsner committed to prepare a narrative of the group's experience based on the letters he received from Abraham. The text was written in Inuktitut and he produced six copies, one for each of the Moravian settlements in Labrador. He received two pounds from the Moravian Church for this work.[225] Two of the six copies have been found to date.[226]

---

[222] Hagenbeck's financial records show that on May 30, 1881, he paid 16 marks to Jacobsen for the trip to Bremen.

[223] Thode-Arora, Hilke (2002). p. 11.

[224] Ibid., p. 12.

[225] Ibid.

[226] The English and French translations are being worked on in collabora-

Elsner also mentioned a manuscript will left by Abraham in which he specified that the repayment of his debt to the mission store was his first priority. Since items identified in this will had been mostly burned or sold, Elsner requested that the document not be returned to Labrador.[227]

When the Moravian Church's ship, *The Harmony,* left London in mid-June 1881, it carried the six copies of Brother Elsner's narrative, a suitcase containing what was left of the group's personal belongings, including Abraham's diary, and the amount of money they had earned for their work in Europe.

Carl Hagenbeck's financial records[228] show that an amount of 1977.16 marks was sent on June 7, 1881, to Pastor Ludwig in Altona, the person in charge of delivering the money to the Moravian Church in London. Converted into pounds sterling it amounted to £96.91.

The financial records also provide the detailed calculation of the income earned by each of the eight *Eskimos.*

Abraham	537.40 marks	(8 days * 2 marks)[229] + (140 days * 3 marks) + 101.40 marks in tips
Tobias	306.80 marks	(139 days * 2 marks) + 28.80 in tips
Tigianniak	355.96 marks	(137 days * 2 marks) + 81.96 in tips
Ulrike	286.00 marks	143 days * 2 marks
Paingu	246.00 marks	123 days * 2 marks
Nuggasak	220.00 marks	110 days * 2 marks
Sara	126.00 marks	126 days * 1 mark
Maria	137.00 marks	137 days * 1 mark
TOTAL	**2,215.16 marks**	

tion with the Torngâsok Cultural Center.
[227] Ibid.
[228] Preserved in the archives of the Tierpark Hagenbeck in Hamburg.
[229] The assumption is that this is the wage earned by Abraham as Jacobsen's interpreter during his trip to Nachvak Fjord.

No written contract was signed in August 1880 between the *Eskimos* and Hagenbeck because of the reluctance of the Moravian missionaries. But according to the August 26, 1880, letter written by missionaries stationed in Hebron, the men should have received a daily wage of 3 shillings, the women, 2 shillings, and the children, 1 shilling. Assuming British shillings and German marks were equivalent, we see that Tigianniak and Tobias were actually given the women's salary.

As for calculating the number of working days for each individual, Hagenbeck seems to have used the period beginning on August 26, the day of their departure from Labrador, until their respective death.

Nuggasak	August 26 to December 14	110 days
Paingu	August 26 to December 27	123 days
Sara	August 26 to December 31	127 days
Maria	August 26 to January 10	137 days
Tigianniak	August 26 to January 11	138 days
Tobias	August 26 to January 13	140 days
Abraham	August 26 to January 13	140 days
Ulrike	August 26 to January 16	143 days

The total accumulated by the eight individuals therefore amounted to 2,215.16 marks. Of this amount, 238 marks, equivalent to an advance that had been paid to them, was deducted by Hagenbeck, leaving a net sum of 1,977.16 marks owed to them.

In his diary, Johan Adrian Jacobsen also mentioned that the income earned by the *Eskimos* was paid to Pastor Ludwig.

> I made a little trip to Bremen because of the deceased Eskimo's things. Saw missionary Elsner. He advised me to give the wages Hagenbeck owed to the deceased to Pastor Ludwig in Altona. The honorarium was indeed paid out to M. Ludwig, who was in charge of the Eskimos' belongings, and transferred to London. I heard afterwards that the ship for Labrador departed in mid-June. (J. A. Jacobsen's diary, June 1881)

On June 13, 1881, as *The Harmony* was about to leave Europe, if it was not already on its way, in Labrador, Johann Heinrich Theodor Bourquin, a missionary in Nain, wrote a letter in which he refers to Abraham's group. After facing the complaints of an Inuk who casted doubt on the integrity of the Moravian Church in the delivery of goods and in the monetary donations coming from Europe, Brother Bourquin told his interlocutor that he should go to Europe to find the truth about all the rumors. Brother Bourquin added:[230]

> In front of such experiences we ask ourselves what has been the fate of the Eskimos hired by Mr. Hagenbeck. Impossible that Europe's easy life will do them any good. Also impossible that, upon their return, they will, once again, take a liking to Labrador's hard life. It would require a miracle.

Brother Bourquin resumed the writing of his letter on July 15 on board the steamer *Kite* en route to Newfoundland. Obviously, *The Harmony* had arrived in Labrador and crossed paths with the *Kite* since Brother Bourquin wrote:[231]

> [...] the steamer taking us brought some initial news from the mother country. It is said that our Eskimos from Hebron all died in Paris! May God grant that it was in faith! What a warning for our Eskimos! What a testimony from above to support our words and our efforts! Who would have suspected such an outcome!

Ten days later, on July 25, *The Harmony* and the news of the tragedy reached the community of Zoar. The missionaries stationed there, Friedrich Rindereknecht and Carl Adolf Slotta, wrote the following summary:[232]

> On July 25th, the first tidings from Europe reached us here, including Br. Elsner's narrative of the death of the Eskimo visitors, who were exhibited in Europe last autumn, and died in Paris in January. As far as we can judge, we are inclined to think that several of our people were impressed by the story of their countrymen's experiences. Several among them

[230] Bourquin, Théodore. (1882). p. 27.

[231] Ibid., p. 30-31.

[232] *Periodical Accounts Relating to the Missions of the Church of the United Brethren Established Among the Heathen*. (1882). p. 114.

have evidently a strong desire to take a trip to Europe: this sad conclusion of their friends' European visit will certainly have a deterrent effect on such.

On August 17, it was Hebron's turn to be dismayed. Missionaries Kretschmer, Haugk and Hlawatscheck summarized the events as follows:[233]

> The intelligence of the death of the Eskimoes in Europe, some of whom were members of this congregation, made a deep impression, and will – we doubt not – for some time to come effectually restrain the longing which some have to go to Europe, in hopes of becoming rich without much trouble. Br. Elsner's narrative of their experience was communicated on the day we received it (August 17th), and we were very thankful for it. The Eskimoes do not think that Abraham was wrong in going to Europe, but they lay the entire blame of their troubles on the circumstances.

The Moravian Church's *Periodical Accounts* summarizing the various events in Labrador between July 1880 and July 1881, published a brief analysis of the events leading to the tragedy:[234]

> The sad end of the Eskimoes, Abraham and Ulrica of Hebron, excited much painful interest in home-circles. Yielding to the persuasions of an agent of Mr. Hagenbeck in Hamburg, they agreed, in consideration of a considerable sum of money, to travel to Europe, in company with a family of heathen Eskimoes, and to allow themselves to be exhibited in various Zoological Gardens. When warned by the missionaries of the perils of such a trip to Europe, Abraham spoke of his poverty and the probability of him being enabled to pay his debts and improve his position by earning liberal wages for little work. In spite of the liberal and scrupulously kind treatment which they received, the poor Eskimoes soon discovered that they had made a great mistake. The long sea-voyage, combined with a secret fear, lest they should never return to their native land, had a fatally depressing effect upon them; homesickness, and a certain feeling of degradation in the part which they had set themselves to play, weighed upon them so heavily that nothing, but a sense of duty could at all reconcile them to

---

[233] Ibid., p. 116.
[234] Ibid., p. 96.

their fate. At the same time, in the Providence of God, they were destined, by contrast with their heathen companions, to prove to the civilized world of Europe that Christianity is the only true civilization, and that it stamps itself on life, character, and conduct, and to bear witness by their death that it can bring peace to the heart of the believing Eskimo, and change the weary pinings of homesickness into resigned aspirations for a better world. After much bodily suffering from smallpox, which attacked them while on their journey, they fell asleep in Jesus at Paris, trusting in the Saviour, and with the hope that through their warnings and entreaties their heathen fellow-countryman had set himself to seek the Lord.

A year later, in 1882, the following letter from the Hebron missionaries was published in the *Missionsblatt aus der Brüdergemeine* and explained how the community of Hebron coped with the loss of the loved ones:[235]

Of course, we never expected at all that the local Eskimos would have to pay with their lives for their undertaking; that they would become homesick, Ulrike had already predicted. We are glad (lieb ist es uns!), because one day everything had to become so serious that Abraham would see his mistake and feel ashamed of it.

Last winter, when there was great poverty, we were often thankful that Abraham did not stay here for our sake. How often would we have had to hear that he had rejected such high profits because of the teachers and that he now had to suffer together with them? The easiest way for us would always be to let the Eskimos live according to their own will. Abraham was our best violin player at church, and we will miss him a lot. We hoped he would profit from Germany, for his own and for our benefit, because he would hear good music for the first time.

Now the Lord decided according to His own will and placed the homesick ones in a better land, saved them from sin and earthly misery, and at the same time taught the locals – the ones lusting for Europe – a lesson; because if they had come back healthy and rich, the craving to go to Europe and to grow rich there would have become an

---

[235] Lutz, Hartmut *et al.* (2005). p. 85-86.

epidemic among the other Eskimos. Many of them, who were looking at Abraham and his companions in envy last year, are now silent and happy not to have gone with them.

Since Mr. Hagenbeck, and in spite of his big losses, paid all earnings honestly, the relatives of the deceased received the commendable sum of 1,120 marks. Unfortunately, suspicion is on the rise and is fomented maliciously by people who were not even involved, maintaining that, besides the suitcase of the deceased arrived from Hamburg – which, as a precaution we had opened immediately on the beach in presence of the helmsman and the Eskimos – another bag had arrived containing belongings of Abraham and Tobias. People believe to have learned this from the captain of the helmsman; there is also talk about 5,000 marks, which they are supposed to have earned. Referring to this, and according to what the crewmembers tell them from the newspapers, they draw their own conclusions; when they hear that thousands came to see them in just one day, they think that all of the money thus taken had belonged to their countrymen.

Now, as everybody knows, Eskimos are not the greatest people at numerical systems or the art of calculation, and so it makes no difference to them if you multiply a number by 4 or 5. But, in spite of their clean conscience, this suspicion hurts our Brothers, and they have to leave it to the Lord to vindicate them in the hearts of the people. For them, unfortunately, this conviction is also a great misfortune. Despite all the things that happened it would not be impossible that, if they were asked again next year to go to Europe, some would again let themselves be seduced by the hope of becoming rich.

Individual Brethren, who knew Abraham and met him again in Europe, express their heartfelt personal grief, but also their trust in divine providence. The missionaries at Hebron were vindicated: The Lord has punished Abraham for his disobedience, and providence had shown that "the outside" was indeed full of lurking dangers.

So, this letter tells us that the families of the deceased received a total of 1,120 marks while Hagenbeck's financial records show that he paid 1,977 marks, a difference of almost 860 marks. What happened to the money raised from the sale of the group's belongings by the Moravian Church in London? Can the difference be explained solely by the deduction of Abraham's debt?

Johan Adrian Jacobsen wrote in his diary that the families were happy with the amount received:

> It had already become quite a handsome sum by Eskimo standards, and the relatives are said to have been heartily delighted, as was reported later to Hagenbeck by the Moravian missionaries. (J. A. Jacobsen's diary, June 1881)

However, the Hebron missionaries' letter allows us to doubt this statement. At present, the evidence required to remove all doubts has not yet been found.

On August 23, 1882, Marie Kretschmer, wife of Brother Kretschmer, who translated Abraham's diary to German, wrote a letter to a friend in which she states that two years after Abraham's death, the community of Hebron was still thinking of him often:[236]

> We often spoke of Abraham, this winter. We miss him greatly, namely as a musician. He was our first violin and played with more feeling than his colleagues who seek only to make as much noise as possible.

Finally, in 1888, a Moravian missionary, Benjamin La Trobe, visited the Labrador missions aboard *The Harmony*. In his diary, he reports having spent eight days in Hebron, during which, on the Sunday after mass, several people were presented to him as members of Abraham's and Tobias' families.[237] Unfortunately, he did not identify them or elaborate on their discussions.

---

[236] Kretschmer, Marie. (1883). p. 120.
[237] La Trobe, Benjamin. (1888).

Fig. 74 Poster *Amerikanishe Völkertypen*
Brockhaus Encyclopédia, 14th edition, 1894–1896, p. 526a.

Fig. 75 Paingu's portrait
Extracted from the top left corner of the above poster.

Paingu's Skullcap

Let's return to Paris in January 1881 to further explore the events that occurred after the *Eskimos'* death.

During the January 6, 1881, meeting of the *Société d'anthropologie de Paris*, Dr. Arthur Bordier,[238] the Société's secretary, presented the skull of a Labrador *Eskimo* who had died recently in Germany. Although there is error on the gender of the person and on the place of death, this skullcap can be no other than Paingu's since, in his diary, Jacobsen admits that he took it when in Crefeld and gave it to a professor in Paris.

> [...] the museum in Paris (Trocadero) had acquired various things, [...] including the skullcap of the woman Paingo, which the physicians in Crefeld had taken off to look for the cause of the sickness, and which I had kept in my suitcase among my clothes (wrapped in paper). However, when I was leaving the hospital, a professor from the museum came to view the grave finds from Labrador. I then offered the skullcap to him because I now wanted to get rid of it. The professor accepted it with great pleasure, stuffed it under his coat, and marched off with it. (J. A. Jacobsen's diary, Additions to page 150)

There is no doubt that Jacobsen gave the skullcap to someone in Paris, but that he did it following his release from the hospital is doubtful. The reasons being that the skullcap was presented to members of the *Société d'anthropologie de Paris* three days before the group was admitted to the hospital, ten days before

---

[238] Arthur Bordier (1841–1910), physician, anthropologist and founder of the *Société de médecine publique*, member of the *Conseil d'hygiène publique et de salubrité*, and of the *Société d'anthropologie de Paris*.

the death of the last survivor, and eleven days before Jacobsen was discharged from the hospital.

The section of Jacobsen's diary where he mentions the skullcap was written at a later date, a date that is unknown to us, and could be several years after the events. So, when and to whom did Jacobsen hand the cap? We do not know, but what is certain is that, on January 6, 1881, the skullcap was in the hands of Dr. Arthur Bordier:[239]

> I present to you the skullcap of an Eskimo who died a few days ago in Frankfurt. Unfortunately, the doctor who performed the autopsy, performed it solely from a medical point of view, and we have only one piece of this individual: his skullcap.
>
> The skull's cephalic index is 76.4 indicating a shallow dolichocephaly [an elongated skull] for an Eskimo. However, the average I have seen in males of this race is 76.
>
> The Eskimos who are currently in the *Jardin d'acclimatation* are from Labrador not Greenland; their type is different: they are taller, have more beard, are less dolichocephalic, and their nose has a different shape; it comes closer to the aquiline nose. It seems they are crossed with Redskins.
>
> I also have, from the same individual, a lock of hair that will be studied in the laboratory.

Dr. Bordier donated the skullcap to the *Laboratoire d'anthropologie de Paris* which later joined the collections of the *Musée Broca*. When the *Musée Broca* was dismantled, the skullcap found its way into the anthropology collection of the *Musée de l'Homme* where it still is today.

As for Paingu's lock of hair, it could not be found, but the *Musée de l'Homme* owns a hair collection inherited from Dr. Paul Latteux who was commissioned in 1876 by Dr. Paul Broca to study the *Musée Broca's* hair collection.[240] In Dr. Latteux's collection are five locks belonging to *Eskimos*. No detail is provided on the origin of these locks except that four of them are identified as follows: the elder, the chief, the woman, and the second. The fifth one has no qualifier.

---

[239] Bordier, A. (1881).
[240] Latteux, Dr. (1877).

Could it be that Dr. Latteux obtained these locks from the Greenlanders who were at the *Jardin d'acclimatation* in November 1877 or from the Labrador group who was there in January 1881? In both cases, the groups consisted of four adults, three men and a woman, which corresponds to the identified locks.

Could the elder be Tigianniak? The chief, Abraham? The woman, Ulrike? The second, Tobias?

For now, the question remains unresolved and the assumption is that the locks belong to the 1877 Greenlanders. Since they were the subject of an anthropologic study by a commission from the *Société d'anthropologie de Paris*, it would have been easy to get the locks at that occasion.

The locks are stored in a box with hair from South America. The colour of some is brown or light brown, i.e. lighter than the black colour reported by 19th century anthropologists who studied both the Greenlanders and the Labrador *Eskimos*. Intriguing!

Fig. 76 Tigianniak, Paingu and Nuggasak, 1886
Illustration by E. Krell. See Ratzel, Friedrich. (1886).

Three Eskimo Brain Casts

When the Greenlanders stayed at the *Jardin d'acclimatation* in 1877, Dr. Paul Topinard[241] and Dr. Arthur Bordier were both part of the commission authorized to go to the *Jardin d'acclimatation* to study and measure them.

Fig. 77 Dr. Paul Topinard
(Courtesy of Bibliothèque de l'Académie de médecine de Paris)

---

[241] Paul Topinard (1830–1911), Secretary General of the *Société d'anthropologie de Paris*, deputy director of the *Laboratoire d'anthropologie de l'École pratique des hautes études*, and professor at the School of Anthropology.

In early January 1881, hoping to repeat the experience with the Labrador group, Dr. Topinard sent a request to the Director of the *Jardin d'acclimatation*. Albert Geoffroy Saint-Hilaire responded favourably to his request:[242]

Bois de Boulogne, January 5, 1881

Sir,

I am entirely at your disposal to facilitate the examination of our Eskimos by the commission delegated by the Société d'anthropologie.

Please tell me the number of people that will be part of this commission and the selected day for its visit to the *Jardin d'acclimatation*. I will quickly send you the permissions to enter the Jardin, and to access the enclosure reserved for the Eskimos.

I am pleased to send you, here enclosed, some tickets for your personal use. I hope you will use them before the little caravan that we host at the moment, leaves Paris to return to Labrador.

Please accept, Sir, the assurances of my highest consideration.

The Director
Albert Geoffroy Saint-Hilaire

A few days later, Albert Geoffroy Saint-Hilaire hastened to write to Dr. Topinard asking him not to convene the commission, all *Eskimos* having been admitted to the hospital:[243]

Bois de Boulogne, January 11, 1881

Sir,·

I received your letter dated the 10th of this month, and I hasten to ask you not to convene the commission that was to come next Thursday to examine our Eskimos.

---

[242] Letter preserved in the archives of the *Société d'anthropologie de Paris* (Box B1, n° U98).
[243] Letter preserved in the archives of the *Société d'anthropologie de Paris* (Box B1, n° U97).

These unfortunate foreigners were too seriously ill for us to keep them longer. We had them transported to *Hôpital Saint-Louis*. I dare not hope for their healing because these poor people are suffering from a truly devastating disease (smallpox).

Please accept, Sir, the new assurances of my highest consideration.

The Director
Albert Geoffroy Saint-Hilaire

Following receipt of this letter, Dr. Topinard went to *Hôpital Saint-Louis* and met Dr. Landrieux. The latter summarized their meeting in the following letter:[244]

My dear friend,

So many letters, so many procedures surrounding these poor Eskimos? Mr. Topinard having come to *Hôpital St Louis* to see them on behalf of G. St Hilaire, I thought it was my duty to donate to him what it was possible for me to have removed by my intern. I therefore had 3 skullcaps and 3 brains sent by the amphitheater boy; these parts were sent to the anthropology laboratory.

Undoubtedly it would have been possible for you to do more, but time was running out. I was receiving many letters from Bordier, Pozzi,[245] etc., but the parts remained in the amphitheater exposed to cold and decay. I cannot be found negligent in any respect.

The five bodies were buried in a common grave at the St Ouen cemetery. I think it would be possible, thanks to your intervention, to proceed with the exhumation.

If you want more information, I am at St Louis every morning from 9 a.m. to 10 a.m.

Yours truly, Landrieux

---

[244] Letter is preserved in the archives of the *Musée de l'Homme*'s anthropology collections.
[245] Samuel Pozzi (1846–1918) was a surgeon, an associate professor at the Faculty of Medicine and member of the *Société d'anthropologie de Paris*.

Dr. Topinard therefore went to the *Hôpital Saint-Louis* on behalf of Albert Geoffroy Saint-Hilaire, but not to see the *Eskimos* and comfort them. It was to ensure that, after their death, the Parisian anthropologists could recover parts of their anatomy that would be useful in their studies of human groups.

The skullcaps and brains of three *Eskimos* were taken. Which ones? The answer is provided in the speech delivered, on May 5, 1881, by Dr. Théophile Chudzinski (1840–1897), head assistant at the *Laboratoire d'anthropologie de l'École pratique des hautes études*, before the *Société d'anthropologie de Paris*:[246]

Fig. 78 Théophile Chudzinski
(© 2014. Musée du quai Branly/Scala, Florence)

The three Eskimo brains arrived at the *Laboratoire d'anthropologie des Hautes-Études* two weeks after death. As they were kept during this time in water with very low alcohol concentration, one can easily imagine the deplorable condition they were in when we received them at the laboratory.

Here are the two hemispheres of Abraham Paulus, which reflect the brain's state of complete decomposition.

---

[246] Chudzinski, Théophile. (1881).

As for the other brains, we were able to harden and preserve them so that the gyri could easily be studied. Of these three Eskimo brains, two belong to men, and the other to a woman.

The first of these brains is that of Tobias Ignatius, 23 years old, who died on January 13, 1881; its weight is 1,398 grams.

The second brain is that of Abraham Paulus, 35 years old, who died January 14 [sic]; the weight of the brain is unknown because of its very advanced state of decomposition.

The third brain is that of the Eskimo woman, Ulrika Henocq, 24 years old, sister [sic] of Abraham Paulus; she died on January 16, and the weight of her brain is 1,236 grams.

We have the honor to present to the *Société d'anthropologie* the plaster casts of these three brains of which the external structures are remarkable in many ways.

Chudzinski continues his presentation with his detailed study of the brains (which can be found in Appendix C).

The brains being those of the last three individuals to die, Dr. Topinard's visit to *Hôpital Saint-Louis* must have taken place on January 12 or 13, 1881, i.e. after the bodies of Maria and Tigianniak had already left for the cemetery, but before Tobias, Abraham, and Ulrike died or at least before their bodies underwent the same fate.

The casts were made on the 2nd floor[247] of the refectory of the Convent of the Cordeliers, which housed, since 1876, the society, the school, and the laboratory of anthropology as well as the *Musée Broca*, the museum which united the collections of the *Société d'anthropologie de Paris* with those of its founder, Dr. Paul Broca. "All anthropologists know the uncomfortable staircase to the second floor of the Cordeliers' Refectory. [...] The long corridor, onto which it comes out, leads to the classroom and to the premises belonging to the school. To the right of this corridor are the *Musée Broca* and the meeting room of the Society; to its left, the laboratory."[248]

---

[247] Third floor for North Americans.
[248] Vallois, H.L. (1940). p. 5.

Fig. 79 Refectory of the Cordeliers' Convent
Photo by Eugène Atget. (© Ministère de la Culture/Médiathèque du
Patrimoine, Distr. RMN-Grand Palais/Art Resource, NY.)

Once completed, the brain casts were integrated into the *Musée Broca*'s collection. They are part of a "remarkable collection of brain casts executed by Chudzinski and which includes no less than 714 casts. Each one represents quite a preparation: the actual casting process only provides the surface of the brain. The fissures and the sulci were carved with an engraving tool on the fresh plaster; such an operation, which can only be performed by a professional anatomist doubled by a very skilled artist, makes it possible to reproduce every detail of the cerebral cortex, and to reveal the various gyri one by one. The parts obtained this way are not only easier to handle than the brain itself, but they allow the permanent display of the arrangements buried deep which could not be looked at on the preserved brain other than by destroying it. No museum in the world has, from this perspective, a collection as extensive as that of the *Musée Broca*. About half of the casts relate to the human brain [...]"[249]

---

[249] Vallois, H.L. (1940). p. 10-11.

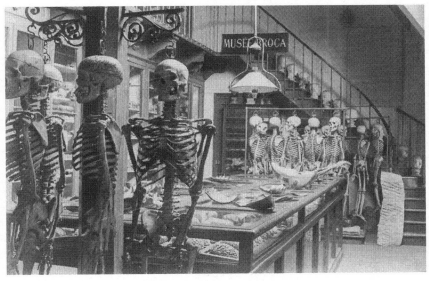

Fig. 80 *Musée Broca*'s skeleton and brain casts collection
(© 2014. Musée du quai Branly/Scala, Florence)

The first use of the brain casts that has been uncovered to date goes back to 1888 when they were studied by Georges Hervé[250] for his book *La circonvolution de Broca* (Broca's gyrus). The full text of his study is provided in Appendix D. Here is the section in which he identifies the three brains he studied:[251]

> We had the good fortune to study the brains of three Eskimos, two males and a female, who died in Paris in January 1881. With his expert skill, Mr. Chudzinski has turned these pieces into valuable casts belonging to the *Musée Broca*.
>
> Paulus Abraham, 35 years old. – Brain extraordinarily simple. Very wide gyri, few tortuosities, with perfectly sharp boundaries. [...]
>
> Tobias Ignatius, 21 years old. – Extremely broad gyri, massive, simple, but irregular.
>
> Henocq Ulrika, 24 years old. – Simple brain, but with narrower and more flexuous gyri than in both men.

---

[250] Physician and professor at the *École d'anthropologie de Paris*.
[251] Hervé, Georges. (1888). p. 134-136.

Fig. 81 Aleš Hrdlička
(Wikimedia Commons)

In 1901, Czech anthropologist, Aleš Hrdlička, published his book *An Eskimo Brain* in which he used Théophile Chudzinski's study of Abraham's, Ulrike's and Tobias' brains and compared them with the brains of a few Inuit from Smith Sounds. Hrdlička wrote:[252]

> The only previous records concerning Eskimo brains of which I could learn are those made by Chudzinski, published in the *Bulletin de la Société d'Anthropologie de Paris*, 1886.[253]

> The brains described by this author were those of Tobias Ignatius, male, 23 years old; Paulus Abraham, male, 35 years old; and Ulrika Hénocq, female, 24 years old. The locality from which these subjects came is not stated, but there are reasons to believe that they belonged to the eastern Greenland Eskimo.

> The three brains present some interesting similarities, but also many characteristics different from those of any of the specimens noted in this paper. [...]

> The similarities in the brains reported upon by Chudzinski and the one described here consist of the large volume of the cerebral hemispheres; long central fissures; sagittal division of the mesial parts of the superior frontal gyri; the large size of the limbic lobe in Tobias, and the large size of the lobe with a tendency toward a longitudinal division in Ulrika.

---

[252] Hrdlička, Aleš. (1901).
[253] The date is incorrect. The text was published in 1881.

The dissimilarities are: the poor differentiation in Chudzinski's specimens of the convolutions and the simple character of the sulci, especially over the frontal lobes; a defective development of the inferior frontal convolution (particularly in Tobias); very large ascending frontal and ascending parietal convolutions; simplicity of parietal convolutions; great slenderness of the superior temporal gyri; and very small cuneus.

The causes of the many dissimilarities are not clear. The morphological inferiority of the two male brains described by Chudzinski, and, on the other hand, the marked superiority of Kishu's and even of Nooktah's [Nuktaq] brain, may be to some extent individual conditions and represent more the extremes than the average of Eskimo brains. At the same time it is possible that Paulus Abraham and Tobias Ignatius belonged to some family of the great Eskimo tribe intellectually less developed than the Smith Sound group to which Kishu [Qisuk] and Nooktah, belonged. The Smith Sound party which Lieutenant Peary[254] brought to New York were by no means dull or incapable people.[255] This is especially well demonstrated in Menee [Minik], the son of Kishu, who has not only shown a remarkable facility for adjusting himself in every way to civilized life, but has made very good progress in the public school.[256] The marked differ-

[254] Robert Peary (1856–1920), an American Arctic explorer known for his controversial claims to be the first to reach the North Pole.

[255] In 1897, Robert Peary brought with him to New York a group of six Inuit from northern Greenland (three adults and three children). Among them were Qisuk and Nuktaq, two men who had worked for Peary in 1891. Qisuk was accompanied by his young son Minik. Very quickly, the three adults and one of the children contracted tuberculosis and died. Minik, orphan, was adopted by William Wallace, curator at the American Museum of Natural History. See Harper, Kenn, (2000).

[256] Minik was about 6 years old when he was taken to the USA. After his father's death, he was educated and raised in the USA. In 1906, he discovered that the funeral of his father, which he attended, was a hoax organized by his adoptive father and the museum. Qisuk's skeleton had been kept and was exhibited in the museum's galleries. Minik returned to Greenland in the early 1910s and then came back to the United States in 1916 where he died two years later in New Hampshire, during the Spanish flu epidemic. The remains of Qisuk, Nuktaq and two other Inuit who died in New York in 1897 were repatriated to Greenland in 1993. Minik's remains are still resting in the United States. See Harper, Kenn, (2000).

ences of the specimens described by Chudzinski and in this paper from those of the whites, as well as among themselves, makes a future acquisition of Eskimo brains very desirable.

Finally, in 1902, Dr. Edward Anthony Spitzka, an American anatomist and author of several texts on brain anatomy, published the first chapter of *Encephalic Anatomy of the Races* in which he studied the brains of three Inuit from Smith Sounds. He also included a summary of Théophile Chudzinski's and Aleš Hrdlička's study of the brain casts of Abraham, Ulrike and Tobias. Dr. Spitzka wrote:[257]

> Only four Eskimo brains have hitherto been described: three by Chudzinski, and one by Hrdlička. Chudzinski's specimens were those of Eskimos who died of small-pox in the Hôpital de Saint-Louis, Paris. The brains had been placed in very weak alcohol for two weeks before Chudzinski obtained them [...]

> Chudzinski nowhere states whence these Eskimos came. One must assume that they were from Greenland, and from an inferior tribe, differing in many respects from the inhabitants around Smith's Sound. Chudzinski states emphatically that with the considerable volume of the cerebrum of his Eskimos, there is a 'notable simplicity in the fissural and gyral pattern'; not only are the gyres said to be quite broad and little marked by 'tertiary fissures and divisions, but they are only slightly flexuous.' This simplicity, he maintains, is especially marked in the frontal lobes, which are rather 'flattened from above below.' The general form was, according to Chudzinski, that of a dolichocephalic brain. The frontal lobe he describes as relatively small, while the parietal especially was considerably well developed. The frontal gyres were of 'very simple configuration – especially in Tobias Ignatius.'

What happened to the casts since these studies were conducted more than 110 years ago? Following the dismantling of the *Musée Broca* in the middle of the twentieth century, we know that part of Théophile Chudzinski's collection of plaster brain casts was acquired by the anatomy laboratory of the Faculty of Medicine, at the Université Paris Descartes, then headed by Pro-

---

[257] Spitzka, Edward Anthony. (1902).

fessor André Delmas. [258] For several years, Professor Delmas worked to restore and expand the collections of the *Musée d'anatomie Orfila* [259] and to integrate it with those of the *Musée Rouvière*. [260] The result of his work was the establishment of the largest French anatomy museum known as the *Musées anatomiques Delmas-Orfila-Rouvière*.

From 1953 until 2011, the *Musées anatomiques Delmas-Orfila-Rouvière* occupied the exhibition hall and galleries on the eighth floor of the Faculty of Medicine, rue des Saints-Pères in Paris. However, the museum was closed in 2011 and its collections were acquired by the Université de Montpellier 1. Currently, the collection is packed and conditioned for long-term storage until the new owner takes possession.

The last curator of the *Musées anatomiques Delmas-Orfila-Rouvière*, Mr. Christian Prévoteau, was nevertheless able to find photographs confirming that *Eskimo* brain casts were indeed part of the museum's collections. They were being exhibited in display C9 when the museum closed. A small card placed beside one of the pieces read 'Ulrika Henocq, 24 years old, Eskimo died on January 16, 1881.'

In the fall of 2013, Mr. Prévoteau was able to recreate the display and confirm beyond any doubt that the brain casts of display C9 belonged to Abraham, Ulrike and Tobias; their names are engraved on the back of each piece. The uncertainty that remains is the origin of the three endocranial casts seen at the top of display C9. Only the word *Eskimo*, sometimes accompanied by the number 2 or 3, is engraved on each cast.

Also, the inscriptions engraved on the brain casts revealed that at least one of them was made, not by Théophile Chudzinski, but by Félix Flandinette, one of the anthropology laboratory's assistant.

---

[258] Minutes of a meeting held on June 2, 1975, to discuss the establishment of the deposit contracts for the collections of the *Société d'anthropologie de Paris*, and the *Laboratoire d'anthropologie biologique de l'EPHE* (Laboratoire Broca). Document kept in the archives of the *Société d'anthropologie de Paris*.

[259] Founded by Mathieu Orfila (1787–1853), Spanish physician, Dean of the Faculty of Medicine from 1831 to 1848.

[260] Founded by the physician and anatomist Henri Rouvière (1876–1952).

Fig. 82 Abraham, J. A. Jacobsen's interpreter, 1880
Photo by Jacob Martin Jacobsen.
(*Nederlands Fotomuseum*)

THE EXHUMATION OF THE
ESKIMOS' REMAINS

Let's return to Dr. Landrieux's letter in which he wrote: "I think it would be possible, thanks to your intervention, to proceed with the exhumation."

The recipient of this letter was not identified, but we believe him to be Armand de Quatrefages, head of the Chair of Anthropology at the *Muséum national d'Histoire naturelle* (MNHN).

Fig. 83 Armand de Quatrefages
(Wikimedia Commons/BNF)

Shortly after the *Eskimos'* death, de Quatrefages made a request to the Prefecture of Police for their bodies to be exhumed and incorporated into the Muséum's anthropology collection.

This request has not yet been found, but the police response is preserved in the archives of the *Musée de l'Homme*'s anthropology collections. It was addressed to de Quatrefages and read as follows:

> Paris, March 10, 1881
>
> Sir,
>
> You have expressed to me your desire to exhume the bodies of five Eskimos who died of smallpox in the month of January in order to place their skeletons in the Muséum's anthropological collection.
>
> I willingly allow this exhumation, in the interest of science, but as there are precautions to be taken from the point of view of public health, I have asked, as per your instructions, Mr. Professor Brouardel to kindly preside over the operation and determine under what conditions and at what time it can be held without inconveniences.
>
> Mr. Brouardel eagerly accepted this mission.
>
> When the time comes, he will come to an arrangement with you, Sir, about all the details of the operation whose costs will naturally be at your expense. The Eskimos were buried in the Saint-Ouen cemetery.
>
> Please accept, Sir, the assurances of my highest consideration.
>
> The Deputy, Prefet of Police.

Dr. Brouardel, pathologist and Chair of the Forensic Medicine at the Faculty of Medicine of Paris, was also a member of the board of the *Conseil d'hygiène et de salubrité* (public health and hygiene board). During the Franco-Prussian War of 1870–1871, he conducted a study on the conditions of contagion and spread of smallpox, and was in charge of the smallpox health service.

Fig. 84 Paul Brouardel
(Courtesy of BIU Santé)

Four years passed before Dr. Brouardel agreed to the exhumation. In 1885, when the Prefecture received his approval, the
Prefect of Police sent a letter to Armand de Quatrefages informing him that he could proceed:[261]

Paris, March 10, 1885

Sir,

You asked me for permission to exhume the bodies of five
Eskimos who died of smallpox in January 1881, in order to
place their skeletons in the Muséum's anthropological collection.

I have the honor to inform you that, based on Professor
Brouardel's favourable opinion, I willingly allow the exhumation in question.

If you would kindly, Sir, discuss the arrangements for the
operation with the curator of the St. Ouen Cemetery in order to safeguard public health. I do not need to add that
the costs of the exhumation will be fully at your expense,
and it is understood that the gravediggers must first be re-
vaccinated.

---

[261] Letter preserved in the archives of the *Musée de l'Homme*'s anthropology collections.

Please accept, Sir, the assurances of my highest consideration.

The Prefet of Police

On March 18, 1885, the Muséum obtained a copy of the five death certificates from the City Hall of Paris' 10th arrondissement. However, another year passed before the exhumation actually took place.

On May 27, 1886, the Prefecture of Police sent, once again, a letter confirming their authorization to exhume the bodies. This time, the authorization, bearing number 7061, was not addressed to Armand de Quatrefages, but to Dr. Delisle, an assistant for the Muséum's Chair of Anthropology.

The exhumation took place on Friday, June 4, 1886. The cemetery's curator wrote and signed the following note written directly on the Prefecture's authorization letter:[262]

Seen and noted the exhumation of the bodies of:

Mrs Henocq, widow Paulus, Ulrika, died on January 16, 1881,
Miss Paulus, Maria, died on January 10, 1881,
Mrs Tigganiak, widow Pengu, died on January 11, 1881,
Mr Ignatius, Tobias, died on January 13, 1881,
Mr Paulus, Abraham, died on January 13, 1881,
who had been buried in the common grave and their departure for the *Muséum de l'histoire naturelle*.

St Ouen, June 4, 1886

The Curator
(indecipherable signature)

How did the gravediggers ensure that the bodies to be exhumed from the common grave were the right ones? Each corpse was carrying a plate bearing its death identification number from the city's vital records and that number was written on each death certificate issued by the city. We therefore assume that the selection of the bodies was made by matching the numbers on the certificate with the ones on the plates attached to the bodies.

---

[262] Authorization preserved in the archives of the *Musée de l'Homme*'s anthropology collections.

The bodies arrived at the *Muséum national d'Histoire naturelle* the next day, Saturday, June 5, 1886. The anthropology laboratory's entrance registry[263] shows that they were recorded under entry No. 13 for the year 1886, and that the skeletons were considered to be a gift from the Prefecture of the Seine.

Each skeleton was assigned an inventory number:

- 10241 – Skeleton of Ignatius (Tobias), Eskimo, 21 years old, born in Hebron, North Labrador coast.
- 10242 – Skeleton of Paulus (Abraham), Eskimo, 35 years old, born in Hebron, North Labrador Coast, married to Ulrika Hénocq, Eskimo woman.
- 10243 – Skeleton of Hénocq (Ulrika), Eskimo woman, 24 years old, born in Hebron, North Labrador coast.
- 10244 – Skeleton of Tigganniak, Eskimo woman, [264] 45 years old, born in Nachvak, North Labrador coast, widow of Pengu.
- 10245 – Skeleton of Paulus (Maria), daughter of Paulus Abraham (n° 10242) and Hénocq Ulrika (n° 10243) 13 months old, young Eskimo girl, born in Hebron, North Labrador coast.

Their record was supplemented by the following paragraph:

These five subjects were exhibited in the *Jardin d'acclimatation* of Bois de Boulogne and they succumbed after a haemorrhagic smallpox epidemic at Hôpital Saint-Louis in January 1881.

As for the Muséum's financial records[265] for the year 1886, they show that the anthropology laboratory paid 115 francs 45 cents to cover the cost of the exhumation.

Finally, in the 1886 annual report for the Muséum's Chair of Anthropology, there was a short paragraph confirming the addition of the skeletons to the collection:

---

[263] Registry is preserved in the archives of the *Musée de l'Homme*'s anthropology collections.

[264] As stated before, this error in Tigianniak's gender results from an error in the city's vital records.

[265] Records kept at the *Bibliothèque centrale* (Central Library) of the *Muséum national d'Histoire naturelle*.

Finally, the Prefecture of the Seine authorized the removal and the entry in our gallery of the skeletons of four adult males[266] and one child, Labrador Eskimos, who died in Paris five years ago.

Fig. 85 Abraham, 1880
Photo by Jacob Martin Jacobsen.
(Moravian Archives, Herrnhut)

---

[266] The text should probably have read "... 4 adults" since they were not all men.

WERE THE SKELETONS
EXHIBITED IN PARIS?

THE ANTHROPOLOGY GALLERY IN THE *BÂTIMENT DE LA BALEINE*

Fig. 86 Exterior view of the *Bâtiment de la baleine*, 1892
Photo by Pierre Lamith Petit. (Bibliothèque centrale du MNHN. ©RMN-
Grand Palais/Art Resource, NY.)

In 1886, when the five skeletons entered the *Muséum national d'Histoire naturelle*, the public rooms of the anthropology collection occupied the whole first floor[267] of the *Bâtiment de la baleine*.[268] The building, located in the north-west section of the

---

[267] This is the floor above the ground floor. North Americans would call it the 2nd floor.

[268] The name means 'the whale's building' in reference to the whale skeleton exhibited in the gallery of comparative anatomy. In front of the building, the skeleton and the bones of a sperm whale, too large to be accommodated in the galleries, could also be seen.

Jardin des Plantes, was shared with the Chair of Comparative anatomy.[269]

To access the anthropological section, one had to first go through the rooms devoted to the comparative anatomy collection. From the second room, a door led onto a long and narrow corridor at the end of which the anthropological museum was located.[270]

Fig. 87 General view – Comparative anatomy gallery, 1880
Photo by Pierre Lamith Petit. (Bibliothèque centrale du MNHN. ©RMN-Grand Palais/Art Resource, NY.)

Originally, disorder reigned in the anthropology galleries. But in 1871, after the Franco-Prussian War, Ernest Théodore Hamy,[271] assistant naturalist for the Chair of Anthropology, worked relentlessly during the summer holidays to catalog the collections ac-

---

[269] Comparative anatomy is the science that aims to identify similarities and differences between the anatomical parts of different species.

[270] *Guide des étrangers dans le Muséum d'histoire naturelle.* (1855).

[271] Ernest Théodore Hamy (1842–1908), assistant naturalist to the Chair of Anthropology at the *Muséum national d'Histoire naturelle* and curator of the *Musée d'ethnographie du Trocadéro*.

cording to a geographical classification. In a speech made in 1907, Hamy described the new structure of the galleries:[272]

> As boxes stored in the basement were brought back [de Quatrefages had them moved there during the war of 1871], we spread the contents on the benches of the anatomy amphitheater which soon took a memorable aspect. I classified everything by country, drew up numbered lists and when the operation was over, I had in hand, the elements of a pro rata distribution among the nine rooms at my disposal. The first two, still separated from the other seven by a staircase that was soon to disappear, received most pieces of European origin; the third one was for Asia and North America, less well represented, the fourth and fifth rooms were reserved for South America, the sixth and seventh for Africa, the eighth and part of the ninth for Oceania, the rest of this last room finally, for the new collections of human paleontology.

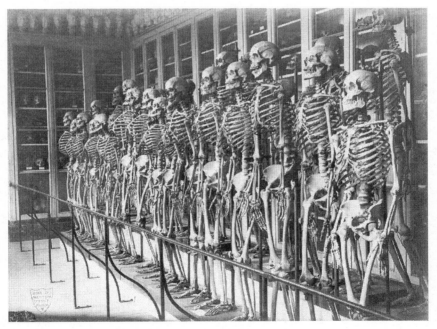

Fig. 88 Group of European skeletons, 1880
Photo by Pierre Lamith Petit.
(Bibliothèque centrale du MNHN. ©RMN-Grand Palais/Art Resource, NY)

---

[272] Hamy, Ernest Théodore. (1907). p. 273.

No record has so far been found which can confirm the exact inventory of the galleries. But we can certainly say that the five skeletons indeed found their place in this museum and were visible to the public. Our confidence comes from a combination of facts. First, we know that the entire anthropology collection was on display. Also, in 1882, in a document aimed for naval officers who wanted to gather natural history collections, the Muséum's professors had expressed an interest in obtaining *Eskimos* from Labrador:[273]

> Labrador Eskimos, which would be full of interest to compare with those of Greenland, of which we have a nice series, are completely lacking [in our collections].

Fig. 89 Ernest Théodore Hamy, 1883
Photo by Eugène Pirou.
(Gallica, Bibliothèque nationale de France)

---

[273] *Instructions pour MM. les officiers de la marine qui voudraient faire des collections d'HN [histoire naturelle] destinées au Muséum de Paris par les professeurs administrateurs du Muséum.* (1882).

Since the Labrador *Eskimos* proved so valuable, the Muséum's professors must have been proud to show off their new acquisition.

Finally, in the Chair of Anthropology's 1886 annual report, Armand de Quatrefages indicated that the exhumation of the skeletons was aimed at adding them to the skeleton gallery. How could it have been otherwise? The assumption is that they were in the third room, the one covering North America.

In 1892, following the death of Armand de Quatrefages, Hamy was put in charge of the Chair of Anthropology whose collection included 9,560 objects. [274] In 1907, that number more than quadrupled to reach over 49,000 objects. Hamy gave the following overview of the collection to his students during the introduction lesson of his 1907 anthropology course:[275]

> These special collections, which increase steadily each year and now exceed the figure of 49,000 objects[276], indeed provide, on most of the topics tackled by the study of descriptive anthropology, demonstration elements of proof both abundant and varied. They consist of long theories of skulls of all races; mounted skeletons in much larger numbers than what can be found elsewhere; anatomical parts of which I would like to increase the number, currently limited by the lack of space; casts made on live people, heads, trunks, limbs, organs, etc.; iconographic documents, busts, statuettes, painting studies, prints; countless negatives and photographs; a first class prehistoric collection, in short, a whole collection for which I do not know any equivalent elsewhere and whose interpretation will keep occupied, for a long time, those who will follow me here.

THE NEW PALEONTOLOGY AND ANTHROPOLOGY GALLERIES

On July 21, 1898, in anticipation of the *1900 Paris Exposition Universelle*, a new building was opened to house the paleontology, comparative anatomy, and anthropology collections. Anthro-

---

[274] Hamy, Ernest Théodore. (1907). p. 274.

[275] Ibid., p. 258.

[276] Note from Hamy: "The collections contained just over 22,000 objects when I was appointed professor; therefore, during my management, they increased by approximately 27,000. "

pology was located on the 2nd floor and occupied two rooms as well as a long balcony that went around overlooking the palaeontology collection. René Verneau, anthropologist and professor at the Muséum, who developed the plans to showcase the anthropology collections with Ernest Théodore Hamy, described the new gallery as follows:[277]

> Although space has been carefully used, displays have been installed on the balcony itself. The space attributed to anthropology is so insufficient that part of the collections, which are housed in the old building on Cuvier Street, . could not fit in the new museum. All major series are represented only by a relatively small number of pieces in the new gallery. The rest will swell the already large inventory of items kept in the warehouses, which are probably too small already.

Fig. 90 Anthropology and paleontology galleries
Photo taken from the west end of the gallery, 1910. (Central Library of the *Muséum national d'Histoire naturelle*)

> Given the space that we were assigned, we have tried to include specimens from the greatest possible number of human groups. Before classifying the current races, we had to consider those who once lived; fossil races, prehistoric races had to come before those that currently populate the globe. [...] Every human group is represented by anything that helps notice its physical characteristics. Apart

---

[277] Verneau, René. (1898). p. 328-332.

from photographic portraits, the displays contain busts, masks, trunks, limbs casted on live individuals, sometimes even whole individuals.[278] They contain samples of hair, skeletons, skulls, trophies, etc. Small maps show the distribution of the groups and communities where the parts are from that make up the collection. Unfortunately, the lighting is so bad that, to clearly distinguish the objects that are on a given side, one must be placed on the opposite balcony.

Fig. 91 René Verneau
(Courtesy of BIU Santé)

Verneau continued his description by going around the balcony. His tour began on the left-hand side with the Black people: the Australians, the Negritos, the Tasmanians, the African Negroes, the tall Negroes, the Sudanese, people from the west coast, and those from the east coast of Madagascar. It ended with the human groups from Southern Africa, the Kaffirs, the Hottentots, the Bushmen, etc. Then came the Malays, the Indonesians, the Micronesians, and the Polynesians who lead the visitor to the Yellow people: the Japanese, the Mongolian, the Indo-Chinese, and the Chinese.

---

[278] Sarah Baartman, the Hottentote Venus, being an example of person whose body was used to make a plaster-cast after her death in 1815.

The visitor moved to America... where the *Eskimos* were used to transition between the Yellow people and the American Indians. Verneau gives no further details on which skeleton(s) represented the Inuit people. But, according to a 1945 inventory of the Muséum's anthropological collections,[279] the five Labrador skeletons were the only mounted skeletons[280] of Inuit origin in the Muséum's collection. The other two skeletons from Greenland Inuit were classified as 'more or less complete' and had probably been gathered during Paul-Émile Victor's mission in the 1930s. It is therefore likely that when the new galleries opened in 1898, the five Labrador skeletons were the only ones of Inuit origin in the Muséum's collection.

Did Abraham, Tobias, Tigianniak or Ulrike represent the Inuit people on the balcony? Nobody knows. But since Verneau mentioned *Eskimos* in his description of the gallery, we can assume that they were represented by at least one skeleton as opposed to skulls which would easily have gone unnoticed among the hundreds, if not thousands, of other skulls. It is also not possible to accurately determine where the skeletons were located, but presumably, they were near the midpoint, the west end of the balcony.

In the gallery, the *Eskimo* people were followed by the tribes of the Northwest Coast of America and other people of the New World: the Indians of California and of the Prairies, the ethnic groups of Mexico, those of Central America and South America, all the way to Tierra del Fuego. The White people were placed in the last displays. They began by Ethiopians and the populations which derived from them. Followed the Egyptians, the Berbers of North Africa, Arabs, Jews, Syrians, and finally, the types from India. Because of a lack of space, the Europeans were relegated to the basement annexes.

Ernest Théodore Hamy and René Verneau were very proud of the result:[281]

> Despite all these shortcomings repeatedly reported in vain, our new gallery has style and the visitor experiences a real

---

279 Vallois, Henri V. (1945).

280 Means that the skeletons were complete and assembled in a standing position.

281 Hamy, Ernest Théodore. (1907). p. 275.

impression when, from the Vibraye room,[282] he walks onto the balcony and can contemplate with a circular glance, the army of methodically aligned skeletons.

MUSÉE DE L'HOMME

In the 1930s, a reorganization was conducted. The first step was the incorporation of the *Musée d'ethnographie du Trocadéro* into the *Muséum national d'Histoire naturelle*'s Chair of Anthropology. Then, in 1937, came the creation of the *Musée de l'Homme* reuniting the Chairs of Anthropology, Ethnology, and Prehistory. The new museum, which also acted as a center of research and education, was to show humanity in all its anthropological, historical and cultural diversity. It opened its doors to the public in June 1938.

After 40 years spent overlooking the paleontology gallery, the skulls and skeletons of the Muséum's anthropological collection left the building that housed them in the *Jardin des Plantes*, and headed to the Passy wing of the new *Palais de Chaillot* built for the 1937 World Exhibition, opposite the Eiffel Tower.

The Anthropology gallery was located on the first floor.[283] The second room, devoted to recent and fossil human races, showcased 'the currently observable races (White, Yellow, Black and their subdivisions), with photographs, skulls, and skeletons.'[284] The *Eskimo* race was one of those on display.

On the upper floor was the Arctic people gallery. A 1975 photograph reveals that the skeleton of an *Eskimo* from the north coast of Labrador was exhibited in a display entitled 'Yellow Races.' This skeleton's inventory number was 10244... The inventory number of Tigianniak's skeleton!

It was not possible to determine the period during which Tigianniak's skeleton was part of the public displays. It was there in the 1970s and, at an unknown date, was withdrawn and headed to the *Musée de l'Homme*'s reserve.

---

[282] Room occupying the north end of the 2nd floor through which one had to walk to reach the balcony. At the time, the prehistory collection of the Marquis Paul de Vibraye (1809–1878) was exhibited in the room.
[283] Ground floor for North Americans.
[284] *Guide du Musée de l'Homme*. (1952).

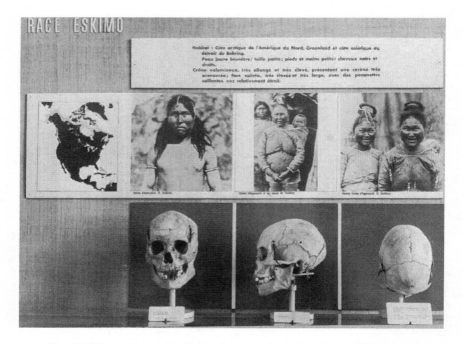

Fig. 92 Eskimo Race. Anthropology gallery, *Musée de l'Homme* Display 39. (© 2014. Musée du quai Branly/Scala, Florence)

What Happened to the Remains of Nuggasak, Paingu and Sara?

In 1892, Dr. Rudolf Virchow published *Crania Ethnica Americana*, a study of various skulls of North American Indigenous peoples whose primary purpose was 'to establish a series of cranial ethnic types as the basis for ethnic classification.'[285]

Three Labrador *Eskimo* skulls were part this study. In Chapter XXI, Virchow presented the skulls of two adults, one of which was that collected in 1880 by Johan Adrian Jacobsen in a Hebron grave. The second was given to Virchow in 1881 by Johann Friedrich Gustav Umlauff, a Hamburg ethnological curiosity dealer, and Carl Hagenbeck's brother-in-law. Virchow wrote:[286]

> In 1880, at Mr. Carl Hagenbeck's request, Captain J. A. Jacobsen brought two Eskimo families to Berlin. One came from the Moravian mission of Hebron (approx. 59° north lat. 60° long. West), the other came from a more northern post. At the same time, we were shown objects coming from hundred year old graves from the Hebron area that Mr. Jacobsen had personally collected. Among them was the skull pictured here that Mr. Jacobsen had kindly offered me. My comments regarding it are in the Acts of the Berlin Anthropological Society (1880, p. 254, 258 and 263).
>
> I present, at the end, the measurements of this skull with those of another skull that Mr. Umlauff handed to me in Hamburg in 1881 with a number of skulls from Greenland. Unfortunately, the lower jaw was missing. It had a persistent

---

[285] Brinton, Daniel G. (1892, November 11).
[286] Virchow, Rudolf. (1892). Chapter XXI.

metopic suture, an almost orthognathic[287] jaw and a palate in the shape of a horseshoe.

Although the first of these skulls is related to Abraham's group, it is not a skull belonging to any of the individuals who made up the group. That said, in the following chapter, Virchow describes the skull of a child who died in Crefeld and whose exhumation was authorized by the local authorities. Virchow introduces this skull as follows:[288]

> The two Eskimo families mentioned in the introduction of Chapter XXI were gradually decimated by diseases during their journey. A child of the Christian family died in Crefeld. Local authorities have kindly authorized the exhumation of the body. A photograph of the whole family with two children is in the bulletin (or, in the Acts) of the Berlin Society of Anthropological (Journal of Ethnology 1880, Vol. XII, fig. 1).

The skull described by Virchow can be none other than Sara's, Abraham and Ulrike's 3-year-old daughter. The photograph Virchow refers to is that of the family of Abraham published in the report of his November 7, 1880, lecture.[289]

Young Sara has therefore been exhumed, at least her skull was. So far, research conducted by the archivists of the City of Krefeld as well as those of the Berlin Society of Anthropology, Ethnology and Prehistory (BGAEU), the organization in charge of preserving Rudolf Virchow's osteological collection, have not been able to locate the request for Sara's exhumation. We do not know when this request was made or whether it asked to obtain the whole skeleton or only the skull.

But we have confirmation that Sara's skull and the other two Labrador skulls described by Virchow in *Crania Ethnica Americana* are still in the collection managed and preserved by BGAEU. Eventually, DNA tests could certainly provide irrefutable evidence that it is indeed Sara's skull.

As for the remains of Paingu and Nuggasak, no evidence that Virchow also asked that they be exhumed has yet been found.

---

[287] A jaw that does not project forward.

[288] Ibid., Chapter XXII.

[289] See Chapter *The Eskimos studied by Rudolf Virchow* for a copy of the said illustration.

However, Virchow knew they had both died a few days earlier. Why was only Sara's skull of interest to him?

Similarly, no document confirming when the remains of Paingu and Nuggasak were removed from the cemeteries has yet been located. The Bockum cemetery became a park more than a century ago. In Darmstadt, the old cemetery still exists, including the division where Nuggasak was buried. However, the cemetery was heavily damaged during the Second World War, and because of the multiple rearrangements over the years, Nuggasak's grave is considered by local authorities as having disappeared.

As for Virchow's study of Sara's skull, here is the table of measures he provided in *Crania Ethnica Americana*:

1. Measurements

Volume	1,210 ccm
Maximum horizontal length	166 mm
Maximum width	128 mm
Vertical height	118 mm
Ear height	103 mm
Occipital length	44 mm
Foramen magnum to the root of the nose	82 mm
Ear canal to the root of the nose	88 mm
Horizontal circumference	471 mm
Frontal Bone circumference	115 mm
Parietal Bone circumference	122 mm
Occipital Bone circumference	104 mm
Sagittal arc (whole)	341 mm
Minimal forehead length	84 mm
Facial height A	87 mm
Facial height B	52 mm
Facial length a	99 mm
Facial length b	74 mm
Facial length c	73 mm
Orbit height	30 mm
Orbit width	34 mm
Nose height	38 mm
Nose width	26 mm
Palate length	37 mm
Palate width	24 mm
Facial angle	75°

2. Calculated Indexes

Length-width index	77.1

Length-height index   71.7
Ear height index   62.0
Occipital index   26.5
Facial index   87.8
Orbital index   88.0
Nasal index   68.4
Buccal index   64.8

Fig. 93 Rudolf Virchow in his laboratory, 1891
Portrait by Hanns Fechner
(Wikimedia Commons)

THE COLLECTION OF ARTIFACTS

MUSÉE D'ETHNOGRAPHIE DU TROCADÉRO

Fig. 94 *Musée d'ethnographie du Trocadéro*
(Polar Horizons Collection)

As mentioned previously, on January 16, 1881, the day Ulrike died, Jacobsen received a telegram from Carl Hagenbeck imploring him to get rid of all the objects related to the *Eskimos*.

Jacobsen therefore did not lose any time and, upon leaving the hospital, a representative of the *Musée d'ethnographie du Trocadéro* met him to assess and acquire the collection of objects he had collected in Labrador graves.

At the time, the *Musée d'ethnographie du Trocadéro* was not yet open to the public. Formally established a few months earlier, by laws voted in June and July 1880, the museum nevertheless had staff: two curators, three security guards and a caster-modeller. The two curators were Armand Landrin and Ernest

Théodore Hamy. The latter was responsible for the scientific classification and installation of collections and also acted as the
museum director while holding concurrently his position at the
Muséum national d'Histoire naturelle's Chair of Anthropology. As
for Armand Landrin, his task was 'to enrich the collections
through the missions he would undertake, purchases and donations, working with correspondents and members of Paris' popu-
lar traditions, geography and anthropology societies.'[290]

Fig. 95 Armand Landrin
(Gallica, Bibliothèque nationale de France)

Who met Jacobsen to assess the collection? Landrin or Hamy?
No documentation has so far been found in the archives of the
museum or in those of the *Ministère de l'instruction publique*
(Ministry of Public Education), under whose authority the museum was falling, confirming the details of the transaction. But Carl
Hagenbeck's financial records show, dated March 13, 1881, and
for the *Ministère de l'instruction publique*, a 300 marks debt for
Eskimo objects.[291] Hagenbeck has never set foot in Labrador;
these objects can be none other than those brought back by

---

[290] Landrin, Armand. [n.d.].
[291] The financial records also show the payment being received on August 27, 1881.

Jacobsen. The fact that Hagenbeck ordered Jacobsen to sell them also confirms he was considered the owner.

In the top right corner of the *Eskimos'* account in the financial registry, one can read two very pale annotations: 'Landrin' and *'Palais du Trocadéro.'* The balance seems to be tilting in favour of Landrin as having been Jacobsen's interlocutor. But we must not eliminate Hamy just yet. In his diary, Jacobsen speaks of a 'professor from the Museum' who came to meet him. Hamy was a professor at the *Muséum national d'Histoire naturelle*. Landrin was an assistant-naturalist.

The *Musée d'ethnographie du Trocadéro*, located in the *Palais du Trocadéro*, officially opened its doors to the public on Sunday, April 16, 1882.

An article published in *Le XIXᵉ siècle* confirms that a room devoted to the Polar Regions was present on the museum's opening day:[292]

Finally, the last room is devoted to the polar regions and northern Europe: Eskimos of Greenland and America, Samoyeds, Laplanders and Scandinavians represented by costumes, models of houses, canoes and utensils of any kind.

It is very likely that some of the artifacts collected by Jacobsen in Labrador were those representing the *Eskimos* of America.'[293] The room, located on the ground floor, was actually the lobby of the right wing, called the Passy wing, and served as a transition between the American and Asian collections.[294]

---

[292] Inauguration du musée d'ethnographie du Trocadéro. (1882, April 14).

[293] Gwénaële Guigon confirms this hypothesis because, in 1881, the most important Arctic collection in France is the one purchased from Carl Hagenbeck. It consists of more than three hundred pieces from Labrador as per the inventory record. There are only five known collections: two pieces of clothing of unknown origin previously preserved at the National Library and probably dating from the eighteenth century; thirty items reported by Alphonse Pinart from the Kodiak Islands; sixty pieces exchanged with the Copenhagen Museum (now the *National Museet*) and less than a dozen items from Greenland bought from a Danish captain.

[294] Dias, Nélia. (1991). p. 180.

Although it attracted thousands of visitors, the *Musée d'ethnographie du Trocadéro* was facing multiple challenges. Following Hamy's death in 1908, it slowly fell into a state of neglect.

> Housed in a palace built for an entirely different purpose, dark and unheated, stocked with improvised displays, poorly protected against dust, moisture and insects, without handling rooms, without work rooms, without a warehouse, without a laboratory, without collections' records, the museum gave the impression of a 'jumble store' (the word is not from us), where valuables accumulated in dark cupboards, went unnoticed by visitors. The labeling was virtually nonexistent. Maps and distribution maps, essential to guide the public, lacked. An even more serious matter: perishable items (wood, wool, cotton, feather, etc.) were exposed to destruction. The lack of security guards made supervision impossible, or at any rate, illusory. No warranty existed against fire or theft. The library without a librarian and no catalog was virtually unusable despite its wealth.[295]

In 1928, its new director, Paul Rivet, professor of anthropology at the Muséum, had the *Musée d'ethnographie du Trocadéro* incorporated into the *Muséum national d'Histoire naturelle*'s Chair of Anthropology. In December 1934, a new gallery on Arctic people was inaugurated. Its main purpose was to highlight the collection of objects brought back by Paul-Émile Victor from his expedition to Greenland. In 1937, as mentioned earlier, the *Musée d'ethnographie du Trocadéro* gave way to the *Musée de l'Homme*. The *Palais du Trocadéro* was demolished and replaced by the *Palais de Chaillot*.

MUSÉE DE L'HOMME

The new *Musée de l'Homme* also had its gallery of Arctic people... the gallery where Tigianniak's skeleton is said to have been exhibited. Were the artifacts collected by Jacobsen also there?

The only evidence gathered so far indicates that the Arctic gallery covered the regions of Alaska, Canada and Greenland:[296]

> '[...] The most numerous objects in this room come from the east coast of Greenland, from the Angmassalik[297] group.

---

[295] Rivet, Paul and Georges Henri Rivière. (1931). p. 478.
[296] Thomas, Philippe and Jean Oster. (1982). p. 23.

The oldest and rarest objects are from Alaska and Canada.'

To date, no information about the contents of the displays in the Arctic gallery of the *Musée de l'Homme* could be found. We dare speculate that some of the items collected by Jacobsen were actually part of these rare and ancient artifacts from Canada.

MUSÉE DU QUAI BRANLY

Since 2006, the *Musée de l'Homme*'s ethnography collection has been moved to the *Musée du quai Branly*. The archives of the *Musée du quai Branly*'s collections show more than 250 artifacts from Labrador and/or Greenland, the vast majority of which were acquired from a certain Hagenbeck! Although 1879 is recorded as the year of acquisition, there is no doubt for Gwénaële Guigon that they are indeed the artifacts Jacobsen collected in 1880. Gwénaële explained that these objects were inherited from the *Musée d'ethnographie du Trocadéro* and that the inventory of the museum was established retroactively. It is plausible that those who compiled the inventory never found any paper trace of the purchase and assumed that all the items were part of the museum's collection from day one of its creation.[298]

---

[297] Community located on the east coast of Groenland now called Ammassalik.

[298] Gwénaële Guigon explains that in 2007, while an *attaché* to the *Musée du quai Branly* in charge of listing all Arctic objects, she had assumed that the seller was Carl Hagenbeck. However, her investigations were not conclusive because of the 1879 inventory acquisition date. Without any other sources available, she could not establish a link with the 1881 Labrador group. She looked into the 1877 Greenlandic group, but to no avail. It was in 2011, when we met, that she learned about the Labrador group. Our discussion raised doubts in her mind about the validity of the inventory's acquisition date. Her suspicions were confirmed by Angèle Martin in charge of documentation at the *Musée du quai Branly*. Gwénaële Guigon adds: "The question is what document did they use to prepare the inventory? Is it possible that negotiations started well before the death of the group? A lack of staff, usually volunteers, did not favor the continuity of knowledge within the *Musée d'ethnographie du Trocadéro*. It was not until the late 1970's that a full-

Artifacts collected by Jacobsen in Labrador are therefore still in Paris! Many of them have now unfortunately disappeared, although they are still identified in the inventory. Is this surprising in light of the various problems the *Musée d'ethnographie du Trocadéro* had to face?

A systematic study of the artifacts, under the guidance of archaeologists specialized in Labrador, would be necessary to confirm their origin, nature and use, especially for the objects that are currently defined as 'indeterminate.' With the many moves and reorganizations over the years, it is also possible that some intruders slipped into the inventory assigned to Hagenbeck.[299]

At present, four ivory rings from Hagenbeck's Labrador collection are shown to the public in the museum's Arctic gallery. But the collection is actually made of several types of objects that Jacobsen reported having collected: oil lamps, arrowheads, grinding stones, ulus (the all-purpose knife traditionally used by Inuit women), kitchen pots, hooks and fishing tools (floats, harpoon heads), beads, etc.

> Since the oil lamps there, as in Greenland, are mostly made of soapstone, they were hence not broken so easily. Therefore, I found several still in good condition, which of course I took along as well. [...]
>
> Many objects of European origin were found. In each second grave there were iron nails, stemming from boat planks, and often iron pots, one bucket, and in two graves I also found pearl necklaces also from Europe, brass buttons, and stained glass framed in brass and even a thimble of brass, all of this in graves that were more than two hundred years old, because there were no traces of human bones to be seen any more. In one grave, I found one of the small wooden puppets, which

time curator was named for the American and Greenlandic collections."

[299] When reviewing the objects in preparation for the creation of the *Musée du quai Branly*'s first inventory, Gwénaële Guigon was surprised to find that many pieces in this collection were incomplete and others seemed contemporary.

are frequently found in graves in Greenland. An English-man *who* had stayed here a long time said that these are carried by the wild Eskimos as pagan idols, also as amulets on the arm. The bows were all so rotten, that none were to be taken along, not [even] one piece. Likewise the arrows, but I kept three pieces of three different arrows; all had iron points made from nails. In several graves, there were also small stones, rounded, very weighty, of a kind of stone that I do not know. I also found a heavy iron stone. Should this perhaps be a meteor stone? I also found stones to whet their knives, as well as fishing gear, /Wicheln/ made of wood, wooden rolls, fishing hooks, mostly of iron, also of bone and iron. I only found few harpoons of bone and iron. Modern ones mounted on wood, as used these days, I found in almost every grave, or in the vicinity of the grave. (J. A. Jacobsen's diary, August 11, 1880)

BERLIN ETHNOLOGY MUSEUM

Although Jacobsen makes no mention in his diary of the sale of Labrador artifacts to the Royal Museum of Ethnology in Berlin, some letters were exchanged between Jacobsen and Adolf Bastian, director of the ethnology department. These letters show that discussions with the museum to purchase objects began before the *Eskimos'* death, the first contact having been made by Adolf Bastian on November 13, 1880, and aimed to ascertain the possibility of acquiring objects from Labrador, Greenland, including items found in graves.[300]

A few days after the *Eskimos'* death, on January 20, 1881, Adolf Bastian contacted Jacobsen once again. He expressed his regrets and then proceeded to ask whether it would be possible for the museum to acquire 'desired things,' such as Labrador snowshoes, a Greenland drum, finds from graves, snow goggles, 'Gods,' idols[301] and scale models. Until March 1881, a series of letters were exchanged between Adolf Bastian, Johan Adrian Jacobsen, Adolf Schoepf and Mr. Bauer, Bastian's assistant, which would have resulted in the purchase of part of the collection by the Berlin museum.[302]

---

[300] Thode-Arora, Hilke. (2002). p. 11.
[301] Small figures representing a deity.
[302] Fienup-Riordan, Ann. (2005). p. 3-5.

Hagenbeck's financial records do show, in the *Eskimos'* account, a sum of 100 marks received on April 6, 1881, from a museum in Berlin. The current hypothesis is that this transaction confirms the purchase, by the Berlin Royal Museum of Ethnology, of artifacts collected in Labrador by Jacobsen, of objects that belonged to, or were crafted by the *Eskimos*.

In 1882, Adolf Bastian showed the museum's *Eskimo* collection to ethnologist Franz Boas, 'much of it brought from Greenland and Labrador by Jacobsen'.[303]

Our communications with the Berlin Ethnology Museum, to confirm whether the items acquired in 1881 are still in their collections, have not yet borne fruit. In October 2013, their curator of American collections having recently retired, we were promised that the new curator would contact us as soon as possible.

Fig. 96 Berlin Royal Museum of Ethnology, ca 1900
(Wikimedia Commons)

---

[303] Baehre, Rainer. (2008). p. 23.

THE IMPACTS OF THE *ESKIMOS'* DEATH

Following this tragedy, newspapers reported that Carl Hagenbeck had committed to end his ethnographic shows.

Nikolsburger Wochenschrif, January 29, 1881

[...] Mr. Hagenbeck in Hamburg, who was devoted like a father to all primitive peoples from north, south, east and west that he has brought to us in recent years, was so shaken by this sad case that, as he announced, he is committed to give up entirely the presentation of such 'ethnological shows.'

Yet, as soon as fall 1881, Carl Hagenbeck resumed the performances with the exhibition of eleven Fuegians from Tierra del Fuego, Chile. Tragedy struck again and more than half of this group was decimated by various diseases. The first victim was a 2 1/2 years old girl who died at the *Jardin d'acclimatation* in Paris on September 29, 1881.[304] Only four of the eleven individuals headed back to Chile.

These two back-to-back tragedies did not spell the death of Hagenbeck's ethnographic shows. From that moment on, Hagenbeck ensured that all hired individuals were examined by a doctor and vaccinated prior to signing their contract.[305]

From 1874 to 1932, Hagenbeck and his enterprise[306] organized nearly 70 ethnographic shows. Even though, starting in the late 1880s, the proliferation of ethnological exhibitions by competitors resulted in a decrease in their profitability, the Hagenbeck family

---

[304] Gontier, Martine. (2010, March 11).

[305] Thode-Arora, Hilke. (2011). p. 84.

[306] Carl Hagenbeck died in 1913.

nevertheless maintained this activity as a source of secondary income.[307]

Le *Jardin d'acclimatation* in Paris maintained its relationship with Carl Hagenbeck until 1891 and one third of the 33 exhibitions that were presented at the Jardin were acquired through Hagenbeck.[308] The vast majority, 29 of them, were presented from 1877 to 1910. According to the *Jardin d'acclimatation*'s website the shows acquired from Hagenbeck were:

- 1877 Nubians and Greenland Eskimos
- 1878 Russian Laplanders
- 1879 Nubians
- 1881 Fuegians
- 1882 Galibi Indians (now known as the Kali'na)
- 1883 Sinhalese, Araucanos, Kalmyks and Redskins
- 1886 Sinhalese
- 1890 Somalis
- 1891 Dahomey

The 1881 Labrador *Eskimos* are notably absent from this list. This probably shouldn't come as a surprise since Hagenbeck himself did not mention them either in his biography. Hopefully, one day, the group will resume its rightful place in the history of the *Jardin d'acclimatation*'s ethnographic shows.

Let's go back for a few moments to the 1881 Fuegians. In 2007, the remains of five of the seven people who died in Europe were found in a laboratory at the University of Zurich, Switzerland. In January 2010, their remains were repatriated to Chile.[309]

Now, what about Johan Adrian Jacobsen? Did he continue to be involved in the recruitment of 'exotic people?' Right after the *Eskimos*' death, Jacobsen abandoned the recruitment activity to devote himself mainly to collecting ethnographic objects. From his various trips on the west coast of North America (1881–1883), Siberia and East Asia (1884–1885) and Indonesia (1887–1889), he brought back more than 12,000 objects for the Berlin Museum of Ethnology. That said, from time to time, he did recruit individuals on behalf of Carl Hagenbeck. For example, in the summer of 1885, while Jacobsen was on the west coast of British

[307] Thode-Arora, Hilke. (2011). p. 82.
[308] David, Philippe. (n.d.).
[309] *CÉRÉMONIE – Des indigènes rapatriés....un siècle plus tard.* (2010, January 15).

Columbia with his younger brother Johan Filip, the two men recruited a group of nine men of the Nuxalc tribe from Bella Coola. Johan Adrian brought them back to Europe and accompanied them on tour until July 1887.

As for the Labrador Inuit, the tragedy did not result in preventing anyone else from agreeing to be exhibited against compensation. In the fall of 1892, a group of 57 Inuit, including 29 women and 19 children,[310] left Labrador for the Chicago's World Fair which was to be held from May 1 to October 30, 1893. The group was recruited to bring to life the 'Eskimo Village' and the Labrador trading post recreated on site.

Life on the coast of Labrador being difficult and often struck by famine, many did not want to take the chance to pass such an opportunity to be housed, fed and to receive pocket money for a period of two years. In addition, at the end of their contract, they were to be returned to Labrador and given a financial compensation of about $100 as well as a rifle, ammunition, pork, flour, bread, tea, molasses, salt, blankets, fishing hooks, etc.[311]

In 1899, Esther Eneutseak, a young Inuk who participated in the Chicago World's Fair came back to Labrador in the company of an American promoter wishing to recruit Inuit for a European tour. Thirty Labrador Inuit, including Esther, her parents and her daughter Nancy Columbia (born during the 1893 Chicago exhibition), left for a two-year tour that took them to London, Madrid, Paris and North Africa. They returned to North America in 1901 to participate in an exhibition in Buffalo.[312]

The tragic stories experienced by many of those who participated in such exhibitions led the Newfoundland government to vote, on March 29, 1911, a law forbidding anyone to take the *Eskimos* or other indigenous peoples away from the colony without the Governor's prior approval. Failure to comply would result in a fine of up to $ 500 or six months imprisonment.[313] However, this law was lifted in 1914 to allow the recruitment of young Inuit as snipers for the First World War.[314]

[310] Forbush, William Byron. (1903). p. 52.
[311] Harper, Kenn and Russell Potter. (2010).
[312] Harper, Kenn. (2009). (2009, August 20).
[313] Expositions and Epidemics. (1986, September).
[314] McGrath, Robin. (2014, May 17).

One of these sad stories is that of Pomiuk, an 8-year-old boy from Nachvak, who returned from the Chicago Fair handicapped with a broken hip. In 1895, George Ford, the Hudson's Bay Company post manager in Nachvak who convinced Abraham to leave for Europe, alerted Dr. Wilfred Grenfell that the boy was in such a poor state that he did not have much longer to live. Dr. Grenfell found the boy "naked and covered with an old caribou skin, [...] his face marked by pain and neglect. His hip was broken and infected."[315] The doctor took the young man under his wing, but despite the care, Pomiuk died in September 1897 as a result of the infection that had invaded his body.

On a happier note, there is at least one case where Inuit participants were able to use these ethnographic shows to change their lives for the better. The most striking example is that of Esther Eneutseak and her daughter Nancy Columbia. After the 1901 European tour, Esther married the American promoter John Caspar Smith, and 'Eskimo shows' became their family's business. They created their own 'Eskimo village' and took it across the United States and they became involved in the burgeoning film industry. Between 1910 and 1920, Esther, Nancy and their families participated in more than 12 films and actually became the first professional actors of Inuit origin.[316]

[315] Forbush, William Byron. (1903). p. 79-81.
[316] Harper, Kenn and Russell Potter. (2010).

NEXT STEPS...

You now know as much as I do about Abraham Ulrikab's tragic story. Being neither a historian, an anthropologist nor an ethnologist, I am pleased, and feel humbled, to have been able to unravel the mysteries surrounding the tragic story of Abraham and his group.

The work is not over yet. The research and documentation processes must continue in parallel with the yet-to-be-written chapter: their potential repatriation to Canada. This essential task will unfold in the months, maybe years, ahead as both the Inuit and other appropriate authorities, including government officials, engage in a dialogue. The publication of this book is therefore seen as the catalyst for that decision-making process.

In the meantime, I'll continue to investigate the remaining unanswered questions, some of which may be held in the still-to-be-translated German, Norwegian or Inuktitut documents. There is also the search for potential descendants that is still in progress, and Abraham's original diary which has yet to be found.

What happened to the many autographs and drawings Abraham offered to visitors in Europe or those that Virchow had in his possession? Could it be that someone somewhere has one hidden in a family photo album or archive? Where is a copy of the group photo taken in Prague and handed to the *Eskimos* for Christmas 1880? Where is the poster that was put up all over Paris announcing the arrival of the *Eskimos* to the *Jardin d'acclimatation*?

Some archives have not yet been found, including that of Albert Geoffroy Saint-Hilaire, director of the *Jardin d'acclimatation*. Did Adolf Schoepf, Mrs. Jacobsen, Captain Bang, or any of the other individuals who crossed the *Eskimos*' path, leave their own writings describing their interactions with them? As for Johan Adrian Jacobsen's archives, they may still hold some secrets which won't be uncovered until the *Museum für Völkerkunde Hamburg* can find the funds and resources to digitize the 5,000 plus documents. Similarly, I have not yet had access to the archives of Berlin Zoological Garden, those of the Berlin Museum of Ethnology or the archives of the anthropological laboratory where the brains of Abraham, Ulrike and Tobias were casted.

Speaking of the brain casts, if the three *Eskimo* endocranial casts that belong to the *Musées anatomiques Delmas-Orfila-Rouvière* are those of Abraham, Ulrike and Tobias then, what were the circumstances that led to these skullcaps being reattached to their respective skeletons? Dr. Émile Landrieux wrote in his note to Armand de Quatrefages that he instructed his intern to send three brains and three skullcaps to the anthropology laboratory. Would the endocranial casts have been made at the *Hôpital Saint-Louis* and the caps put back on the bodies before they were sent to the cemetery? Hopefully, the question will be resolved one day.

So, the research does not stop here with the publication of this book. Indeed, a revised and expanded version may soon be required.

Even though I will not be one of the decision-makers, it must be obvious that my fervent wish is for Abraham, Maria, Sara, Tigianniak, Tobias and Ulrike to eventually return to their homeland, as they so dearly hoped. The past cannot be changed. But, it seems to me that bringing their remains back home where they can be buried in a dignified manner, and be with their ancestors who inhabit the *Torngait*, the place of spirits, is the ultimate way to ensure that a sense of closure is brought to this tragic late 19th century episode. The Inuit elders and the community are the only people who can decide what is best. It is their story. These are their ancestors, not mine. My role is to bring them all the information they need to make an informed decision.

I suspect that if he were still among us, the Vicomte de Challans would not hesitate to tell us what he is thinking. If you too want to share your opinion or thoughts, if you have questions that have not been answered, if you think you may have a lead to uncover a new piece of the puzzle, or if you feel that some of the information provided in this book is inaccurate, please, do not hesitate to write to me at france@horizonspolaires.com. All constructive comments and suggestions will be appreciated.

Thank you! Nakkumek!
France Rivet

Appendix A – Abraham's Diary

We reproduce here the entire translation of Abraham's diary so that you can read it exactly as Abraham wrote it. The English translation was based on the 19th century German translation by Brother Kretschmer, a Moravian missionary who was stationed in Hebron when Abraham's original diary (written in Inuktitut) was returned to Labrador. The original has yet to be uncovered.

All parentheses included in his translation are those of Brother Kretschmer.

Diary of Hebron Eskimo Abraham about his stay in Europe 1880 Translated by Brother Kretschmer

In 1880, the family Abraham Ulrike was taken to Europe by Mr. Jacobsen, the agent of M. Hagenbeck. With them the unmarried Tobias, also from Hebron, as well as the heathen family Tirrianniakat from the North. All died in Europe. Abraham's diary was sent back to Hebron together with some other things. There it says:

In Berlin, it is not really nice since it is impossible because of people and trees, indeed, because so many children come. The air is constantly buzzing from the sound of the walking and driving; our enclosure is filled up immediately.

It was not until Oct. 22 that we heard that *The Harmony* had arrived, when two acquaintances from Hlawatscheck came to us. They were two teachers (missionaries), and they were so happy when they saw us that they knew us immediately and called our names, told us to sing, and because we are not without knowing various things, they were very happy and even thanked us greatly and invited us to their house and their church. We really want to, but are not able to, as there are too many people. Indeed, going out by daytime is impossible because of all the people, because we are totally surrounded by them, by many very different faces.

On Oct. 23, snow was falling all the time, the *Kablunat* are freezing; even we are freezing very much.

On Oct. 25, we saw teacher Kern and one of the <u>great teachers</u> ([von] Dewitz) who send out teachers.

Oct. 27. Storm and rain. Yesterday on the 26, we went to church, and prayed and sang together. We were all very greatly cheered (blessed), also all our *Kablunats*, very greatly we have been inspired. We people sang together in the church, *Jesu ging voran* (Jesus Still Lead On) and then recited the Lord's Prayer. The assembly was greatly inspired by our voices. And again, we were recommended pleadingly to the Lord. And again, there was choir: *Wir stehen getrost auf Zion fest* (*We rely confidently on Zion*). Then we were at loss because of all the blessings, even the *Kablunat*, too. When the choir had finished, the man at the table called upwards, then the trumpets started playing; *Kommst Du, Jesu, vom Himmel herunter auf Erden*[317] (*Come Thou, Jesus, from Heaven to Earth*) and other melodies. When we had finished, we were given an enthusiastic welcome, our hands were shaken greatly. Before the table we sat. After this event, the teachers often appeared in our house (in the zoo) and sang (and prayed); even women who came into our hut have joined in the singing and recommended us greatly to Jesus.

One day in the evening, us wearing big coats and shoes, we went to see things (the wax works) exhibited in a large house,[318] we drove there (sitting) in a house.[319] When we arrived, we went in and saw many people gathered there, – but – they only looked like people; they looked so much like real people that you did not notice anything. Yes indeed, some of them even took breath, and some were moving, and all that from the inside, indeed, to name all is impossible. We also saw Napoleon's wagon, it had been brutally snatched from him during the war. And all sorts of rifles, indeed, they really looked like humans, of

[317] Written by Johann Sebastian Bach.
[318] The French translation of Abraham's diary published in 1883 in the *Journal des frères de l'unité chrétienne* specifies that this house was a panopticon. See Notes de voyages d'Abraham, l'Esquimau. (1883).
[319] The French translation of Abraham's diary published in 1883 in the *Journal des frères de l'unité chrétienne* clarifies that this house was in fact a tramway. See Notes de voyages d'Abraham, l'Esquimau. (1883).

great diversity. Nubians, Africans we have also seen, and Chinese and Indians and Americans and Californians. Yes indeed, the inhabitants of the earth, very many did we see in Berlin. All Sundays there were violin concerts in front of us, in a great house.

Our fellowmen, the fox family (Terrianiak) stopped to be cheerful, because they are tired of the people. And we in the other house have been very patient, although we have also been greatly tired. Constantly in the evenings, we pray, wanting to be helped. This thing (our praying) also seems to achieve something within us.

Some *Kablunat*, some Catholics (?) laugh at us, but this did not make us tired, as their souls are also to be laughed at. To some of them, who were talking about us, I have even given answers often, as they could speak English. Often, some of them were even horrified by our Northlanders[320]. Every day I have consistent work drawing people, Labrador and Nain.

Nov. 3. We heard that many ships sank at Heligoland and London because of storm.

Nov. 7. Had sorrow again. Our companion, the unmarried Tobias, was beaten with a dog whip by our master, Mr. Jacobsen. (Mr. Jacobsen) was immediately furious because, as he said, Tobias never obeyed him and had got himself into trouble too often. He was nearly not taken and sent away. If Mr. J. does that twice I shall write to England as I am told. Afterwards, he was very friendly towards me so that I don't write. Even our two wives were immediately bought silken ribbons. If Tobias is frequently as stubborn, he won't get paid, but if he is nice, he will get greatly paid. After this incident, Tobias was very sick.

The pond on which we kayak around is very cold; we always have to get rid of the ice before we can kayak. At times there is a great cold. We also saw the animals of the Berliners, fish, a seal Netsek[321] and nearly all kinds of sea animals. Meat (seal meat) we miss very greatly, let be, some of it is probably not very good, but that's what we mostly eat: coffee and rusk in the morning, codfish, potatoes, beer and ship cookies for lunch. Coffee and ship bread at 4 p.m. Tea, herring, beer and ship bread at 6 p.m.

---

[320] Tigianniak and his family.
[321] In Inuktitut 'natseq' means 'ringed seal.'

The *Kablunat* (the audience) always take delicious things with them to treat us with; all kinds of things to chew, which they give to us, and big fruits, which even have juice (fresh fruits).

On some days I have also played violin outdoors, as the *Kablunat* wished it so greatly, even if I am not very good at it they don't mind. I was constantly told to write my name, occasionally, there were many voices, one always took it away from the other; to please them all was impossible, there were too many.

Nov. 10. It was snowing greatly, even in Berlin.

Daily we heard the voices of the canons very loud. But it is very easy to get sick with a bad cold; I am still quite well, although I have a badly running nose. But the daily work is getting hard due to indisposition, because our child Sara is ill, and because we all have to suffer; that is certainly difficult. That (Sara) has to stay alone is regrettable, but she herself does not complain, because she is already able to understand that it can't be any different.

Sometimes we are given some money, sometimes two pence, sometimes one mark, sometimes 50 pence, sometimes 20 pence, also cigarettes every day.

It is too long until the year is over because we would very much like to return to our country, because we are unable to stay here forever, yes indeed, it is impossible! It buzzes and roars day and night because of the rattling of the sleighs and the constant voices of the steam whistles.

When we were travelling with steam, we were faster than flying. We always occupied (places) that are reserved for grand gentlemen. The train was so long that there was a great distance between both ends. We were in the middle in a very nice house (a wagon), we could not close the windows in order to see, looking out was impossible because of the wind; my eyes were bad and swollen with seeing, although I hardly stuck my head out.

[While we were travelling, our countryman Fox (Terrianiak) worked [his] magic quite exceptionally. Although he was in the beautiful steam wagon, he was extremely distressed by his witchcraft and couldn't smile at anyone, when we arrived.][322]

---

[322] The following note can be found in the right margin of Brother Kretschmer's manuscript: "The passage in square brackets [...] was crossed out, perhaps with an eye to readers in Europe. It is also possible,

Saturday, Oct. 15 or 16, we arrived in Berlin by means of the marvelous steam. At 9 p.m. we had left Hamburg, at 6 a.m. we arrived in Berlin at our house that we built ourselves; a beautiful house although only of boards. To wipe the floor of our house was nearly impossible because of all the people. Although they were thrown out by our masters, others quickly took their place. Between some trees we have a house. Nearly is a music house, a cause for astonishment. A lot of people wish to see our house, but it is impossible to be seen by all of them. Only a few have seen it, our masters even did not know whether we should ask someone in (or not). When the teachers came they were the first ones in, but not immediately, because it was impossible due to all those people. Our enclosure was often broken by the throng.

One day a great gentleman from Berlin came to see us and had many gentlemen with him. They all came into our enclosure to see the kayak, but immediately everything was filled with people and it was impossible to move anymore. Both our masters Schoepf and Jacobsen shouted with big voices and some of the higher-ranking soldiers left, but most of them had no ears. Since our two masters did not achieve anything, they came to me and sent me to drive them out. So I did what I could. Taking my whip and the Greenland seal harpoon, I made myself terrible. One of the gentlemen was like a crier. Others quickly shook hands with me when I chased them out. Others went and jumped over the fence because there were so many. Several thanked me for doing this and our masters also thanked me very much. Ulrike had also locked our house from the inside and plugged up the entrance so that nobody would go in, and those who wanted to look in through the windows were pushed away with a piece of wood.

Nov. 11. Few people. We got no money, because they were too few.

Nov. 12. I saw Elsner who came (from Bremen) to see us. He came with (Emperor) Wilhelm's teacher (court preacher Stöcker) and another one. They prayed because of us that we don't turn from the Lord and may not get lost. Also some religious women

---

however, that it was crossed out in the original. (?)". This note suggests that the manuscript is not that of Kretschmer, but a copy by a third party (another Moravian brother?) who did not have access to Abraham's original diary.

came to our hut and sang and led the prayers very greatly. Yes indeed, we have the believers here in Germany as our brothers and sisters, they even called us 'brothers' and 'sisters,' even cried in front of us that we might not get lost through Satan, they even knelled down in front of us reverentially, by greeting they often strengthen us greatly; many times they brought us good things to eat and thought that, by doing so, they would strengthen our souls.

Esdraige (Austria)

Nov. 26. I am writing in Prague here far away, in Austria, in the country of Catholics, in a big city. We are here for two weeks, inside a big long house. To go out is impossible, so that we may not be caught by the Catholics. Yes indeed, we are highly regarded and have a house in the big house. It also has a seal, coming from Holland for us to eat, but it only is allowed to be stabbed with the seal harpoon. But until now I still have seen few believers, those, which are not from us. They sang with little voice because of their fear of the Catholics.

We too with a little voice can sing and pray to get help from the Lord, so that nothing happens to us through the Catholics, because they are always asking if we are believers; we are unable to deny and claim it constantly while we wonder if they will do us harm. Yes indeed, because everything is to be feared here, we feel that we need a lot of help.

One day in the afternoon at 4 o'clock, countless soldiers came; the big ways were totally filled. They carried fire[323] as well as lanterns with a handle; the horses had fire as well. But they have also made beautiful voice (music), most delightful to hear, with the trumpets.

Nov. 27. Have caught a seal (netsek) in Prague in a pond, while there were enormously many people, yes indeed countless. When I harpooned it with the seal harpoon, everybody clapped their hands greatly like the eider ducks. When I was done with it (when I killed it), the voice makers sang greatly with violins, drums, trumpets, and flutes. Yes indeed, to talk to each other was impossible because of the many voices.

---

[323] The French translation of Abraham's diary published in 1883 in the *Journal des frères de l'unité chrétienne* specifies that these were torches. See Notes de voyages d'Abraham, l'Esquimau. (1883).

From Prague, we left for Frankfurt, where it has many people. There we had two houses in the open in an enclosure. In our whole village grove, we were guarded day and night by soldiers who took turns. There are many Jews there; the Catholics are very greatly despised there. But there we very often paddled the kayak even on a pond. From there, we went away again in a sleigh with wheels and horses in the night, all of us, to Darmstadt.

In Darmstadt, we had a beautiful house in a beautiful big round house, which is a playground for ice-skating on wheels. There we often sleighed round and round inside the house, all of us sitting on it. There one of us, Terrianiak's daughter, Nochasak, stopped living (died) very fast and suffered terribly greatly. After her, in another country, in Krefeld, her mother also died, greatly suffering as well. After her, also little Sara stopped living, peacefully, with a great rash and swellings, because she was swollen all over. After two days of being sick, she died in Krefeld.

While she was still alive, she was brought to hospital, where I went with her. She still had her mind, while I was there. She still prayed the song *Ich bin ein kleines kindelein* (*I am a little child, you see*). When I wanted to leave, she sent her greetings to her mother and little sister. When I left her, she slept; from then on, she did not wake up anymore. For this we both had reason to be thankful. While she was still alive, we went to Paris and travelled the whole day and the whole night through.

Abraham Ulrikab

Fig. 97 Herman Frederik Carel ten Kate
(Wikimedia Commons, *Bibliothèque nationale de France*)

Dutch anthropologist (1858–1931) who visited the *Eskimos* at the Berlin zoo in the fall of 1880 and purchased several of their *cartes-de-visite*. Ten Kate donated these photos to the *Museum voor Volkenkund* in Rotterdam. They are now preserved at the *Nederland Fotomuseum* also in Rotterdam. Ten Kate studied anthropology in Paris with Paul Topinard and Armand de Quatrefages, and in Berlin with Rudolf Virchow. Was he part of the audience during Virchow's conference on the *Eskimos*?

APPENDIX B – CHRONOLOGICAL SUMMARY OF EVENTS

Date	Description of the event
1880-08-10	Jacobsen arrives in Hebron, Labrador.
1880-08-15	Jacobsen hires an interpreter, Abraham, to go to Nachvak recruit non-Christian *Eskimos*.
1880-08-16	Jacobsen accompanied by Abraham leaves for Nachvak.
1880-08-18	Arrival in Nachvak.
1880-08-19	A non-Christian family accepts Jacobsen's offer.
1880-08-20	George Ford, the HBC post manager, discusses with Abraham and convinces him to go to Europe.
1880-08-22	Departure from Nachvak.
1880-08-25	Arrival in Hebron at 3 a.m.
1880-08-26	Departure from Hebron for the trans-Atlantic crossing.
1880-09-22	The *Eisbär* anchored in Heligoland near the mouth of the Elbe River.
1880-09-23	Stop in Cuxhaven to send a telegram announcing their arrival.
1880-09-24	Arrival in Hamburg at 6 a.m. The group is taken to Carl Hagenbeck's residence at 13 Neuer Pferdemarkt street.
1880-10-02	The exhibition opens at Hagenbeck's Thierpark.
1880-10-04	Jacobsen is admitted to the hospital. Adolf Schoepf takes charge of the group.
1880-10-15	Night train from Hamburg to Berlin. Departure from the Berliner train station at 9 p.m.
1880-10-16	Arrival at the Hamburger station in Berlin at 6 a.m.
1880-10-22	Two Moravian missionaries visit the group at the Berlin Zoo.
1880-10-25	Eight Moravian brothers and sisters visit the group

	at the Berlin Zoo.
1880-10-26	Abraham and his family visit Berlin's Moravian church for the first time.
1880-10-27	Jacobsen joins the group in Berlin.
1880-10-28	Dr. Rudolf Virchow studies the *Eskimos* and takes various anthropometric measurements.
1880-11-07	Abraham reports that Tobias was beaten by Jacobsen. Dr. Rudolf Virchow gives a conference to share the results of his study.
1880-11-09	Brother Elsner receives Abraham's first letter.
1880-11-12	Brother Elsner visits Abraham at the zoo.
1880-11-13	Adolf Bastian of the Berlin Ethnology Museum writes to Jacobsen asking if it would be possible for the museum to acquire some of the artefacts collected in Labrador and Greenland.
1880-11-13 or 14	Abraham and his family visit Berlin's Moravian church for the second time.
1880-11-15	Departure from Berlin at 8 a.m. Arrival in Prague in the evening.
1880-11-17 to 28	The *Eskimos* are exhibited at the Kaufmann Menagerie in Prague.
1880-11-29	Departure from Prague.
1880-11-30	Arrival in Frankfurt where the exhibition is set up at the Frankfurt Zoo.
1880-12-12	Nuggasak starts feeling sick. Departure for Darmstadt accompanied by Mrs. Jacobsen.
1880-12-14	Nuggasak dies at the Orpheum in Darmstadt at 8 a.m.
1880-12-16	Nuggasak's funeral is held in the afternoon.
1880-12-17	Departure from Darmstadt in the morning. Arrival in Bockum/Crefeld at 7 p.m.
1880-12-24	Christmas celebration.
1880-12-25	Paingu starts showing the same symptoms as Nuggasak.
1880-12-26	Sara gets ill.
1880-12-27	Paingu dies at the Bockum Zoo at 7 p.m.
1880-12-28	During Paingu's autopsy, Jacobsen takes her skullcap and hides it in his luggage. Paingu's funeral is held in the evening.
1880-12-29	Sara is admitted to the hospital. Dr. Jacobi informs Crefeld's burgomaster of the little girl's illness. The Bockum Zoo is closed for a few days.
1880-12-30	Departure from Crefeld around 9 a.m. Crefeld's burgomaster sends a telegram to the authorities

	in Paris informing them that the group has left behind a child with smallpox.
1880-12-31	Arrival at the Gare du Nord in Paris at 4:45 a.m. Sara dies in Crefeld at 10 a.m.
1881-01-01	The *Eskimos* are vaccinated by the *Jardin d'acclimatation*'s doctor. Sara is buried in the Crefeld cemetery.
1881-01-01 to 06	The exhibition is on at the *Jardin d'acclimatation* in Paris.
1881-01-05	The director of the *Jardin d'acclimatation* sends a letter to Dr. Paul Topinard confirming that he can come examine the *Eskimos* with his colleagues of the *Société d'anthropologie de Paris*.
1881-01-06	Dr. Arthur Bordier shows Paingu's skullcap to the members of the *Société d'anthropologie de Paris*.
1881-01-07	The *Eskimos* are vaccinated a second time.
1881-01-08	Abraham writes his last letter to Brother Elsner.
1881-01-09	The five *Eskimos* as well as Jacobsen are admitted to the *Hôpital Saint-Louis* in Paris. A notice is published in various newspapers to inform the population that the *Eskimos* have left Paris and are on their way back to Labrador.
1881-01-10	Maria dies at 2 p.m.
1881-01-11	Tigianniak dies at 6 p.m. The director of the *Jardin d'acclimatation* sends a letter to Dr. Paul Topinard telling him to cancel the examination of the *Eskimos* by the anthropologists.
1881-01-12	Maria is buried in Saint-Ouen cemetery.
1881-01-13	Tobias dies at 2 a.m. Tigianniak is buried in Saint-Ouen cemetery. Abraham dies at 6 p.m.
1881-01-12 or 13	Dr. Paul Topinard visits the Hôpital Saint-Louis on behalf of Albert Geoffroy Saint-Hilaire. Dr. Landrieux commits to having three brains and skullcaps removed and sent to him.
1881-01-14	Tobias is buried in Saint-Ouen cemetery. Dr. Landrieux presents, to the medical society, his observations on the condition of the *Eskimos* when they were admitted to the hospital as well as the autopsy results on the first three bodies.
1881-01-15	Abraham is buried in Saint-Ouen cemetery.
1881-01-16	Ulrike dies at 3 a.m. Hagenbeck sends a telegram to Jacobsen asking him to get rid of all *Eskimo* things.

1881-01-17	Ulrike is buried in Saint-Ouen cemetery. Jacobsen is discharged from the hospital.
1881-01-17, 18 or 19	Jacobsen meets with a professor from the *Musée d'ethnographie du Trocadéro* who buys the artifact collection.
1881-01-17 (on or about)	Dr. Landrieux writes to the *Muséum national d'Histoire naturelle* suggesting that their intervention could allow the bodies to be exhumed.
1881-01-18	Brother Elsner sends a letter to Brother Reichel to inform him of the death of the Eskimos.
1881-01-20	Jacobsen, Schoepf and Mrs. Jacobsen leave Paris by train. Adolf Bastian writes to Jacobsen expressing his regrets following the *Eskimos'* death and asking about acquiring some of the artifacts.
1881-01-21	Dr. Léon Colin is mandated to conduct the inquiry into the death of the *Eskimos*.
1881-01-29	An article announcing the death of all eight individuals appears in a Prague newspaper.
End of January 1881	The brains of Abraham, Ulrike and Tobias are received at the *Laboratoire d'anthropologie de l'École pratique des hautes études*.
1881-02-04	Dr. Léon Colin delivers his report on the death of the *Eskimos*.
1881-02-08	First article announcing the death of all eight individuals appears in a Paris newspaper.
1881-03-07	During a session of the French legislative Assembly, the death of the *Eskimos* is given as an example to justify the need for the proposed law on compulsory vaccination.
1881-03-10	The Prefecture of Police of Paris acknowledges receipt of Armand de Quatrefages' request to exhume the remains. However, a study must first be conducted by Dr. Brouardel to determine when it will be safe to proceed.
1881-03-13	Carl Hagenbeck records an amount of 300 marks owed by the Musée d'ethnographie du Trocadéro for *Eskimo* things.
1881-04-06	Carl Hagenbeck receives a payment of 100 marks from the Berlin Ethnology Museum for some *Eskimo* things.
1881-05-05	Théophile Chudzinski shows the plaster casts of the brains of Abraham, Ulrike and Tobias to the *Société d'anthropologie de Paris*.

1881-05	Jacobsen visits Brother Elsner in Bremen.
1881-06-07	Carl Hagenbeck sends the *Eskimos'* wages to Pastor Ludwig in Altona.
1881-07-15	The news of the group's death arrives in Labrador on the Moravian ship *The Harmony* as reported in a letter written by Brother Bourquin.
1881-07-25	*The Harmony* arrives in the community of Zoar bringing the sad news and the narrative written by Brother Elsner.
1881-08-17	*The Harmony* arrives in Hebron with the group's personal belongings and Abraham's diary.
1881-08-27	Carl Hagenbeck records a payment of 300 marks from the Trocadero museum for the purchase of *Eskimo* things.
1882-04-16	Official opening of the *Musée d'ethnographie du Trocadéro* in Paris. Artefacts acquired from Jacobsen by the museum may have been on display from the museum's opening on.
1885-03-18	The city of Paris issues the five death certificates needed to proceed with the exhumation.
1886-05-27	The authorization to proceed with the exhumation of the bodies is sent by the Prefecture of Police to the *Muséum national d'Histoire naturelle*.
1886-06-04	The remains are exhumed from the Saint-Ouen cemetery.
1886-06-05	The remains are received at the *Muséum national d'Histoire naturelle*.
1888	Publication by Georges Hervé of his book *La circonvolution de Broca* in which he provides the details of his study of the brain casts of Abraham, Tobias, and Ulrike.
1892	Rudolf Virchow publishes *Crania Ethnica Americana* in which he mentions the exhumation of Sara and provides the details of his study of her skull.
1898-07-21	Opening of the new gallery of anthropology at the *Muséum national d'Histoire naturelle*.

Fig. 98 Poster *Amerikanische Völker*
Meyers Konversationslexikon, 5th edition, page 457e, 1897.
(Wikimedia Commons)

Fig. 99 Nuggasak and Tigianniak's portrait
Extracted from above poster (first row, 3rd and 4th from the left)

APPENDIX C – STUDY OF THE BRAINS BY THÉOPHILE CHUDZINSKI

We present here the full text of the speech delivered by Dr. Théophile Chudzinski on May 5, 1881 before the *Société d'anthropologie de Paris* and published in the Society's Bulletin, as well as the discussion that ensued.[324]

About the brains of the three Eskimos who died of smallpox from January 10 to 16, 1881, in M. [L]Andrieux's department at the Hôpital Saint-Louis.

The three Eskimo brains arrived at the *Laboratoire d'anthropologie des Hautes-Études* two weeks after death. As they were kept during this time in water with very low alcohol concentration, one can easily imagine the deplorable condition they were in when we received them in the laboratory.

Here are the two hemispheres of Abraham Paulus, which reflect the brain's state of complete decomposition.

As for the other brains, we were able to harden and preserve them so that the gyri could easily be studied. Of these three Eskimo brains, two belong to men, and the other to a woman.

The first of these brains is that of Tobias Ignatius, 23 years old, who died on January 13, 1881; its weight is 1,398 grams.

The second brain is that of Abraham Paulus, 35 years old, who died on January, 14;[325] the weight of the brain is unknown because of its very advanced state of decomposition.

---

[324] Chudzinski, M. (1881).
[325] This date is incorrect. Abraham died on January 13, 1881.

The third brain is that of the Eskimo woman, Ulrika Henocq, 24 years old, sister[326] of Abraham Paulus; she died on January 16, and the weight of her brain is 1,236 grams.

We have the honor to present to the *Société d'anthropologie* the plaster casts of these three brains of which the external structures are remarkable in many ways.

First, when the brains are examined, we notice the considerable volume of their cerebral hemispheres; then one can see that the gyri constituting the external surface are wide, simple, and have very few secondary divisions, and that there are few tortuosities of the gyri.

This simplicity is especially evident on the frontal lobes of the brains of our Eskimos; the lobes are at the same time flattened from top to bottom. The general form of these brains is frankly dolichocephalic.

Now let's move on to the more detailed study of the peculiarities found in the sulci and gyri of these three brains.

The Sylvian fissure appears to be shorter than usual, nearly horizontal, and with very simple contours, except in the woman Ulrika Henocq, where it is more complex, especially on the right side.

Generally, its external branch is very short and is even totally hidden by the temporal lobe in the brain of Paulus Abraham.

The fissure of Rolando is very long; indeed, this fissure starts a few millimeters away from the superior portion of the Sylvian fissure, where it begins with three incisures in Tobias Ignatius, and on the left hemisphere in Abraham Paulus; it then travels obliquely up and back towards the large interlobar fissure; it then goes along the superior portion of the hemisphere, turns into the inner surface of the hemisphere and ends on the surface of the oval lobule, so aptly named by Mr. Pozzi.

This portion of the fissure of Rolando which enters the inner surface of the hemisphere is especially remarkable in Tobias Ignatius, in which it forms a kind of hook, the concavity of which is turned backwards and divides into two parts.

---

[326] As we know, Ulrike was not Abraham's sister, but his wife.

It is true that at the bottom of the intra-hemispheric part of the fissure of Rolando, there is a tiny *pli de passage*, which seems to delineate the lunate sulcus characteristic of the oval lobule and of the fissure of Rolando itself. Nevertheless, its length on the inner face of Tobias' left hemisphere is 11 millimeters. Yet the fissure of Rolando is flexuous, and its flexures are very sharp in Paulus Abraham's brain. The occipital sulcus is very short in its extra-hemispheric portion; the intra-hemispheric part is indistinguishable from the calcarine fissure, which is long and flexuous, especially in Ulrika Henocq.

The sub-frontal sulcus is also long, and has several incisures, especially in Tobias Ignatius.

In Ulrika Henocq's brain, the sub-frontal fissure is interrupted in the middle, by a broad *pli de passage* (19 mm wide), exactly as in the schematic hemisphere of my revered teacher Mr. Broca. The posterior part of this fissure delineates the oval lobule exactly. In the anterior portion, two new *plis de passage*, much smaller and somewhat hidden, interrupt its path again.

The sub-frontal fissure in Paulus's left hemisphere is strangely organized; the posterior superior section is simple, then at the oval lobule, it divides into two branches; the superior branch divides the entire inner surface of the first frontal gyrus. The inferior branch follows the regular path. However, note that the superior branch of our fissure is separated from the main gyrus by a small *pli de passage*, hidden at the bottom of the sub-frontal fissure in the fresh state, and which we have deliberately exposed when casting this hemisphere.

Let's now quickly review the main sulci of our Eskimos' brains.

The pre-rolandic sulcus is almost as long as the fissure of Rolando: it is almost uninterrupted over Paulus Abraham's left hemisphere. Ordinarily, in our Eskimos, the pre-rolandic sulcus is divided in two by the anastomotic segment of the second frontal gyrus. On the right hemisphere, as the second frontal convolution has two anastomotic segments, therefore the pre-rolandic sulcus is cut into three distinct parts.

The pre-rolandic sulcus is parallel to the fissure of Rolando; it is not interrupted on Abraham Paulus' left hemisphere, on Tobias' left hemisphere and on Ulrika's two hemispheres.

The first frontal sulcus is clean and simple, with the exception of Paulus' right hemisphere. The orbital lobule's sulci are few and far between in Paulus' left hemisphere, and the natural consequence of this arrangement of the sulci is the unusual width of the cerebral gyri of that lobe.

Finally, allow me to enter the examination of certain features of the gyri.

The frontal lobe is relatively short; but the other lobes are, to the contrary, highly developed, especially the parietal. There are very few meandering gyri of the frontal lobe, and this arrangement of the frontal gyri is remarkable, especially in Tobias Ignatius.

The first frontal gyrus is very wide and, in Tobias, it has very few incisures.

The second gyrus is very well developed, especially in Paulus. Indeed, this gyrus, among the other peculiarities, has two anastomotic folds connecting it to the ascending frontal gyrus. The second frontal gyrus is very simple in Tobias.

The third frontal gyrus is underdeveloped; it is short and curled up on itself.

In Tobias, it is reduced to a small mass, almost completely smooth, without the convolutions usually found on superior brains. In its posterior portion, we can see a thin *pli de passage*, which in Tobias does not exceed two and one half millimeters and which connects it to the lower portion of the pre-central gyrus. However, this gyrus is more developed in the woman Ulrika.

The ascending frontal gyrus is very wide. The ascending parietal gyrus is very flexuous in Paulus; is very wide in Tobias. On the other hand, these two gyri are slender in Ulrika.

The two parietal gyri are generally simple and very wide in our three Eskimos. The second parietal gyrus distinguishes itself by its width and the simplicity of its structure.

Usually, among the Eskimos in question, the occipital lobe is very simple, and this simplicity is most obvious on Tobias' brain.

As for the temporal lobe, two points are to be made; 1° the extreme slenderness of the first gyrus; it is so rudimentary that we find such gyri only in the inferior races; and 2° the unusual width of the second frontal gyrus.

The internal surface of the cerebral hemispheres of these three Eskimo brains has the following features: the enormous development in breath of the internal portion of the first frontal gyrus, especially in Tobias; the division of this gyrus into two secondary gyri by an uninterrupted sulcus on the left hemisphere in Paulus, and as we noted above, this sulcus seems to be continuous with the sub-frontal fissure; on the right, we see the same sulcus, very well marked, but interrupted in several places by anastomotic gyri. In Ulrika, the internal portion of the first frontal gyrus is largely anastomosed by an extensive *pli de passage*, with the gyrus of corpus callosum. The gyrus of the corpus callosum is well developed, in general, in our Eskimos; but its width is quite remarkable, in Tobias, in its posterior portion, and in the anterior portion in Ulrika, in whom it seems to divide itself in the middle section, into two secondary gyri.

The oval lobule is very developed; its development is enormous in Ulrika; on the other hand, the cuneiform lobule is small, and even in Ulrika, it is reduced to a single *pli de passage*, largely hidden in the depth of the calcarine and occipital fissures.

Discussion

Mr. Pozzi. I would not allow the communication just made by Mr. Chudzinski to pass without insisting on its relevance. It shows that the brains of these Eskimos have a somewhat schematic simplicity, and that this simplicity is observed especially in the frontal lobe. It exists, especially in the third frontal gyrus, where, as Broca demonstrated, is located the cerebral organ of articulate language. No doubt this anatomical inferiority corresponded, for the Eskimos, to a physiological inferiority, to an inferiority of the phonetic function. It is remarkable to see that simplicity of the frontal lobe coinciding here with an exaggerated development of parts known to be the motor of the brain, including ascending frontal and parietal gyri and the oval lobule; so that there is striking contrast between the great development of the so-called motor parts of the brain, the ones less important from a psychic point of view, and the simplicity of the most human parts, so to speak.

Mr. Dally.[327] It is not accurate to call the third left frontal gyrus, the organ of articulate speech: that portion of the brain usually plays the role of a center that presides over the articulate language; but this is not a reason to name it the organ of language.

---

[327] Eugène Dally (1833–1887), physician and professor at the School of Anthropology.

298   Appendix C – Study of the Brains by Théophile Chudzinski

The substitution of certain parts of the brain by other parts is too clearly established for us to qualify any part of the brain as an organ.

Mr. Pozzi. Mr. Dally will agree with me in if I say: the usual organ.

Mr. Auburtin.[328] What does Mr. Dally mean by "the substitution of certain parts of the brain by other parts?" I do not know that positive developments have been reported, showing that a part of the brain can be substituted in its functions.

Mr. Dally. These facts exist, and in large numbers. Mr. Aubertin will be able to find them in M. Parant's thesis. They were found in a number of cases of aphemia. Besides, mutual substitution of various brain regions is accepted by Brown-Sequard.[329] It is therefore no longer a question of finding organs in the brain, but rather, parts adapted in various ways to one function or another, according to the circumstances and in particular based on education.

Mr. Coudereau.[330] Some parts of the brain may be supplemented in their function by other parts, but not by any part; this does not mean that all parts of the brain, without distinction, are able to fulfill a specific function. The third left frontal convolution can be substituted, in its special function, by the third right convolution, but not by other parts of the brain, as far as I know.

Mr. Auburtin. This is precisely what I meant earlier and to which Mr. Dally did not answer.

Mr. Dally. I obviously cannot quote specific facts out of the blue; but these facts exist, and I can cite them another day, if Mr. Aubertin so desires.

Mr. President. Perhaps it would be better to postpone this discussion to another meeting, where everyone can support his opinion, evidence in hand.

---

[328] Simon Alexandre Ernest Auburtin (1825–1893), French neurologist.
[329] Charles Édouard Brown-Séquard (1817–1894), French neurologist.
[330] Charles Auguste Coudereau, pharmacist and member of the *Société d'anthropologie de Paris*.

APPENDIX D – BROCA'S GYRUS

Here is our English translation of the section of the book *La circonvolution de Broca* (Broca's Gyrus) in which Georges Hervé describes his study of the brain casts of Abraham, Tobias, and Ulrike. Please note that we have translated this section to the best of our knowledge. It may nevertheless contain some inaccuracies.

We had the good fortune to study the brains of three Eskimos, two males and a female, who died in Paris in January 1881. With his expert skill, Mr. Chudzinski has turned these pieces into valuable casts belonging to the *Musée Broca*.

1. Paulus Abraham, 35 years old. – Brain extraordinarily simple. Very wide gyri, few tortuosities, with perfectly sharp boundaries.

On the left, F³ is separated from F²ᵘ by the sulcus *f²*, extended without interruption from the pre-rolandic sulcus at the reflection point of the third frontal on the orbital lobe, where it ends by curving. – The simple foot, which is low, arises from that of the ascending frontal; it is separated from the rest of the gyrus by a deep vertical sulcus coming off *f2* and going beyond the lower edge of the hemisphere it convolutes. – At the bottom follows a thicker loop straddling a single external cerebral branch which, at the concave side of the loop, is divided at an acute angle into two smaller secondary branches, isolating a small cuneal lobule taken from this loop. – The origin of the orbital portion forms a wide operculum with a rounded top that extends in front of the insula, and forms a meander with a convexity in the opposite direction of the previous loop; this meander bypasses the external branch of the H incisure. – Four levels are visible on the frontal lobe as a result of the uninterrupted rostral sulcus.

On the right, the lower region of the gyrus is unclear; the cap is coated on the cast by the temporal lobe. The frontal lobe has more anastomoses than on the other hemisphere, and the rostral sulcus cannot be followed on its full length.

2. Tobias Ignatius, 21 years old. – Extremely broad gyri, massive, simple but irregular.

On the left (See Plate III, fig. 1), the foot of F^3 is minimized: high, but singularly narrow, it is represented only by a very thin strip, 2.5 mm wide, smothered between the ascending frontal and the very wide and triangular cap. The ascending branch of the Sylvian fissure, 20 mm long, separates it from the cap. The horizontal branch, very short and bifurcated, notches the origin of the orbital portion. An incisure coming from f^2 runs through the cap almost to its top; behind this incisure, the posterior branch of the cap sends F^{211} a wide anastomosis which cuts f^2. From the origin of the orbital portion starts another big anastomosis which gets lost in F^{211} and in the orbital lobule: the outer branch of the H incisure keeps it inside.

There are only three frontal roots; but F^2, simple at its origin, soon splits into two separated folds by the rostral sulcus. At the starting point, f^2 is only separated from the latter by a very narrow fold from F^2, so that the two sulci seem to originate from a common origin of the pre-rolandic sulcus.

On the right, we can only distinguish the foot, separated from the rest of the gyrus by a Sylvian fissure which, at the top, bends forward and extends far enough along f^2. It measures 27 mm: in front of it, there was a complete fusion between F^3 and F^2.

3. Henocq Ulrika, 24 years old. – Simple brain, but with narrower and more flexuous gyri than in both men.

On the left, F^3 is clearly separated from F^2 by a second frontal sulcus. The gyrus is very wide, extremely rough and confused. A 23 mm branch, which goes down into the Sylvian fissure, limits in the front the very long and narrow foot. Then comes a triangular and cuneal portion with a lower top: it is a pseudo-cap. The real cap is in front, small and confined between an ascending sylvian branch of

15 mm and a 6 mm horizontal branch: in the middle of the cap we see a long sulcus, almost horizontal at the back, which emanates from the front end of f^2. The rostral sulcus only decomposes the external portion of F^2.

On the right, F^3 is extremely reduced in height and length. At the top, the foot is merged with the ascending frontal; a descending incisure coming from f^2 separates it from a triangular portion with a frontal summit which should perhaps be attached to it. The cap, small, opercular, with a summit directed downward and backward, is circumscribed by the two external sylvian fissures, which seem to continue by rounded contour and to arise from a common trunk behind the summit.

Mr. Chudzinski had already very well noted the characteristic features of these three brains: the little relative length of their external lobes, the other lobes being on the other hand very developed, especially the parietal lobes; the reduction of Broca's gyrus 'short and as curled up on itself.' It is not unreasonable to suggest that this anatomical inferiority corresponded to an inferiority in the phonetic function. Among the Eskimos, in fact, the vowel system is simple; certain consonants lack; the language does not suffer, at the end of words, of groups of consonants.

Fig. 100 Entrance door to the Berlin Zoo in 1880
(© France Rivet, Polar Horizons, 2013)

APPENDIX E – VARIOUS MENTIONS OF ABRAHAM'S STORY

Over the years, Abraham's story has been mentioned in various books and articles. Usually the mention is in very general terms. Here are a few examples where the facts are not quite accurate:

In *Zoo: A history of Zoological Gardens in the West*[331], the author states that the *Eskimos* died on their return trip to Labrador.

> [...] five adult Eskimos from Labrador and their children, visitors in 1880–81, died of smallpox on their return. Hagenbeck wrote to Jacobsen: "You know to what extent I am a friend to all men, and you can imagine how this tragedy affects me," but he did not suspend his shows.

In *Eskimos in Europe: How they got there and what happened to them afterwards*[332], the author identifies all eight Inuit as originating from Nachvak. He also makes Carl Hagenbeck the sole owner of the *Eisbär* and Johan Adrian Jacobsen the captain of the ship.

> After having taken the Inuit back to Greenland, Adrien Jacobsen was commissioned in 1879 to fetch more Eskimos. For this, Hagenbeck purchased a special schooner of which the young man was appointed Captain. [...] [Jacobsen] returned with Eskimos, this time from Labrador. They were from the Moravian mission in Hebron and consisted of a married couple with two children and an adult male, as well as another couple with their daughter. They were eight in all from Nachvak, a village situated some fifty miles north of Hebron. When they reached Germany they too were

---

[331] Baratay, Eric and Elisabeth Hardouin-Fugier. (2004). p. 28.
[332] Bonnerjea, René. (2004). p. 362.

measured – by the well-known ethnologist Rudolf Vir-
chof [sic]. Hardly anything is known about them except
that they were exhibited in several German towns and
were found interesting because of their similarity with the
American Indians. Unfortunately they all died of smallpox,
some in Germany and the rest in France, which was the last
country on their touring programme. Hagenbeck and
Leutemann were very saddened. Up to that point not one
of their invited natives had perished in their hands.

In *Their souls were to be laughed at*[333], the author pretends that
Hagenbeck ordered Jacobsen to head to Labrador to recruit
Eskimos and that Abraham is the one who convinced Jacobsen
to take him along to Europe.

But when the Greenlanders returned home, Hagenbeck
faced a dilemma. He knew he needed more Inuit to keep
the public coming to his zoo, but Greenland's Danish authorities refused to send any more Inuit abroad. So, he sent
Jacobsen to Labrador. [...] When Ulrikab led Jacobsen
north, he found what, to the European mind, were heathens – a godless people who'd rejected the civilizing influence of white men. Yet Ulrikab had no problem convincing
three of them – Terrianiak, Paingo and Noggasak – to travel
to Hamburg. What's more, he convinced Jacobsen to take
him along as well. [...]

In *Captured Heritage: The Scramble for Northwest Coast Artifacts*[334], the author states that only one *Eskimo* died in Paris.

Then tragedy struck at the Jardin d'Acclimatisation [sic] in
Paris: one of the Eskimos died. The Labradorian's death was
a severe blow to a larger and already crippled enterprise.
Jacobsen and Hagenbeck had put money into a ship, the
Eisbär, for the Labrador voyage, but things had gone badly. [...] Now the death of the Eskimo cast a pall over the entire scheme; Hagenbeck, no doubt feeling the double effect of guilt and adverse publicity, had lost heart for further
ethnic expositions. His family, moreover, was hostile to Jacobsen, blaming him for the whole Eskimo-Eisbär imbroglio.

---

[333] Hames, Elizabeth. (2012, June).
[334] Cole, Douglas. (1995). p. 60.

Acknowledgments

A research project of this scale, and spread over four years, could not have been completed without the support of many people. Even the smallest gestures which may seem insignificant sometimes have a decisive impact on the course of history.

Thank you to master photographer Hans-Ludwig Blohm, met in July 2009, during a cruise along the Labrador coast. If Hans had not put on a hat identical to mine, we perhaps would never have spoken and I would never have heard of Abraham's story. Hans had been carrying the story of Abraham in his heart for several years and he contributed his photographs to two books published by Professor Hartmut Lutz. His support, encouragement and wise advice have been most valuable.

Thank you to Mechtild and Wolfgang Opel, a German couple also met on the Labrador cruise. It is following their suggestion that I traced Dr. James Garth Taylor, the person who, in 1980, rediscovered Abraham's diary and brought it to the attention of the 20th century public.

Thank you to James Garth Taylor for agreeing to answer my questions about his discovery of Abraham's diary and for suggesting that I see his writings on the Labrador Inuit kept at the Canadian Museum of Civilization's Library.[335]

Thank you to Anneh Fletcher of the Canadian Museum of Civilization's Library, for taking the initiative to delve into their databases looking for the *Eskimos*. It was she who found a short text published in 1881 in the British Medical Journal[336] which was the first text uncovered providing the name of a physician and of a Paris medical institution linked to the *Eskimos*.

---

[335] The museum has since been renamed *Canadian Museum of History*.
[336] *The Esquimaux at Paris.* (1881, April 2).

Thank you to Marianne Adato, secretary of the *Société médicale des hôpitaux de Paris* for referring me to Dr. Loïc Guillevin, who holds a copy of their archives.

Thank you to Dr. Loïc Guillevin for delving into his archives and for suggesting that I contact the *Bibliothèque Interuniversitaire de Santé* (BIU Santé).

Thank you to Guy Cobolet, librarian at BIU Santé, for providing me with the address of their research database. A few minutes later, I was looking at a dozen articles related to the 1880 group. These articles revealed the existence of the brain casts and confirmed that Paingu's skullcap was presented to the *Société d'anthropologie de Paris*. A turning point in the research.

Thank you to Christine of the Central library of the *Muséum national d'Histoire naturelle* for routing my request for information about the brain casts and skullcap to the persons in charge of the Musée de l'Homme's Department of Anthropology.

Thank you to Philippe Mennecier, in charge of the Biological Anthropology collections at the Musée de l'Homme, for responding to my request so promptly and in such great detail, but especially for having taken the initiative to reveal the presence of the fully mounted skeletons of five Labrador *Eskimos* in their collections! Never ever had this possibility crossed my mind! I was in shock when I read Mr. Mennecier's email. It is at this precise moment that the research project took a totally unexpected turn. It was no longer simply a matter of uncovering the events of 1880–1881, but an opportunity opened to change the course of history.

If any of the above persons had not taken the action specified, as insignificant as it may seem, chances are that you would not be reading this book and that it would still be several decades before today's Labrador Inuit found out the whole truth of what happened to eight of their fellow countrymen.

Thank you to Christian Prévoteau, curator of *Musées anatomiques Delmas-Orfila-Rouvière*, for agreeing to meet with me despite the fact that his museum had been dismantled. Mr. Prévoteau took the *Eskimos*' story so much to heart that he did the impossible... gain access to the brain casts even though they were in the midst of nearly 200 pallets of boxes packed for an extended storage period. It is his actions and efforts that have allowed us to confirm that the casts are indeed those of Abraham's, Ulrike's and Tobias' brains.

Thank you to Gwénaële Guigon, historian and museographer specializing in Arctic collections, for her interest in this project, for sharing her knowledge and for her valuable advice provided at various levels throughout this research.

Thank you to Hartmut Lutz for volunteering, despite his busy schedule, to translate Johan Adrian Jacobsen's diary from German to English, and for recruiting Jacqueline Thun to do the French translation. The unusual language used by Jacobsen combining German, Norwegian and Danish proved a challenge. I also thank him for allowing me to reprint the English translation of Abraham's diary and excerpts of various texts that he and his students at the University of Greifswald published in 2005 in the book *The Diary of Abraham Ulrikab: Text and Context*. The students who worked on these translations are: Claudia Albrecht, Dorothea Buchholz, Karen Ebel, Jennifer Felkel, Kathrin Grollmuß, Nadine Hiepler, Karin Hinckfoth, Jana Jerchel, Sabine Ihlow, Martina Lange, Andrea Mages, Axel Nieber, Jana Schnorfeil, Susanne Rumpoldin, Verena Sachse, Anja Weidner and Susanne Zahn.

Thank you to Jacqueline Thun for her conscientious work, for the quality of her German-French translations and for her willingness to always respond positively to new translation requests.

Thank you to Philippe Gendron and Hans-Josef Rollmann for their help in translating various newspaper articles and texts from German.

Thank you to Belinda Niedieck for translating to English the part of Jacobsen's 1879 diary written in Norwegian.

Thank you to Dr. Louise Lefort for reviewing the English translation of Théophile Chudzinski's talk to ensure the accuracy of the neurologic terms used.

Thank you to Martin Zeilig and Anders Lafon for their recommendations to improve the English manuscript.

Thank you to Line Fortin for the countless hours spent proofreading so carefully both the French and English manuscripts, despite the short deadlines.

Thank you to Diane Mongeau for taking the initiative, after reading *Voyage With the Labrador Eskimos, 1880–1881*, to prepare the two geographical maps allowing us all to visually locate the places linked to the story.

Thank you to Jamie Brake, archaeologist for the Nunatsiavut Government, for taking the time to read the manuscript and for clarifying certain aspects of Inuit culture and life in Labrador.

Thank you to Louise Metcalfe for visiting the *Nederlands Fotomuseum* in Rotterdam on our behalf and uncovering the interesting details about Herman Frederick Carel ten Kate.

Thank you to Christelle Patin for sharing the 1886 annual report of the Muséum's Chair of Anthropology as well as the document *Instructions pour MM. les officiers de la marine qui voudraient faire des collections d'HN destinées au Muséum de Paris par les professeurs administrateurs du Muséum.*

Thank you to the following individuals who contributed their time and / or shared their knowledge in the search for new information or photographs relating to Abraham's story. In some cases, the search was unsuccessful but it was no less important since it allowed us to eliminate potential leads.

In Canada

Avataq Cultural Institute (Montréal)	Christelle Cuilleret
Historian	Kenn Harper
Historian – Ford family	Frederick Ford
Hudson's Bay Company Archives	Maureen Dolyniuk Mandy Malazdrewich Tara Sadler
Labrador history enthusiasts	Carol Brice-Bennett Susan Felsberg Louise Metcalfe Denis Saint-Onge
Memorial University (St. John's)	Tom Gordon Bert Riggs Hans-Josef Rollmann Linda White
Them Days (Happy Valley-Goose Bay)	Aimee Chaulk

Université Laval (Centre interuniversitaire d'études et de recherches autochtones (CIERA) / Anthropology Departement)

Bernard Saladin d'Anglure
Francis Lévesque

In Germany

Alexianer Hospital (Krefeld)

Barbara Krause

Berlin Ethnology Museum

Viola König

Berlin Zoo

Heiner Klös

Berliner Gesellschaft für Anthropologie, Ethnologie und Urgeschichte (Berlin Society for Anthropology, Ethnology and Prehistory)

Nils Seethaler

Customs Museum (Hamburg)

Juergen Hegemann

Darmstadt City Archives

Friedrich W. Knieß
Sabine Lemke

Dresden Zoo

Kerstin Eckart

Frankfurt Zoo

Sabine Binger
Caroline Liefke

Hagenbeck Tierpark (Hamburg)

Klaus Gille

Hamburg State Archives

Barbara Koschlig

Hessian Departmental Archives (Darmstadt)

Marion Coccejus
Ars Zimmerman

Humboldt University Berlin

Britta Lange

Institut für Stadtgeschichte Frankfurt

Volker Harms-Ziegler

Krefeld Municipal Archives

Daniela Gillner
Michael van Uem

Moravian Archives (Herrnhut)

Rüdiger Kröger

Museum für Völkerkunde Hamburg (Museum of Ethnology)

Anja Battefeld
Jantje Bruns
Wulf Köpke

Museum für Vor- und Frühges-
chichte (Museum for prehistory
and early history) (Berlin)

Alix Hänsel
Horst Junker

von der Linden Publisher

Marga von der Linden
Herbert von der Linden
Ragnhild von der Linden

In Belgium

SNCB Archives (Brussels)

Miek Somers

In France

Les Arts Décoratifs (Paris)

Michele Jasnin

Académie nationale de médecine (Paris)

Damien Blanchard
Dr. Emmanuel Alain Cabanis
Jérôme van Wijland

Anthropologist and author

Christelle Patin

Archives de l'Assistance publique
– Hôpitaux de Paris (Paris)

Marie Barthelemy
Patrice Guérin
Maïlys Mouginot

Archives départementales du
Nord (Lille)

Michel Vangheluwe

Archives nationales de France
(National Archives) (Paris)

Armelle Le Goff
Cloé Viala

Archives de Paris (Paris Municipal
Archives)

Gérald Monpas
Solène Simon

Augustines de Notre-Dame de
Paris (Paris)

Sr Jeanne and their archivist.

Central Library of the Muséum
national d'Histoire naturelle (Paris)

Hélène Foisil
Alice Lemaire
Antoine Monaque
Julie Randriambao
and staff of the reserve area.

Bibliothèque Forney (Paris)

Isabelle Sève

Bibliothèque historique de la ville de Paris (Paris)	Marie-Françoise Garion-Roche Frédéric Lions Laura Minh Hong Séverine Montigny
Bibliothèque nationale de France (National Library) (Paris)	Evelyne Bréjard Nadège Danet Valérie Sueur-Hermel
Carnavalet Museum (Paris)	Jocelyne Van Deputte
Centre des archives historiques de la SNCF (Le Mans)	Jean-Paul Berthet Sandrine Coulibeuf Didier Houlbert
École pratique des hautes études (Paris et Bordeaux)	Jacques Berchon Olivier Dutour
Expert-merchant – photography from its origins to 1940 (specializing in the exhibitions held at the *Jardin d'acclimatation*)	Gérard Lévy
Historian	Pascal Blanchard
Jardin d'acclimatation (Neuilly-sur-Seine)	Marie-Laurence Jacobs-Pirajean
Médiathèque de l'architecture et du patrimoine (Paris)	Emmanuel Marguet
Musée de l'Homme (Paris)	Aurélie Fort Alain Froment
Musée des moulages de l'Hôpital Saint-Louis et Bibliothèque Henri Feulard (Paris)	Françoise Durand
Musée du quai Branly (Paris)	André Delpuech Carine Peltier-Caroff Almudena Hitier Angèle Martin

Neuilly-sur-Seine Municipal Archives	Elise Dosquet Virginie Poullilian
Préfecture de police du département de la Seine (Paris)	Richard Wagner
Préfecture du Nord (Lille)	Isabelle Gruber
Société d'anthropologie de Paris (Paris)	François Marchal
Société de géographie de Paris (Paris)	Sylvie Rivet
Saint-Ouen Cemetery (Saint-Ouen)	Véronique Gautier

In Norway

Jacobsen Family	Anne Kirsti Jacobsen
Historian	Kirsten K. Kotte Holiman
Museum of Cultural History (Oslo)	Anne Britt Halvorsen Arne Røkkum Tone Wang
National Library of Norway (Oslo)	Staff of the reading room
Polar Museum (Tromsø)	Juliane Seidl

In The Nederlands

Nederlands Fotomuseum (Rotterdam)	Anneke Groeneveld Carolien Provaas

In the Czech Republic

National Library of the Czech Republic (Prague)	Šárka Nováková

In Switzerland

Basel Municipal Archives	Sabine Strebel

Historian   Nicolas Bancel

International Museum of Refor-   Simona Sala
mation (Geneva)

In the United States

Anthropologist   Ann Fienup-Riordan

Moravian Church Archives   Paul Peucker
(Bethlehem, Pennsylvania)

Thank you to the 'Friends of Abraham' whose contribution to the spring 2013 crowdfunding campaign covered the costs of two research trips to Europe, and turned the publication of this book and of the translation of Johan Adrian Jacobsen's diary, into reality:

Distinguished Benefactress
- Line Fortin

In Abraham's honour
- Annalise and Kurt Biedermann and friends
- Steve Bouthillette
- Suzanne Rivet
- Nicole Vallée

In Tigianniak's honour
- Hans-Ludwig Blohm
- Louise Poliquin
- Benoit Rivet
- Jean Rivet

In Paingu's honour
- Anonymous
- Raymonde Arsenault
- Gilles Baron
- Ingeborg Blohm
- Louise Boulay
- Daniel Denis
- Nadine Fortin
- Stephen Gurman and Ann Thomson
- Rozanne Junker
- Claire Lavigne
- Gina Njolstad and Pierre Lalonde
- Sylvie Pinsonneault
- Jean-Marie Philippe
- Rock Poulin

In Ulrike's honour
- Pierre Bélanger
- Carole Brodeur
- Joyce and Jon Clarke
- Carole Leroy
- Gilbert Troutet

In Tobias' honour

- Anonymous
- Suzanne Aubin
- Julie Dechenault
- Josée Labelle
- Albert Mougeot

- Bruce Raby
- Riffou-Loomes Family
- Yvette Rivet
- Peggy Waterton

In Nuggasak's honour

- Anonymous
- Shelley Ball
- Manon Francoeur
- Josée Morin

- Harry Nowell
- Ingo Peters
- Jérémy Rivet
- Philip Schubert

In Sara's honour

- Anonymous
- Raymond Aubin
- Michel R. Beaudry
- Michel Y. Bédard
- Suzane Carrière
- Claire Charron
- Nathalie Côté
- Renaud Cyr
- Luc Fortin

- André Geick
- Carole Gobeil
- Lisa Goren
- Robert Gravel
- Jean and Lise Leclerc
- Diane Mongeau
- Thérèse Mongeau
- Madeleine Parisien

In Maria's honour

- Anonymous
- Diane D'Aragon

- Roxann Dalpé-Morin
- Raymond Savard

As for the project's component which aims to assess the possibility of repatriating to Canada the Inuit remains currently on European soil:

Thank you to Zipporah Nochasak for initiating the contact with the Nunatsiavut Government.

Thank you to Johannes Lampe and Dave Lough, respectively Nunatsiavut's Minister and Deputy Minister of Culture, Recreation and Tourism, for their support and their trust.

Thank you to the former Consul General of Canada for identifying the right people at the Department of Foreign Affairs Canada to bring up the issue with.

Thank you to the Department of Foreign Affairs Canada and to the Embassy of Canada in Paris for taking this 'story of Inuit skeletons' seriously and for taking the initiative to request that the possible repatriation be included in the cooperation agreement signed on June 14, 2013, by Prime Minister Stephen Harper and French President François Hollande. I never crossed my mind that the project could get support at such a high level and on both sides of the Atlantic.

Thank you to the Embassy of Canada in Berlin, to the Embassy of the Federal Republic of Germany in Ottawa and to the French Embassy in Ottawa for their interest and support.

Thank you to Yvonne Uthurralt, Manon Francoeur and Renald Gilbert who hosted me during my stays in Paris, as well as to Lorraine and Jean Lepage, my neighbours, who, on several occasions, have allowed me to go off in the footsteps of Abraham with piece of mind.

Thank you to my whole family as well as to my friends who, for the last four years, have been encouraging me, have been lending me their support and have been listening to me talk about Abraham's story.

Thank you to 25 free designers from around the world who took the time to submit their views on the book cover, as part of the contest launched on the 99designs platform. Thank you to Sumit Shringi for his excellent work and patience.

Thank you to all the people working behind the scene to digitize public domain books and to make them available through searchable engines. The depth of this research and the variety of documents uncovered was attained as a result of your work.

Is there a better proof of the extraordinary things that can be accomplished when a spirit of collaboration prevails?

Bibliographic References

Archival Sources

Moravian Archives, Bethlehem, Pennsylvania, United States

Ulrikab, Abraham. (1880). *Tagebuch des Hebroner Eskimos Abraham von seinem Aufenthalt in Europa 1880/1881, übersetzt von Br. Kretschmer.* Records of the Labrador Mission Station, 13557–13571.

Hagenbeck Tierpark Archives, Hamburg, Germany

1881 Financial records.

Museum für Völkerkunde Library, Hamburg, Germany

Johan Adrian Jacobsen's journal. *Tagebuch no 1 – May 1877- Dec 1881.* Pages 54 to 158.

Moravian Archives, Herrnhut, Germany (The original documents have not been consulted. We reprinted, with permission, the published English translations versions (Lutz, Hartmut, (2005))

Missionsblatt aus der Brüdergemeine. (1880, December). Nr 12. [*Contains Abraham's first letter to Brother Elsner and Brother von De Witz's account of his visit to the Berlin zoo (p. 223-226)*].

Missionsblatt aus der Brüdergemeine. (1881). Nr 3. [*Contains Abraham's second letter to Brother Elsner*].

Missionsblatt aus der Brüdergemeine. (1882). Nr 1. [Contains the missionaries' account of the events in Hebron following the death of the group.].

Brief an die UAC von der Hebroner Conferez 1880-08-16. R 15 K b. 17 h. N° 111 [Letter from the missionaries in Hebron to the UAC].

Brief an Br. Connor von Br. Kretschmer, Hebron. 1880-08-20. R 15 K. b. 17 h. N° 114. [Brother Kretschmer's letter to Brother Connor].

Brief an Br. Reichel von Br. Elsner. 1880-11-10. R 19 Bf. 16b. [Brother Elsner's letter to Brother Reichel].

Brief an Br. Reichel von Br. Elsner. 1881-01-18. R 19 Bf. 16b. [Brother Elsner's letter to Brother Reichel].

DARMSTADT CITY ARCHIVES + HESSIAN STATE ARCHIVES, DARMSTADT, GERMANY

Stamdesamt Darmstadt Sterbenebenregister 1881 (HStAMR Best. 901 N° 293). [Nuggasak's death certificate].

Historical maps of the city of Darmstadt.

Collection of photos and articles on the Orpheum. (Da/B/2.77.04)

Folder: Zirkus Völkerschauen, Varieté: 2 C/2 Zeitgeschehen: allgemein und diverse, bis 1999. Sub-folder 'Eskimos in Darmstadt.' [Internal folder about the 'Labrador Eskimos' containing correspondance with various researchers. Covers the period 1997 to 2010].

KREFELD CITY ARCHIVES, KREFELD, GERMANY

Standesamt Bockum C. N° 148/1880 – December 27, 1880 [Paingu's death certificate].

Standesamt Krefeld C. N° 2037/1880 – December 31, 1880 [Sara's death certificate].

StadtA KR 4/1665, Bl. 75. – December 30, 1880 [Notice from the city of Crefeld to the Bergisch-Märkischen railway company about the *Eskimos*. Letter has not yet been fully transcribed and translated].

StadtA KR 6/290, Bl. 7. – December 27, 1880 [Note from Dr. Jacobi to the burgomaster].

StadtA KR 6/290, Feuillet 7. [Note stating the the zoo was closed for a few days after Paingu's death].

StadtA KR 6/290 – Events section.

Map of the city of Bockum(1894).

ARCHIVES DE L'ASSISTANCE PUBLIQUE – HÔPITAUX DE PARIS, PARIS, FRANCE

1Q 2/169 – Registre des entrées – *Hôpital Saint-Louis*, 1881. [Admission Log Book]

3Q 2/39 – Registre des décès– *Hôpital Saint-Louis*, 1881. [Death Registry]

C-2235 – Photography collection – *Hôpital Saint-Louis* (1885–1918).

3Fi4 – Saint-Louis – Fonds iconographiques

9L 11 – *Hôpital Saint-Louis* – Maladies contagieuses – Administration et règlementation – Activité et fonctionnement – Variole.

9L 11 – *Hôpital Saint-Louis* – Maladies contagieuses – Administration et règlementation – Documentation et publication – Variole.

9L 11 – *Hôpital Saint-Louis* – Maladies contagieuses – Administration et règlementation – Règlement et instructions – Variole.

9L 12 – *Hôpital Saint-Louis* – Maladies contagieuses – Travaux, hygiène et salubrité – Hygiène et salubrité – Isolement.

9L 12 – *Hôpital Saint-Louis* – Maladies contagieuses – Travaux, hygiène et salubrité – Hygiène et salubrité – Conseil d'hygiène publique et de salubrité.

9L 13 – *Hôpital Saint-Louis* – Maladies contagieuses – Malades hospitalisés – Varioleux.

9L 141 – *Hôpital Saint-Louis* – Services hospitaliers – Service des varioleux, 1879.

9L 141 – *Hôpital Saint-Louis* – Services hospitaliers – Service des varioleux, 1887.

ARCHIVES DE LA PRÉFECTURE DE POLICE DE LA SEINE, PARIS, FRANCE

BA90 – Rapport quotidien du préfet de police 1881.

DA38 – Secours publics – Attribution de voitures pour le transport dans les hôpitaux des personnes atteintes de maladies contagieuses (1881–1886.

DA39 – Secours publics – Transport dans les hôpitaux des personnes atteintes de maladies contagieuses.

DA127 – Exhibitions d'enfants phénomène, femme singe, la machine parlante, ... 1876–1883.

DB202 – Exhibitions de peuplades étrangères.

DB440 – Moulages, embaumements – Momification de cadavres, amphithéâtres de médecine et de chirurgie, cours de dissection, écoles d'anatomie, ...

DB459 – Hygiène publique – typhoïde, variole.

DB6 – Préfet de police – Travail avec les chefs de services, signature de pièces, départ correspondance.

ARCHIVES DE LA SOCIÉTÉ D'ANTHROPOLOGIE DE PARIS, PARIS, FRANCE

SAP 43 – Registre des correspondances – Entrées [Incoming Mail Log Book]

SAP 8 (1), Lettre B.2698 : Correspondance – Entrées – Carton B1 – N° U98 [January 5, 1881 letter from Albert Geoffroy Saint-Hilaire to Dr. Paul Topinard]

SAP 8 (1), Lettre B.2697 : Correspondance – Entrées – Carton B1 – N° U97 [January 11, 1881 letter from Albert Geoffroy Saint-Hilaire to Dr. Paul Topinard]

Fonds Paul Topinard (8 boxes)

ARCHIVES DE LA VILLE DE NEUILLY-SUR-SEINE, NEUILLY-SUR-SEINE, FRANCE

2556R – Folder on the *Jardin d'acclimatation*.

4Fi3/53 – Illustration of the 1877 Greenlanders at the *Jardin d'Acclimatation*.

1C GA 1 – Newpaper *Gazette de Neuilly et de Courbevoie* (February 6, 1881, February 13, 1881, March 6, 1881)

Newspaper *L'Écho de l'arrondissement de Saint-Denis*, No 51 to 61 (January 21 to March 13 1881)

ARCHIVES DE PARIS, PARIS, FRANCE

V3D1 – Mémoires du Préfet de la Seine.

V4E 3814 – Registre des décès du 10e arrondissement, 10 au 16 janvier 1881. [Death register for Paris' 10th arrondissement]

2484 W3 – Registres de transports des corps. [Register of the transportation of bodies]

ARCHIVES DÉPARTEMENTALES DU NORD, LILLE, FRANCE (Search conducted by M. Michel Vangheluwe, Conservateur du patrimoine (Heritage Curator)).

Documents related to border surveillance, epidemics and smallpox: M 178/2, M 303/59, M 321, M 403, M 184/90 à 93).

Newspapers *Écho de la Frontière* et *La Vraie France*.

ARCHIVES DES COLLECTIONS D'ANTHROPOLOGIE – MUSÉE DE L'HOMME, PARIS, FRANCE

Registre des entrées (1881). [Entry Log Book]

Registre d'inventaire (1881). [Inventory Register]

Documentation associée aux pièces d'inventaire n° 1886-13. [Documents associated to inventory n° 1886-13.]

- March 10, 1881 letter from the Préfecture de police de la Seine to Armand de Quatrefages.
- Handwritter letter by Dr. Landrieux.
- March 10, 1885 letter from the Préfecture de police de la Seine to Armand de Quatrefages.

- Exhumation Autorization N° 7061 – May 27, 886 – from the Préfecture de police de la Seine to Dr. Délisle.

- Death certificates for Abraham, Ulrike, Tobias, Maria and Tigianniak.

ARCHIVES NATIONALES , PIERREFITTE-SUR-SEINE, FRANCE

AJ/15 – Muséum national d'Histoire naturelle

AJ/15/555 – Dossiers du personnel – Jules Louis Dédoyart, préparateur au laboratoire d'anthropologie, 1877–1923.

AJ/15/551A – Dossier personnel d'Armand de Quatrefages, 1842–1892.

F/8 – Police sanitaire

F/8/168-171 and -172 – Conseils et commissions de la Seine, 1807–1903.

F/17 – Ministère de l'instruction publique

F/17/3846-1 and -2 – Correspondance 1833–1895.

F/17/3847-1 and -2 – Comptabilité, 1879–1893.

F/17/3886 – Minutes des assemblées des professeurs, 1880–1889.

F/17/4001 – École pratique des hautes études, 1881–1884

F/21 – Beaux-Arts

F/21/4490 – Musée d'ethnographie du Trocadéro.

BIBLIOTHÈQUE DE L'ACADÉMIE NATIONALE DE MÉDECINE, PARIS, FRANCE

Review of the folders of the following members of the Académie: Léon Colin, Paul Brouardel, Ernest Théodore Hamy and Paul Topinard.

BIBLIOTHÈQUE HISTORIQUE DE LA VILLE DE PARIS, PARIS, FRANCE

Poster Collection [Searched by M. Frédéric Lions].

Newspaper *Le Monde Illustré* [from January 1 to April 30, 1881].

Newpaper L'Illustration [1881].

Newspaper L'Univers Illustré [from January 1 to May 21, 1881].

CP 3411 – *Jardin d'acclimatation* – Various handwritten documents

Ancienne collection des actualités – Série 38 – Press clippings on the *Jardin d'acclimatation*. (2 boxes)

BIBLIOTHÈQUE NATIONALE DE FRANCE (DÉPARTEMENT DES CARTES ET PLANS), SITE RICHELIEU-LOUVOIS, PARIS, FRANCE

Histoire de France (1880–1881)

Photos sous Eichtal/Potteau, Rousseau

Va 92a fol, t. 12. B 20199, B20198, B201200, B201201

Esquimaux du Groenland 20302, 20303, 20304

CENTRAL LIBRARY OF THE MUSÉUM NATIONAL D'HISTOIRE NATURELLE, PARIS, FRANCE

AM 37 – Minutes des procès-verbaux des assemblées des professeurs (1881).

AM 38 – Minutes des procès-verbaux des assemblées des professeurs (1882).

AM 42 – Minutes des procès-verbaux des assemblées des professeurs (1886–1887).

AM 65 – Procès-verbaux des assemblées des professeurs (1886–1887).

2AM1K47a – Correspondance à l'arrivée [Échanges avec Carl Hagenbeck (neveu). 11 documents de 1932–1933.]

AM 93 – Correspondance au départ (1er semestre 1881)

AM 103 – Correspondance au départ (1er semestre 1885)

AM 104 – Correspondance au départ (2e semestre 1885)

AM 105 – Correspondance au départ (1er semestre 1886)

AM 106 – Correspondance au départ (2e semestre 1886)

AM 314 – Enregistrement des pièces justificatives des dépenses (1881)

AM 317 – Relevé général par service des dépenses (1886)

AM 390 – Enregistrement des pièces justificatives de dépenses (1886).

MS 2255 – Correspondance d'Ernest Théodore Hamy (1878–1883).

MS 2256 – Correspondance d'Ernest Théodore Hamy (1884–1887).

MS 2258 – Correspondance d'Armand de Quatrefages.

MS 2312 – Correspondance scientifique d'Ernest Théodore Hamy

MS 3317 – Collection de cartes postales du Muséum national d'Histoire naturelle

MUSÉE DU QUAI BRANLY – SERVICES DES ARCHIVES ET DE LA DOCUMENTATION, PARIS, FRANCE

Consultation de la base de données TMS (collections).

D000553 *Registre d'inventaire II des numéros d'entrées du MET* (typed version).

D000563 *Registre d'inventaire I des numéros d'entrées du MET* (typed version).

Notices des artefacts du Labrador conservés au Musée du quai Branly. [Description of the Labrador artefacts kept at the museum]. Document created on November 14, 2011 by the Service des archives et de la documentation.

DA001350–15437 – *Laboratoire d'anthropologie inventaire des collections ostéologiques.*

D000524/13273 – *Catalogue des clichés photographiques, conservés au Laboratoire d'Anthropologie. 1879 à 1890 et collection Potteau.*

D000524/7719 – *Collections des clichés photographiques du* laboratoire d'Anthropologie *du Muséum national d'Histoire naturelle de Paris: récapitulatif.*

ARCHIVES OF THE MUSEUM OF CULTURAL HISTORY, OSLO, NORWAY

Innkomme brev, 1877–1890 [incoming letters]

HUDSON'S BAY COMPANY ARCHIVES, WINNIPEG, CANADA

RG3/40B/1 – George Ford's personal file.

D.38/55 folio 140 – George Ford's Character report, 1897–1908.

LIBRARY AND ARCHIVES CANADA, OTTAWA, CANADA

Microfilm 1M1257 – Drawing of the HBC Post in Nachvak, 1895.

Microfilm 510 – 1837–1907 – Minutes regarding the spiritual affairs and large business projects of the Hebron Mission.

Microfilm 512 – 1881–1927 – From the Society for the Furtherance of the Gospel, London, to the Hebron Mission. Annual Conference letters, etc.

PUBLICATIONS (BOOKS, ARTICLES, WEB PAGES,...) CITED AS A REFERENCE IN THIS BOOK

Annales de la chambre des députés – Débats parlementaires. (1881). Tome I (11 janvier au 12 avril 1881). Paris: Imprimerie du Journal Officiel. 443-447. Retrieved from
http://books.google.ca/books?id=k6hDAQAAIAAJ&pg=PA442

Bahere, Rainer. (2008). Early anthropological discourse on the Inuit and the influence of Virchow on Boas. *Études/Inuit/Studies*, 32(2), 13-34. Retrieved from http://id.erudit.org/iderudit/038213ar

Baratay, Eric and Elisabeth Hardouin-Fugier. (2004). *Zoo: A History of Zoological Gardens in the West*. London: Reaktion Books. 127-128.

Berlin-Hamburg Railway. [n.d.]. From *Wikipedia*. Accessed on April 21, 2014 at http://en.wikipedia.org/wiki/Berlin%E2%80%93Hamburg_Railway

Besnier, Ernest. (1881, May 13). Rapport sur les maladies régnantes (janvier, février et mars 1881). *Bulletin et mémoires de la Société médicale des hôpitaux de Paris*. 152-183. Retrieved from http://gallica.bnf.fr/ark:/12148/bpt6k5440212z

Bohemia. (1880, November 15). (Prague). N° 317. p. 6.

Bohemia. (1880, November 19). (Prague). N° 323. p. 14.

Bonnerjea, René. (2004). *Eskimos in Europe: How they got there and what happened to them afterwards*. London and Budapest: Biro Family Ltd. 355-363.

Bordier, Arthur. (1881). Calotte cérébrale d'un Esquimau du Labrador. *Bulletin de la Société d'anthropologie de Paris*, 3(VI), 16-19. Retrieved from http://gallica.bnf.fr/ark:/12148/bpt6k639174

Bourquin, Théodore. (1882). Correspondance du Labrador. Première lettre du missionnaire Bourquin, président. *Journal des frères de l'unité chrétienne*. Quarante septième année. 25-31.

Brinton, Daniel G. (1892, November 11). Crania Ethnica Americana. Book Review. *Back Matter Science*, 20 (510), 279. Retrieved from http://www.jstor.org/stable/1765100

Bulletin épidémiologique. (1881). *Revue d'hygiène et de police sanitaire*. Vol. 3. p. 176. Retrieved from http://www.biusante.parisdescartes.fr/histmed/medica/page?90113x1881x03&p=179

Bulletin hebdomadaire de statistiques. (1881, January 16). *Le Siècle*. (Paris). p. 3. Retrieved from http://gallica.bnf.fr/ark:/12148/bpt6k735849s

CÉRÉMONIE – Des indigènes rapatriés....un siècle plus tard. (2010, January 15). *Le petit journal.com*. (Santiago). Retrieved from http://www.lepetitjournal.com/santiago/societe/52062-ceremonie-des-indigs-rapatriun-sie-plus-tard

Charlottenburger Zeitung. (1880, October 19). (Berlin). p. 2.

Charlottenburger Zeitung. (1880, October 24). (Berlin). p. 2.

Charlottenburger Zeitung. (1880, November 2). (Berlin). p. 2.

Charlottenburger Zeitung. (1880, November 17). (Berlin). p. 2.

Chudzinski, Théophile. (1881). Sur les trois encéphales des Esquimaux morts de la variole, du 13 au 16 janvier 1881, dans le service de M. [L']Andrieux, à l'hôpital Saint-Louis. *Bulletin de la Société d'anthropologie de Paris*, 3(IV), 312-318. Retrieved from http://gallica.bnf.fr/ark:/12148/bpt6k639174

Colin, Léon. (1881a). *Rapport sur l'épidémie de variole à laquelle ont succombé les Esquimaux arrivés le 31 décembre 1880 au* Jardin d'Acclimatation *de Paris*. Paris: Imprimerie centrale des chemins de fer. 16 p. Accessed at the Service des archives de la Préfecture de police de la Seine. (DB459 – Hygiène publique)

Crefelder Zeitung. (1880, December 24). N° 304. p. 2. Accessed at the Krefeld City Archives.

Crefelder Zeitung. (1880, December 29). N° 307. Accessed at the Krefeld City Archives.

Crefelder Zeitung. (1881, January 4). N° 3. Accessed at the Krefeld City Archives.

Darmstädter Tagblatt. (1880, December 15). (Darmstadt). Accessed at the Hessian State Archives.

Darmstädter Tagblatt. (1880, December 16). (Darmstadt). Accessed at the Hessian State Archives.

Darmstädter Zeitung. (1880, December 16). (Darmstadt). Accessed at the Hessian State Archives.

David, Philippe. (n.d.). *55 ans d'exhibitions zoo-ethnologiques au* Jardin d'acclimatation. Retrieved from http://www.jardindacclimatation.fr/article/le-jardin-vu-par/

De Challans, Vicomte. Chronique parisienne. Nécrologie. (1881, February 16). *La Presse*. (Paris). p. 2. Retrieved from http://gallica.bnf.fr/ark:/12148/bpt6k543602d

Départ des Esquimaux. (1881, January 9). *Le Figaro*. (Paris). p. 4. Retrieved from http://gallica.bnf.fr/ark:/12148/bpt6k277706f

Départ des Esquimaux. (1881, January 9). *Le Gaulois*. (Paris). p. 4. Retrieved from http://gallica.bnf.fr/ark:/12148/bpt6k523694s

Départ des Esquimaux. (1881, January 9). *Le journal des débats politiques et littéraires*. (Paris). p. 3. Retrieved from http://gallica.bnf.fr/ark:/12148/bpt6k4613976

Départ des Esquimaux. (1881, January 10). *Gil Blas*. (Paris). p. 4. Retrieved from http://gallica.bnf.fr/ark:/12148/bpt6k7515980k

Départ des Esquimaux. (1881, January 10). *La Presse*. (Paris). p. 3. Retrieved from http://gallica.bnf.fr/ark:/12148/bpt6k5435659

Départ des Esquimaux. (1881, January 10). *Le Siècle*. (Paris). p. 4 Retrieved from http://gallica.bnf.fr/ark:/12148/bpt6k735843h

Départ des Esquimaux. (1881, January 10). *Le Temps*. (Paris). p. 4. Retrieved from http://gallica.bnf.fr/ark:/12148/bpt6k228254x

Départ des Esquimaux. (1881, January 10). *Le XIXe siècle*. (Paris). p. 4 Retrieved from http://gallica.bnf.fr/ark:/12148/bpt6k7563531g

Dias Nélia. (1991). *Le musée du Trocadéro (1878–1908) : Anthropologie et muséologie en France*. Paris: Centre national de la recherche scientifique. 310 p. (+ pl. XV).

Die Eskimos im Zoologischen Garten zu Berlin. (1880, October 21). *Magdeburgische Zeitung*. (Berlin). No. 493.

Doulas, Cole. (1995). *Captured Heritage: The Scramble for Northwest Coast Artifac*ts. Vancouver: UBC Press. 60-62.

Elliot, Hugh S.R. and Thacker, A.G. (1912). *Beasts and Men: Being Carl Hagenbeck's experiences for half a century among wild animals (an abridged translation)*. London: Longmans, Green and Co. xi, 299 p. Retrieved from http://ia600504.us.archive.org/22/items/beastsmenbeingca00hage/beastsmenbeingca00hage.pdf

Elliott, Deborah L. and Susan K. Short (1979, September). The Northern Limit of Trees in Labrador: A Discussion. *Arctic*. 32(3), 201-206. Retrieved from http://pubs. aina.ucalgary.ca/arctic/Arctic32-3-201.pdf

The Esquimaux. (1881, May 21). *The Sunday at Home Family Magazine for sabbath reading*. (Londres). 328-331.

The Esquimaux at Paris. (1881, April 2). *The British Medical Journal*. (Londres). p. 526.

Les Esquimaux du Jardin d'acclimatation. (1881). Extrait des travaux publiés par La Revue Britannique. Paris: Librairie du *Jardin d'acclimatation*. Accessed at the Bibliothèque nationale de France.

Les Esquimaux en Europe. (1881, March 6). *Feuille religieuse du canton de Vaud*. (Lausanne). 56e année. 104-109. Retrieved from http://books.google.ca/books?id=aDQpAAAAYAAJ

The Esquimaux in Paris. (1881, January 17). *Dundee Courier and Argus*. p. 4.

The Esquimaux in Paris. (1881, January 18). *Northern Warder and bi-weekly courrier and argus*. p. 7.

Expositions and Epidemics. (1986, September). *Them Days*. (Happy Valley-Goose Bay). 12(1), s.p.

Faits divers. *Le XIXe siècle.* (1881, January 10). (Paris). p. 3. Retrieved from http://gallica.bnf.fr/ark:/12148/bpt6k7563531g

Feuerschiff Elbe 1. [n.d.]. From *Wikipedia.* Accessed on January 25, 2014 at http://de.wikipedia.org/wiki/Feuerschiff_Elbe_1

Fienup-Riordan, Ann. (2005). *Yup'ik elders at the Ethnologisches Museum Berlin: Field work turned on its head.* Seattle: University of Washington Press . xv, 337 p.

Forbush, William Byron. (1903). *Pomiuk, A waif of Labrador: A brave boy's life for Brave Boys.* Boston: The Pilgrim Press. 156 p. Retrieved from https://archive.org/details/pomiukwaifoflabr00forb

Ford, Henry. (2000). Labrador and Baffin Trading Company. *Them Days.* 25(4). s.p.

Frankfurter Nachrichten. (1880, December 3). (Francfort).

Garnier, M.P. (1882). Vaccine internationale. *Dictionnaire annuel des progrès des sciences et institutions médicales.* Paris: Imprimerie Germer Baillière. p. 573. Retrieved from http://books.google.ca/books?id=2O0EAAAAQAAJ

Gontier, Martine. (2010, March 11). *Un livre, un acte, un article : décès d'une Fuégiene en 1881 à Neuilly-sur-Seine.* Retrieved from http://racinesenseine.fr/curiosites/pages/lectures0001.html

Guide des étrangers dans le Muséum d'histoire naturelle. (1855). Paris: Museum national d'Histoire naturelle. p. 70-73. Retrieved from http://books.google.ca/books?id=zj1PAAAAYAAJ

Guide du Musée de l'Homme. (1952). Paris: Muséum national d'Histoire naturelle. p. 5.

Guigon, Gwénaële, (2006). *Historique et présentation des collections inuit dans les musées français au XIXe siècle,* Mémoire de recherche de l'Ecole du Louvre, under the direction ofAndré Desvallées and Michèle Therrien, 474 p.

Hagenbeck, Carl and M. Hoffmann. (1880). *Beiträge über leben und treiben der Eskimos in Labrador und Grönland.* Berlin: Im Selbstverlage des Herausgebers. 24 p. Retrieved from http://books.google.ca/books?id=90Q-AAAAYAAJ

Hames, Elizabeth. (2012). Their souls were to be laughed at. *Up Here Magazine. 28(4).* 72-75.

Hamy, Ernest Théodore. (1907). La collection anthropologique du Muséum national d'Histoire naturelle, leçon d'ouverture du cours d'anthropologie faite le 11 avril 1907. *L'Anthropologie.* Tome XVIII. 257-276. Retrieved from http://gallica.bnf.fr/ark:/12148/bpt6k5433874s

Harper, Kenn. (2000). *Give me my Father's Body: The life of Minik, the New York Eskimo*. London : Profile Books. 277 p.

Harper, Kenn. (2009, August 20). Nancy Columbia: The first Inuit Queen. *Nunatsiaq Online*. Retrieved from http://www.nunatsiaqonline.ca/stories/article/taissumani_aug._28/

Harper, Kenn and Russell Potter. (2010). *Early Arctic Films of Nancy Columbia and Esther Eneutseak*. s.p. Retrieved from http://www.academia.edu/2324918/_With_Kenn_Harper_Early_Arctic_Films_of_Nancy_Columbia_and_Esther_Eneutseak

Harper, Stephen. Prime Minister of Canada. (2013, June 14). *Programme de coopération renforcée Canada-France*. Retrieved from http://www.pm.gc.ca/fra/nouvelles/2013/06/14/programme-de-cooperation-renforcee-canada-france

Hrdlička, Aleš. (1901). *An Eskimo Brain*. New York: The Knickerbocker Press. 47-49. Retrieved from https://archive.org/details/eskimobrain01hrdl

Hervé, Georges. (1888). *La circonvolution de Broca : étude de morphologie cérébrale*. Paris: Lecrosnier et Babé. 134-136, 183. Retrieved from http://gallica.bnf.fr/ark:/12148/bpt6k6210185d

Human zoos: The Invention of the Savage. [n.d.] Musée du quai Branly. Retrieved from http://www.quaibranly.fr/en/programmation/exhibitions/last-exhibitions/human-zoos.html

Inauguration du musée d'ethnographie du Trocadéro. (1882, April 14). *Le XIXe siècle*. (Paris). 1-2. Retrieved from http://gallica.bnf.fr/ark:/12148/bpt6k7567387d

Instructions pour MM. les officiers de la marine qui voudraient faire des collections d'HN destinées au Muséum de Paris par les professeurs administrateurs du Muséum. (1882). Paris. p. 8.

Jacobsen, Johan Adrian and Adrian Woldt. (1977). *Alaskan Voyage 1881–83: An expedition to the Northwest Coast of America*. English translation by Erna Gunther from Adrian Woldt's German text (1884). Chicago: University of Chicago Press, 1977. xii, 266 p.

Jacobsen, Johan Adrian. (1894). *Eventyrlige Farter, Fortalte for Ungdommen*. Bergen: John Griegs Forlag. Traduction de Ingeborg v.d . Lippe Konow. 43-50. Accessed at the National Library of Norway (Oslo).

Jacobsen, Johan Adrian. (2014). *Voyage With the Labrador Eskimos, 1880–1881*. English translation of the German text by Hartmut Lutz. Gatineau: Horizons Polaires. 86 p.

Kremers, Elisabeth. (2002). *Vom Boulevard zum Biotop: Die Geschichte des städtischen Grüns in Krefeld*. Krefeld: City of Krefeld. 154 p.

Kretschmer, Marie. (1883). Correspondance du Labrador. Lettre de Madame Kretschmer (extraits). *Journal des frères de l'unité chrétienne.* Quarante huitième année. 118-120.

La Presse. (1881, January 8). Paris. p. 3 Retrieved from http://gallica.bnf.fr/ark:/12148/bpt6k543563j

La santé publique. (1881, January 26). *Le Siècle.* (Paris). p. 2. Retrieved from http://gallica.bnf.fr/ark:/12148/bpt6k7358594

La Trobe, Benjamin. (1888). *With the Harmony to Labrador: A visit to the Moravian mission stations on the North East Coast of Labrador.* London: Moravian Church and Mission Agency. 56 p. Retrieved from https://archive.org/details/cihm_01302

Laborde, Dr. (1881, January 26). Esquimaux morts de variole. *Société de médecine publique et d'hygiène professionnelle.* 145-146.

Landrieux, Dr. (1881, January 14). Relation de quelques cas de variole hémorragique observés chez des esquimaux à l'hôpital Saint-Louis. *Bulletin de la Société médicale des hôpitaux de Paris.* 9-12. Retrieved from http://gallica.bnf.fr/ark:/12148/bpt6k5440212z/f13.image

Landrin, Armand. [n.d.]. From *Wikipédia.* Accessed on February 25, 2014 at http://fr.wikipedia.org/wiki/Armand_Landrin

Latteux, Dr. (1877). Sur la technique microscopique dans ses applications à l'étude de la chevelure dans les races humaines. *Bulletin de la Société d'anthropologie de Paris.* 2(12), 193-195. Retrieved from http://gallica.bnf.fr/ark:/12148/bpt6k639143

Les On-Dit. (1881, February 9). *Le Rappel.* (Paris). p. 2. Retrieved from http://gallica.bnf.fr/ark:/12148/bpt6k7534391j

Lutz, Hartmut, Alootook Ipellie, Hans-Ludwig Blohm. (2005). *The Diary of Abraham Ulrikab: Text and Context.* Ottawa: University of Ottawa Press. xxvii, 100 p.

Lutz, Hartmut et al. (2007). *Abraham Ulrikab im zoo: Tagebuch eines Inuk 1880/1881.* Wesel: M.u.H. von der Linden GbR. 167 p.

Martin, A.-J. (1881, February 9). Académie et corps savants. Revue de médecine et d'hygiène. *Journal officiel de la République Française. Lois et décrets.* 13(39), p. 713. Retrieved from http://gallica.bnf.fr/ark:/12148/bpt6k6222565x

Menus extravagants et bizarreries culinaires. [n.d.]. Retrieved from http://www.jardindacclimatation.fr/histoire/

Neue Preussische Zeitung. (1880, October 23). (Berlin). No. 249.

Norddeutsche Allgemeine Zeitung. (1880, October 18). (Berlin). No. 487.

330   Bibliographic References

Norddeutsche Allgemeine Zeitung. (1880, October 21). (Berlin). No. 492. p. 2.

Norddeutsche Allgemeine Zeitung. (1880, October 23). (Berlin). No. 496. p. 2.

Norddeutsche Allgemeine Zeitung. (1880, October 26). (Berlin). No. 501. p. 2.

Notes de voyages d'Abraham, l'Esquimau. (1883). *Journal des frères de l'unité chrétienne.* (Peseux, Suisse). 148-155.

Nouvelles & Échos. (1881, February 8). *Gil Blas.* (Paris). p. 1. Retrieved from http://gallica.bnf.fr/ark:/12148/bpt6k75160030

Periodical Accounts Relating to the Missions of the Church of the United Brethren Established Among the Heathen. (1881, December). London: The Brethren's Society for the Furtherance of the Gospel Among the Heathen. XXXI(329). Retrieved from http://collections.mun.ca/cdm4/document.php?CISOROOT=/cns_perm orv&CISOPTR=8814&REC=5

Periodical Accounts Relating to the Missions of the Church of the United Brethren Established Among the Heathen. (1882). XXXII(333). London: The Brethren's Society for the Furtherance of the Gospel Among the Heathen. Retrieved from http://collections.mun.ca/cdm4/document.php?CISOROOT=/cns_perm orv&CISOPTR=6268&REC=11

Petit, André. (1881, January 21). Observations de M. Landrieux. *Gazette hebdomadaire de médecine et de chirurgie.* (Paris). 40-41. Retrieved from http://www.biusante.parisdescartes.fr/histmed/medica/page?90166x18 81x18&p=42

Ratzel, Friedrich. (1886). *Völkerkunde. Zweiter Band. Die Naturvölker Ozeaniens, Amerikas und Afiens.* Leipzig: Berlag des Bibliogrphichen Instituts. p. 768. Retrieved from http://books.google.ca/books?id=eL8sAAAAYAAJ

Rollmann, Hans-Josef. [n.d. a] *Establishments of the Moravian Mission in Labrador.* Religion, Society and Culture in Labrador and Newfoundland. Retrieved from http://www.mun.ca/rels/hrollmann/morav/

Rollmann, Hans-Josef. [n.d. b]. *Preliminary alphabetical checklist of Moravian missionaries, teachers and traders in Labrador (with years of their service) 1752 – ca 1900.* Retrieved from http://www.mun.ca/rels/morav/texts/checklist.html

Rollmann, Hans-Josef. (2013, November 7). Labrador Inuit Workship in Berlin. *The Telegram.* (St. John's). Retrieved from http://www.thetelegram.com/Living/2013-11-07/article-3469736/Labrador-Inuit-worship-in-Berlin/1

Rothfels, Nigel. (2008). *Savages and Beasts: The Birth of the Modern Zoo*. Baltimore: The Johns Hopkins University Press. xii, 268 p.

Sad faith of Esquimaux. (1881, February 9). *Manchester Courrier and Lancaster General Advertiser*. p. 6.

Sad faith of Esquimaux. (1881, February 10). *Edinburg Evening News*. p. 3.

Sad faith of Esquimaux. (1881, February 11). *The Belfast News-letter*. p. 8.

Sad faith of Esquimaux. (1881, February 12). *Manchester Courrier and Lancaster General Advertiser*. p. 3.

Siderey. M.A. (1881). Recherches anatomo-pathologiques sur les lésions du foie dans les maladies infectieuses. *Bulletin de la Société anatomique de Paris*. 46e année. 4(6), 631-638. Retrieved from http://gallica.bnf.fr/ark:/12148/bpt6k6333622b

Situation financière du Jardin [d'acclimatation]. (1882). *Bulletin de la Société Nationale d'acclimatation*, 3(9), CXVII-CXXVI. Retrieved from http://gallica.bnf.fr/ark:/12148/bpt6k5453568k

Spitzka, Edward Anthony. (1902, November 29). Contributions to the encephalic anatomy of the races. First paper: – three Eskimo brains, from Smith's sound. *American Journal of Anatomy*. 2(1), 28-29. Retrieved from http://onlinelibrary.wiley.com/doi/10.1002/aja.1000020104/abstract

The Spread of Small-pox. (1881, April 30). *The Evening News*, Portsmouth. p. 2.

Taylor, James Garth. (1981). An Eskimo abroad, 1880: His diary and death. *Canadian Geographic*. Oct/Nov 1981, 38-43.

Thode-Arora, Hilke. (2002). Abraham's Diary – A European Ethnic Show from an Inuk Participant's Viewpoint. *Journal of the Society for the Anthropology of Europe*, 2(2), 2-17.

Thode-Arora, Hilke. (2011). Hagenbeck et les tournées européennes: L'élaboration du zoo humain. *Zoos humains*. Paris: La Découverte Poche/Sciences humaines et sociales. 150-159.

Thomas, Philippe and Jean Oster. (1982). *Le Musée de l'Homme*. Rennes: France-Ouest. 22-24 .

Vaccinated to death. (1881, January). *The Vaccination Inquirer and Health Review*. (Londres). 2(22), p. 179.

The Vaccination Inquirer and Health Review. (1881, September). (Londres). III(30), p. 103.

Vallin, E. (1881a). Les varioleux en wagon. La trichine à Paris. *Revue d'hygiène et de police sanitaire*. Vol. 3. 89-93. Retrieved from

http://www.biusante.parisdescartes.fr/histmed/medica/page?90113x18
81x03&p=92

Vallois, H. L. (1940). Le Laboratoire Broca. *Bulletin et mémoires de la
Société d'anthropologie de Paris.* IX(1), 1-18. Retrieved from
http://www.persee.fr/web/revues/home/prescript/article/bmsap_0037-
8984_1940_num_1_1_2761

Vallois, Henri V. (1945) *Inventaire des collections ostéologiques du Département d'anthropologie du Musée de l'Homme.* (Cote
DA001350/15437). Accessed at the Service des archives et de la documentation, Musée du quai Branly.

Verneau, René. (1898). Les nouvelles galeries du Museum.
L'Anthropologie. IX(3). 319-336. Retrieved from
http://gallica.bnf.fr/ark:/12148/bpt6k5433873c

Virchow, Rudolf. (1880). Ausserordentliche Zusammenkunft im zoologischen Garten am 7. November 1880. Eskimos von Labrador. Zeitschrift
für Ethnologie. (Berlin). Vol. 12. 253-274. Retrieved from
http://www.jstor.org/stable/23026564

Virchow, Rudolf. (1892). *Crania Ethnica Americana: Sammlung
auserlesener amerikanischer schädeltypen.* Berlin: A. Asher & Co. (4 p.-
33-[53] p.-XXVI pl.) Accessed at the Médiathèque d'étude et de recherche (Reserve), Musée du quai Branly.

Wöchentliche Anzeigen. (1880, December 3). (Francfort). p. 2.

Wöchentliche Anzeigen. (1880, December 14). (Francfort). p. 2.

OTHER ADDITIONAL PUBLICATIONS

Bancel, Nicolas, Pascal Blanchard and Sandrine Lemaire. (n.d.). *Ces
zoos humains de la république coloniale.* Paris: s.n. 11p. Retrieved from
http://www.jardindacclimatation.fr/article/le-jardin-vu-par/

Bassler, Gerhard. (2006). *Vikings to U-Boats: The German Experience in
Newfoundland and Labrador.* Montreal: McGill-Queen's University Press,
80-83.

Barthélemy, Toussaint. (1880). *Recherches sur la variole.* Paris: Delahaye
et Lecrosnier. 288 p. Retrieved from
http://gallica.bnf.fr/ark:/12148/bpt6k5672779s

Bertrand, Émilie. (2010). *La présentation des crânes préhistoriques : de
l'Exposition universelle de 1878 à la création du Musée de l'Homme de
1937.* Paris: Muséum national d'Histoire naturelle. (Thesis). 101 p. Retrieved from
http://www.ipt.pt/teses.digitais/emilie.bertrand/emiliebertrand.pdf

Blanchard, Pascal *et al.* (2011). *Zoos humains et exhibitions coloniales: 150 ans d'invention de l'Autre*. Paris: La Découverte Poche/Sciences humaines et sociales. 598 p.

Blanckaert, Claude *et al.* (2013). *La Vénus Hottentote, entre Barnum et Muséum*. Paris: Muséum national d'Histoire naturelle. 478 p.

Bordier, Arthur. (1877a). Les Esquimaux du *Jardin d'Acclimatation*. *Mémoires de la Société d'anthropologie de Paris*. 448-461.

Bordier, Arthur. (1877b). Rapport de la commission nommée par la Société pour étudier les esquimaux du *Jardin d'Acclimatation*. *Bulletin de la Société d'anthropologie de Paris*. 575-586. Retrieved from http://gallica.bnf.fr/ark:/12148/bpt6k639143

Borlase, Tim. (1993). First Inuit Depiction by Europeans. *Labrador Studies: The Labrador Inuit*. Happy Valley-Goose Bay: Labrador East Integrated School Board. s.p.

Bouchardat, A. (1881) *Rapport sur la marche de la variole à Paris, depuis l'année 1860 jusqu'à ce jour, et sur les moyens d'en atténuer les ravages*. Paris: Conseil d'hygiène publique et de salubrité du département de la Seine. 19 p. (DB459 – Hygiène publique) Accessed a the Service des archives de la Préfecture de police de la Seine.

Bulletin hebdomadaire de statistiques. (1881, January 24). *Le Siècle*. (Paris). p. 3. Retrieved from http://gallica.bnf.fr/ark:/12148/bpt6k735857c

Callet, A. (1898). Le jardin des plantes et les nouvelles galeries du Museum. *La Science française*. 357-358. Retrieved from http://gallica.bnf.fr/ark:/12148/bpt6k116380r

Carvajal, Doreen. (2013, May 24). *Museums Confront the Skeletons in Their Closets*. *The New York Times*. Retrieved from http://www.nytimes.com/2013/05/25/arts/design/museums-move-to-return-human-remains-to-indigenous-peoples.html?_r=0

Colin, Léon. (1881b). L'épidémie de variole des Esquimaux. *Annales d'hygiène publique et de médecine légale*. 225-237. Retrieved from http://www.biusante.parisdescartes.fr/histmed/medica/page?90141x18 81x05&p=225

Colin, Léon. (1881c) L'épidémie de variole des Esquimaux et de la réceptivité spéciale des nouveaux venus dans les foyers épidémiques. *Bulletin de l'Académie nationale de médecine*. 2(X), 356-371. Retrieved from http://gallica.bnf.fr/ark:/12148/bpt6k408671n

Colin, Léon. (1881d) Épidémie de variole des Esquimaux. *Bulletin général de thérapeutique médicale et chirurgicale*. (Paris). N° 100. p. 272. Retrieved from http://www.biusante.parisdescartes.fr/histmed/medica/page?90014x18 81x100&p=276

Colin, Léon. (1881e) L'épidémie de variole des Esquimaux. *La Revue scientifique de la France et de l'étranger*. 2(19), 614-618. Retrieved from http://gallica.bnf.fr/ark:/12148/bpt6k215096c

Colin , Léon. (1881, March). L'épidémie de variole des Esquimaux et de la réceptivité spéciale des nouveaux venus dans les foyers épidémiques. *Archives générales de Médecine*. (Paris). Volume I. VIIe série, Tome 7. 498-499. Retrieved from http://www.biusante.parisdescartes.fr/histmed/medica/page?90165x1881x07&p=498

Corbey, Raymond. (1993). Ethnographic Showcases, 1870–1930. *Cultural Anthropology*, 8(3), 338-369. Retrieved from http://www.jstor.org/stable/656317

Coutancier, Benoit and Christine Barthe. (2004). Exhibition et Médiatisation de l'autre : Le jardin zoologique d'acclimatation (1877–1890). *Zoos humains*. Paris: La Découverte Poche/Sciences humaines et sociales. p. 306-314.

Darmstädter Zeitung. (1881, January 4). (Darmstadt).

De l'épidémie de variole des Esquimaux et de la réceptivité spéciale des nouveaux venus dans les foyers épidémiques. (1881, March 18). *Gazette hebdomadaire de médecine et de chirurgie*. p. 169. Retrieved from http://www.biusante.parisdescartes.fr/histmed/medica/page?90166x1881x18&p=171

De Ranse, F. (1881, March 19). *Gazette médicale de Paris*, 52e année, 6e série, Tome III, Nº 12, p. 154-155,160-161. Retrieved from http://www.biusante.parisdescartes.fr/histmed/medica/page?90182x1881x03&p=156

De Rialle, Girard. (1877, November 19). Les esquimaux au *Jardin d'acclimatation*. *La Nature, revue des sciences et de leurs applications aux arts et à l'industrie*. 390-395. Retrieved from http://cnum.cnam.fr/CGI/fpage.cgi?4KY28.9/394/100/432/0/0

De Witte, A.F. (1898, August 6). Le Muséum du Jardin des Plantes. Nouvelles galeries. *La France illustrée. Journal littéraire, scientifique et religieux*. 112-113. Retrieved from http://gallica.bnf.fr/ark:/12148/bpt6k5764632m

Au jour le jour. Académie de médecine. (1881, March 17). *Le Temps*. (Paris). p. 2. Retrieved from http://gallica.bnf.fr/ark:/12148/bpt6k228320p

Derex, Jean-Michel. (2012). *Les zoos de Paris : Histoire de la ménagerie du Jardin des Plantes, du* Jardin d'Acclimatation *et du zoo de Vincennes*. Parhecq: Éditions Patrimoines & médias. 124 p. Accessed at the Archives of Neuilly-sur-Seine.

Decaisne, E. (1881, March 12). Rapport de M. Léon Colin sur l'épidémie de variole qui a décimé la caravane d'Esquimaux du *Jardin d'acclimatation*. *L'Univers illustré*. (Paris). 166-167. Retrieved from http://gallica.bnf.fr/ark:/12148/bpt6k57382866

Dias, Nélia. (1989). Séries de crânes et armée de squelettes : les collections anthropologiques en France dans la seconde moitié du XIXe siècle. *Bulletins et Mémoires de la Société d'anthropologie de Paris*. 1(3-4), 203-230. Retrieved from http://www.persee.fr/web/revues/home/prescript/article/bmsap_0037-8984_1989_num_1_3_2581

Ditrich, Lothar and Annelore Rieke-Müller. (1998). *Carl Hagenbeck (1844–1913) Tierhandel und Schaustellungen im Deutschen Kaiserreich*. Frankfurt-am-Main: Peter Lang. 157-158.

Duckworth, W.L.H. and B.H. Pain. (1900). A contribution to Eskimo craniology. *The journal of the Anthropological Institute of Great Britain and Ireland*. 30(3). 125-140. Retrieved from www.archive.org/details/v30t1journalofro30royauoft

Épidémie de variole des esquimaux, réceptivité des nouveaux venus dans les foyers épidémiques. (1881, May). *Journal de médecine, de chirurgie et de pharmacologie*. (Bruxelles). 39e année. 72e volume. p. 516.

Épidémiologie : Relation des quelques cas de variole hémorragique observés chez des Esquimaux. (1881, February 12). *L'Union médicale: journal des intérêts scientifiques et pratiques, moraux et professionnels du corps médical*. 35(22), 256-258. Retrieved from http://www.biusante.parisdescartes.fr/histmed/medica/page?90068x18 81x31&p=260

Feest, Christian F. (1989). *Indians and Europe: An Interdisciplinary Collection of Essays*. Aix-la-Chapelle: Alsno Verlag. p. 337.

Felsberg, Susan. (2010). People: Labrador's Very First Export. In *Very Rough Country: Proceedings of the Labrador Exploration Symposium*, edited by Martha MacDonald. Happy Valley-Goose Bay: Labrador Institute of Memorial University. 214-227.

Frank, Edmond. (1898, July 22). Les nouvelles galeries du Museum. *L'Illustration*. 22-23.

Glangeau, Ph. (1898, April 23). Les nouvelles galeries du Museum. *L'Illustration*. 287-288.

Gosling, W. G. (1911). The Moravian Brethren. *Labrador: its discovery, exploration and development*. New York: John Lane Company, 309-313. Retrieved from http://www.ourroots.ca/e/toc.aspx?id=1205

Grimard, Edouard. (1877). *Le Jardin d'Acclimatation : Le tour du monde d'un naturaliste*. Paris: Bibliothèque d'éducation et de récréation. 392 p.

Guide du promeneur au Jardin d'Acclimatation *du Bois de Boulogne*. (1877). Édition 16a. Paris: Librairie spéciale du jardin zoologique d'Acclimatation. Retrieved from http://gallica.bnf.fr/ark:/12148/bpt6k5401443d

Hamy, Ernest Théodore. (1890). *Les origines du Musée d'ethnographie : histoire et documents*. Paris: Ernest Leroux. 321 p. Retrieved from https://archive.org/details/lesoriginesdumus01hamy

Hamy, Ernest Théodore. (1988). *Les origines du Musée d'ethnographie*. Paris: Éditions Jean-Michel Place. iv, 321 p. (facsimile of the 1890 edition with a preface by Nélia Dias). Accessed at the Médiathèque, Musée du quai Branly.

Hayem, Georges *et al.* (1883). Pathologie interne et clinique médicale. *La Revue des sciences médicales en France et à l'étranger*. Tome XXII. 114-115. Retrieved from https://archive.org/details/revuedesscience47unkngoog

Joltrain, A. (1881, March 3). Bulletin des conseils d'hygiène – La variole des esquimaux du *Jardin d'Acclimatation* de Paris. *Journal d'hygiène*. Paris: Société française d'hygiène. 100-103. Retrieved from http://books.google.ca/books?id=7O4DAAAAYAAJ

Kotte Holiman, Kirsten K. (2012). *Adrian Jacobsen, fra polarkulden og inn i varmen? en biografisk beretning om etnografen, eventyrerendog polarpionereren norge glemte*. Tromsø: University of Tromsø. (Thesis). 103 p. Retrieved from http://munin.uit.no/bitstream/handle/10037/4289/thesis.pdf

La collection anthropologique du Muséum d'Histoire naturelle. (1875, May 29). *La Nature, revue des sciences et de leurs applications aux arts et à l'industrie*. 408-410.

The Esquimaux at Paris. (1881, April 12). *The Evening News*. (Portsmouth). p. 3

Landrieux, Dr. (1881, June 11). Du transport des corps des varioleux décédés dans les hôpitaux. *Le Progrès médical*. 9(24), 472-473. Retrieved from http://www.biusante.parisdescartes.fr/histmed/medica/page?90170x1881x01x09&p=477

Landrieux, Dr. (1881). La variole des Esquimaux. *Bulletin général de thérapeutique médicale et chirurgicale*. N° 100. 139-140. Retrieved from http://www.biusante.parisdescartes.fr/histmed/medica/page?90014x1881x100&p=143

Lereboullet, L. (1881, February 25). L'épidémie de variole observée à Paris sur des Esquimaux venus du Labrador. *Gazette hebdomadaire de médecine et de chirurgie*. 116-119. Retrieved from http://www.biusante.parisdescartes.fr/histmed/medica/page?90166x1881x18&p=118

Lespès, Léo. (1874). *Une visite au* Jardin d'Acclimatation *du Bois-de-Boulogne*. Paris: La librairie du *Jardin d'Acclimatation*. 72 p. Accessed at the Archives of Neuilly-sur-Seine.

L'invention du sauvage. Exhibitions. Musée du quai Branly. (2012, Janvier). *Beaux-Arts*. Issy-les-Moulineaux : TTM Éditions. 48 p.

Lutz, Hartmut. (2005). Unfit for the European Environment: The tragedy of Abraham and other Inuit from Labrador in Hagenbeck's Völkerschau, 1880/81. *Canadian environments: essays in culture, politics and history*. Brussels: Peter Lang. 53-70.

Manouvrier, L. (1897). Notice sur Théophile Chudzinski. *Bulletin de la Société d'anthropologie de Paris*. IV(8). 664-670. Retrieved from http://www.persee.fr/web/revues/home/prescript/article/bmsap_0301-8644_1897_num_8_1_5741

Martin, A.-J. (1881, January 1). La vaccination obligatoire. *La Revue Scientifique de la France et de l'étranger*. 5-10. Retrieved from http://gallica.bnf.fr/ark:/12148/bpt6k215096c/f8.image

Martin, A.-J. (1881, March 19). Réceptivité spéciale des nouveaux venus dans les foyers épidémiques. *Journal officiel de la République Française*. *Lois et décrets*. 13(77), 1518-1519. Retrieved from http://gallica.bnf.fr/ark:/12148/bpt6k6223038m

Martin, A.-J. (1883, June 18). Prophylaxie de la fièvre typhoïde. *Journal officiel de la République Française*. *Lois et décrets*. 15(165), p. 3021. Retrieved from http://gallica.bnf.fr/ark:/12148/bpt6k6224114v

M. Bourgeois au Museum. L'inauguration d'aujourd'hui. *La Presse*. (1898, July 22). p. 1. Retrieved from http://gallica.bnf.fr/ark:/12148/bpt6k548871f

Petrone, Penny. (1992). *Northern Voices: Inuit writing in English*. Toronto: University of Toronto Press. 108-112.

Ritsema, Alex. (2007). *Heligoland, Past and Present*. S.l.: Lulu. 113 p.

La santé publique. (1881, February 2). *Le Siècle*. (Paris). p. 3. Retrieved from http://gallica.bnf.fr/ark:/12148/bpt6k735866b

Seurat, M. (1898, May 21). Les nouvelles galeries du Museum d'Histoire naturelle à Paris. *Le génie civil : Revue générale hebdomadaire des industries françaises et étrangères*. XXXIII(3), 37-40. Retrieved from http://gallica.bnf.fr/ark:/12148/bpt6k6476618q

Sociétés savantes. Société d'anthropologie. Séance du 5 mai 1881. (1881, June 4). *Le Progrès médical*. 9(23), p. 449. Retrieved from http://books.google.ca/books?id=S9ZCAQAAIAAJ

Sociétés savantes. Société médicale des hôpitaux. Séance du 15 janvier 1881. (1881, January 29). *Le Progrès médical*. 9(5), p. 84. Retrieved from http://books.google.ca/books?id=S9ZCAQAAIAAJ

Spehl, E. (1891). Contribution à l'étude de la « variole hémorragique ». *Journal de médecine, de chirurgie et de pharmacologie*. 49e année, 92e volume. 713-726. Retrieved from http://books.google.ca/books?id=KvKfAAAAMAAJ

Trautmann-Waller, Céline. (dir). (2004). *Quand Berlin pensait les peuples : Anthropologie, ethnologie et psychologie (1850–1890)*. Paris: CNRS Éditions. Web. Retrieved from http://books.openedition.org/editionscnrs/2190

Travaux académiques. Académie de médecine. (1881, March 19). *Gazette médicale de Paris*, 52e année, 6e série, Tome III, N° 12, 160-161. Retrieved from http://www.biusante.parisdescartes.fr/histmed/medica/page?90182x18 81x03&p=162

Vallin, E. (1881b). Sur l'épidémie de variole à laquelle ont succombé les Esquimaux arrivés le 31 décembre au *Jardin d'acclimatation* de Paris, rapport fait au Conseil d'hygiène de la Seine par M. Le Dr Léon Colin. *Revue d'hygiène et de police sanitaire*. Vol. 3. 247-248. Retrieved from http://www.biusante.parisdescartes.fr/histmed/medica/page?90113x18 81x03&p=250

Vallin, E. (1881c). De l'épidémie de variole des Esquimaux et de la réceptivité spéciale des nouveaux venus dans les foyers épidémiques. *Revue d'hygiène et de police sanitaire*. Vol. 3. p. 337. Retrieved from http://www.biusante.parisdescartes.fr/histmed/medica/page?90113x18 81x03&p=340

Vallin, E. (1881d). Du transport des corps des varioleux décédés dans les hôpitaux. *Revue d'hygiène et de police sanitaire*, Vol. 3. p. 619. Retrieved from http://www.biusante.parisdescartes.fr/histmed/medica/page?90113x18 81x03&p=622

Vallin, E. (1881, June 11). Du transport des corps des varioleux décédés dans les hôpitaux. *Le Progrès médical*, Vol. 3. 472-473. Retrieved from http://www.biusante.parisdescartes.fr/histmed/medica/page?90170x18 81x01x09&p=477

Virchow, Rudolf. (1881). Ausserordentliche Zusammenkunft am 14. November 1881 im Saale des zoologischen Gartens. *Zeitschrift für Ethnologie*. (Berlin). Vol. 13. 375-394

Von Kuenheim, Haug. (2009). *Carl Hagenbeck*. Hamburg: Ellert & Richter Verlag. 216 p.

Von Peter, Kummer. (2013). *Von der 'Lehrstätte für die Jugend' zur modernen Tierhaltung. Zoobiläum – Die besten Geschichten aus 75 Jahren*. (Krefeld: Zoo Krefeld gGmbh). p. 4.

Index of Names Cited

Folios in italics refer to footnotes.
Those in bold refer to illustrations and their captions.

A

Abraham, 15, 16, 17, 18, 19, 21, 38, 45, 46, 47, 49, 50, 51, 53, **56**, 65, 69, 70, 71, 72, 73, 74, 75, *76*, 78, **82**, 83, 84, 85, 89, 92, 93, 95, 96, 97, 98, 99, 100, 101, 102, 103, 107, 110, 121, 122, 124, 127, 129, 134, 136, *137*, 139, 143, 146, 149, 151, 154, 155, 159, 160, 161, 164, 166, **167**, 171, 172, 173, 175, 176, 178, 179, 180, 181, 182, **194**, 195, 199, **200**, 204, 219, 220, 221, 222, 223, 224, 225, 226, 227, 231, 236, 237, 239, 240, 241, 242, 243, **244**, 248, 249, **250**, 258, 262, 276, 277, 278, 279, *280*, **284**, 285, 287, 288, 289, 290, 291, 293, 294, 295, 299, 303, 304
Alice (Princess), 149
Atget, Eugène, **238**
Auburtin, Simon Alexandre Ernest, 298

B

Baartman, Sarah, *257*
Bach, Johann Sebastian, *100*, *280*
Baehre, Rainer, *106*, *272*
Bang (captain), 31, 32, 46, 277
Baratay, Eric, *303*
Bastian, Adolf, 271, 272, 288, 290
Bauer (Mr.), 271
Besnier, Ernest, 191, 192
Bessels, Emil, 112

Blohm, Hans-Ludwig, 16, 17, **47**
Boas, Franz, 272
Bodinus, Heinrich, **98**
Bonaparte, Napoleon, 76
Bonnerjea, René, *303*
Bordier, Arthur, 229, 230, 233, 235, 289
Bourdel (Mr.), 192
Bourquin, Johann Heinrich Theodor, 223, 291
Brinton, Daniel G., *261*
Broca, Paul, *118*, 230, 237, 295, 297
Brouardel, Paul, 214, 246, **247**, 290

C

Challans (Vicomte de), 11, 15, 278
Christensen (Mr.), 32
Chudzinski, Théophile, **236**, 237, 238, 239, 240, 241, 242, 243, 290, 293, 297, 299, 301
Colin, Léon, *163*, *165*, **201**, 202, 212, 213, 216, 290
Columbia, Nancy, 275, 276
Columbus, Christopher, 203
Connor (Brother), 50
Coudereau, Charles Auguste, 298

D

Dally, Eugène, 297, 298
David, Philippe, *274*
Delisle (Dr.), 248
Delmas, André, 243
Dias, Nélia, *267*

E

Elizabeth (Abraham's mother), *49*
Elliot, Hugh S.R., *25*, *26*
Elliott, Deborah L., *111*
Elsner, Augustus Ferdinand, 51, 89,
    92, 93, 95, 102, 103, 171, 172, *202*,
    219, 220, 221, 222, 223, 283, 288,
    289, 290, 291
Elsner, Bertha, 92
Eneutseak, Esther, 275, 276
Erdmann (wife of Friedrich), 51
Erdmann, Friedrich, 52

F

Faust (Dr.), 86
Fechner, Hanns, **264**
Fienup-Riordan, Ann, *27*, *271*
Fischer, J.H., **10**
Flandinette, Félix, 243
Fleischer, Carl, 46
Forbush, William Byron, *275*, *276*
Ford, George, 45, **46**, 276, 287
Ford, Henry, *46*

G

Garnier, M. P., 216
Gay, Eugene, 179, 182
Geoffroy Saint-Hilaire, Albert, 164,
    196, 210, 234, 235, 236, 277, 289
Girard (Mr.), 164
Giroux, Alphonse, 13
Gontier, Martine, *273*
Grenfell, Wilfred, 276
Guigon, Gwénaële, *130*, *214*, *267*,
    269, *270*
Gulliksen (captain), 32

H

Hagenbeck, Carl, 16, **24**, 25, 26, 27,
    28, 29, *34*, **36**, 38, 41, 42, **60**, 62,
    63, **64**, 65, 66, 70, 83, 91, 97, 98,
    113, 129, 133, 136, 141, 145, 151,
    155, 160, 166, 181, 182, 195, 197,
    202, 219, 220, 221, 222, 223, 224,
    226, 261, 265, 266, 267, 269, 270,
272, 273, 274, 279, 287, 289, 290,
    291, 303, 304
Hagenbeck, Claus Gottfried Carl, 62
Hames, Elizabeth, *304*
Hamy, Ernest Théodore, 252, *253*,
    254, 255, 256, 258, 266, 267, 268
Hardouin-Fugier, Elisabeth, *303*
Harper, Kenn, **66**, *241*, *275*, *276*
Harper, Stephen, 19
Haugk, W., 37, 42, 224
Hendrik, Hans, 28
Hervé, Georges, 239, 291, 299
Hlawatscheck, Gustav Adolf, 42, 95,
    224, 279
Hoffmann, M., **28**, **36**, **60**, 63
Hoffmann, Philippe, 161
Hollande, François, 19
Hrdlička, Aleš, **240**, 242

I

Ipellie, Alootook, *16*

J

Jacobi (Dr.), 156, 159, 288
Jacobsen (Mrs.), 66, 69, 149, 156,
    159, 162, 183, 277, 288, 290
Jacobsen, Anne Kirsti, **30**
Jacobsen, Jacob Martin, 27, 29, **48**,
    56, 62, 65, **66**, **104**, **157**, **244**, **250**
Jacobsen, Johan Adrian, 16, 22, 26,
    27, 28, 29, **30**, 31, 32, 33, 34, 35,
    37, 38, 39, 41, 42, 43, 44, 45, 46,
    47, 49, 50, 51, 57, 58, 59, 62, 63,
    65, 66, **67**, 72, 75, 83, *90*, 95, 109,
    110, 113, 117, 128, *129*, 138, 139,
    141, 142, 150, 151, 153, 155, 156,
    157, 159, 160, 161, 164, 165, 166,
    173, 174, 176, 178, 180, 181, 182,
    220, *221*, 222, 227, 229, 230, **244**,
    261, 265, 266, 267, 268, 269, 270,
    271, 272, 274, 275, 277, 279, 281,
    283, 287, 288, 289, 290, 291, 303,
    304
Jacobsen, Johan Filip, 275
Jenner, Edward, *214*
Jonas (Abraham's brother), *49*

K

Kaufmann, C., 136
Kern, Carl Gotthelf, 51, *90*, 96, 97, 98, 280
Kirchenpauer, Gustav Heinrich, *61*
Kokkik, Hans, 27, 33
Koppmann, Georg, **62**
Kraatz, Leopold, **40**
Kranich (Mr.), 151
Krell, E., **232**
Kremers, Elisabeth, *154*
Kretschmer, Carl Gottlieb, 15, 22, 37, 42, 50, 52, *69*, 224, 227, 279, *282*
Kretschmer, Marie, 227
Kujanje, Heinrich, 27, 33, 34

L

La Trobe, Benjamin, 227
Laborde (Dr.), 213, 215
Landrieux, Émile, 175, **185**, *186*, *187*, 191, 192, *193*, 204, 215, 235, 245, 278, 289, 290
Landrin, Armand, 265, **266**, 267
Latteux, Paul, 230, 231
Leutemann, Heinrich, **25**, 304
Linder, Carl, 51
Liouville, Henri, 213, 215, 216, 217, **218**
Louis IV (Grand Duke of Hesse), 149
Lubbock, John (Sir), 128
Lubineau, René, 179, 182
Ludwig (Pastor), 221, 222
Lutz, Hartmut, 16, 21, *41*, *50*, *92*, *96*, *219*, *225*
Lyon, Julien, 179, 182

M

Maggak, Juliane, 27, *34*
Maria, 18, 22, 49, **56**, 71, 96, 143, 146, 171, 173, 176, 177, 178, 182, **190**, 193, **194**, **200**, 204, 221, 222, 237, 248, 249, 278, 289
Martin, A.-J., *214*, 216
Martin, Angèle, *269*
Martinet (Mr.), 183
McGrath, Robin, *275*
Mendelssohn-Bartholdy, Felix, 102

Merrifield, Harriet, **46**
Meyer, W.A., **104**
Minik [Menee], 241
Molenaar, Gustav, 153
Mongeau, Diane, **54**, **55**
Müller-Kuchler, Carl, 153

N

Niccodemius (Abraham's brother), *49*
Niemeyer, Günter, *34*
Nochasak, Zipporah, 17
Nuggasak, 17, 18, 22, 47, **48**, 52, 57, 71, 96, 110, 144, 147, **148**, 149, 150, 151, 155, 158, *164*, 165, **184**, 205, 206, 221, 222, **232**, 262, 263, 285, 288, **292**, 304
Nuktaq [Nooktah], *241*

O

Okabak, Anne, 27
Okabak, Caspar Mikel, 27, 33, 34
Okabak, Katrine, 27
Orfila, Mathieu, *243*
Oster, Jean, *268*

P

Paingu, 18, 22, 47, **48**, 52, 71, 83, 84, 96, 106, 107, 109, 110, **120**, 121, 122, 123, 124, 127, 144, 147, 151, 155, 156, **157**, 158, 161, *164*, 165, 166, 182, **184**, 206, 207, 221, 222, **228**, 229, 230, **232**, 248, 262, 263, 288, 289, 304
Panneval (Dr.), 165, 204, 208
Paulus (Abraham's father), *49*
Peary, Robert, *241*
Petit, André, *185*
Petit, Pierre Lamith, **251**, **252**, **253**
Pinart, Alphonse, *267*
Pirou, Eugène, **254**
Pomiuk, 276
Potter, Russell, *275*, *276*
Pozzi, Samuel, 235, 294, 297
Prévoteau, Christian, 243

Q

Qisuk [Kishu], 241
Quatrefages, Armand de, **245**, 246, 247, 248, 253, 255, 278, 286, 290

R

Ratzel, Friedrich, **232**
Réaumur, René-Antoine Ferchault de, *87*
Reichel, Levin Theodor, **40**, 92, 219
Rindereknecht, Friedrich, 223
Rivet, France, **14**, **103**, **145**, **152**, **158**, **302**
Rivet, Paul, 268
Rivière, Georges Henri, *268*
Rochard, Jules, 216
Rollmann, Hans-Josef, **10**, *89*, *95*, *96*, 102, 103, *110*
Rothfels, Nigel, *26*, *34*
Rouvière, Henri, *243*

S

Sabine (Abraham's sister), *49*
Sara, 18, 19, 22, 49, **56**, 71, 75, 96, 101, 102, 143, 144, 146, 156, 159, 160, 161, 162, *164*, 165, 166, **194**, **200**, 206, 221, 222, 262, 263, 278, 282, 285, 288, 289, 291
Schneider, Johann Georg, 37, 42
Schoepf, Adolf, 66, **67**, 69, 72, 83, 95, 151, 159, 160, 173, 183, 220, 271, 277, 283, 287, 290
Schoepf, Albin, *183*
Schuiler (Mr.), 163, 205
Short, Susan K., *111*
Siderey, M. A., 188, 189
Sinéty (Mr. de), 189
Slotta, Carl Adolf, 223
Smith, John Caspar, *276*
Spitzka, Edward Anthony, 242
Stechmann, Hermann, *153*, 157
Stöcker, Adolf, 93, **94**, 102, 283

T

Taylor, James Garth, 15, 16
ten Kate, Herman Frederik Carel, **286**

Thacker, A.G., *25*, *26*
Thode-Arora, Hilke, 16, *83*, *95*, *182*, *220*, *271*, *273*, *274*
Thomas, Philippe, *268*
Tigianniak, 18, 22, 47, **48**, 52, 59, **60**, 69, 71, 73, *74*, 77, 78, 82, 83, 84, 85, 96, 109, 110, 119, 121, 122, 124, 127, 144, 147, 149, 151, 154, 157, 158, 166, 171, 173, 176, 178, **179**, 182, **184**, 193, 204, 206, 221, 222, 231, **232**, 237, 248, 249, 258, 259, 268, 278, 281, 282, 285, 289, **292**, 304
Tobias, 18, 22, 49, **56**, **66**, 71, 75, 77, 78, **82**, 83, 84, 96, 99, 100, 101, 102, 103, 110, 118, 121, 122, 123, 124, 126, **127**, 143, 146, 154, 155, 157, 166, 171, 173, 175, 176, 180, 181, 182, 193, **194**, **200**, 204, 221, 222, 226, 227, 231, 237, 239, 240, 241, 242, 243, 248, 249, 258, 278, 279, 281, 288, 289, 290, 291, 293, 294, 295, 296, 297, 299, 300
Topinard, Paul, **233**, 234, 235, 236, 237, 286, 289

U

Ulrike, 18, 21, 22, 49, 50, 52, **56**, 70, 73, 84, 92, 96, 101, 102, 110, 118, 121, 122, 124, 126, 127, **128**, 143, 146, 166, 172, 175, 176, 178, 179, 181, 182, 185, *186*, *187*, 189, **190**, 193, **194**, **200**, 204, 219, 221, 222, 224, 225, 231, 237, 239, 240, 242, 243, 248, 249, 258, 262, 265, 278, 279, 283, 289, 290, 291, 294, 295, 296, 297, 299, 300
Umlauff, Johann Friedrich Gustav, 261

V

Vallin, E., *164*
Vallois, H. L., *237*, *238*
Vallois, Henri V., *258*
Verneau, René, 256, **257**, 258
Vibraye, Paul de, *258*
Victor, Paul-Émile, 258, 268
Victoria (Queen), 149

Virchow, Rudolf, **104**, **105**, 106, 107,
    110, 111, *112*, 113, 114, 128, *129*,
    132, 133, 197, 261, 262, 263, **264**,
    277, 286, 288, 291, 304
von Dewitz, August, *90*, 96, 99, 280
Von Kuenheim, Haug, *65*

W

Wallace, William, *241*

Walter (Mr.), 151
Weiz, Samuel, 42, 52
Wilhelm I (Emperor), **28**, 63, 93
Woldt, Adrian, *27*

Z

Zimmermann (Dr.), 156

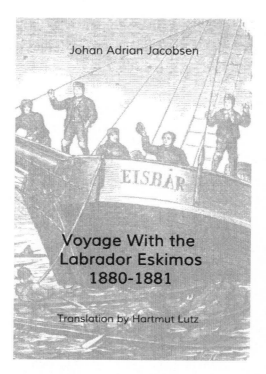

Johan Adrian Jacobsen

EISBÄR

**Voyage With the
Labrador Eskimos
1880-1881**

Translation by Hartmut Lutz

In September 1880, when Johan Adrian Jacobsen returns to Hamburg with two Labrador Inuit families, he's confident that the European public will come in large numbers to see these "exotic" people. Never had he imagined that he was actually taking them to their death.

Discover the moods, thoughts and qualms of the 23 year old Norwegian through the diary he kept, from June 1880 to January 1881, during his travels with Abraham and the Labrador *Eskimos*.

Original manuscript by Johan Adrian Jacobsen
English translation by Hartmut Lutz

86 pages, 14 illustrations/photographs
6" X 9" (15.5 cm X 23 cm)

Also available in French.

For more information:

abrahamulrikab.com

Made in the USA
San Bernardino, CA
20 February 2016